INSURGENT VEINS

ILLUMINATIONS: CULTURAL FORMATIONS OF THE AMERICAS SERIES

Jorge Coronado, Editor

INSURGENT VEINS

Indigenismo, Indigenous Literatures, and Decolonial Cracks

JOSÉ CARLOS DÍAZ-ZANELLI

University of Pittsburgh Press

Published by the University of Pittsburgh Press, Pittsburgh, Pa., 15260
Copyright © 2026, University of Pittsburgh Press
All rights reserved
Manufactured in the United States of America
Printed on acid-free paper
10 9 8 7 6 5 4 3 2 1

Cataloging-in-Publication data is available from the Library of Congress

Hardcover: 978-0-8229-4875-9
Paperback: 978-0-8229-6782-8

Cover image: C.Clavijo, Unidentifed Woman, after 1868, albumen carte de visite, Department of Image Collections, National Gallery of Art Library, Washington, DC
Cover design: Melissa Dias-Mandoly

Publisher: University of Pittsburgh Press, 7500 Thomas Blvd., 4th floor, Pittsburgh, PA 15260, United States, www.upittpress.org
EU Authorized Representative: Easy Access System Europe, Mustamäe tee 50, 10621 Tallinn, Estonia, gpsr.requests@easproject.com

CONTENTS

Acknowledgments
vii

INTRODUCTION:
Indigenista Inquiries and the Formation of Cracks
3

PART I

CHAPTER 1.
Arguedas and Gamio: Sensing the Criollo Failure
21

CHAPTER 2.
Vasconcelos and Valcárcel: Historicizing Peripheral Cultures
48

CHAPTER 3.
Mariátegui's Indo-Marxism and Arguedas's Cultural Program
74

INTERLUDE:
The Indigenous Turn of the Mid-Twentieth Century
99

PART II

CHAPTER 4.

Indianismo: Reinaga's Indianization of Revolutionary Dialectics

111

CHAPTER 5.

Marcos and the Zapatista Writing: Authority Upside-Down

135

CHAPTER 6.

Poetics of Buen Vivir: Political Ontology of Indigenous Poetry

161

AFTERWORD:

An Indigenous Decolonial Critique

190

Notes

197

Bibliography

221

Index

239

ACKNOWLEDGMENTS

Finding adequate words to express the affective and intellectual debts entailed in writing a manuscript is difficult. This book went through several stages, and at each one I was accompanied by colleagues, friends, and loved ones whom I like to think of as coauthors. This is how I see the names in this section—not as a professional network but as a constellation of coauthors whose comments, suggestions, and emotional support made the writing process an enjoyable journey.

Although the seminal idea for this manuscript came to me while having coffee in the Plaza de Armas of Cuzco, Peru, in 2018, and reflecting on the significance of that historical site for Andean history, the actual writing process was supported by numerous institutions that positively influenced my professional development. The first of these was Rutgers University, where I was fortunate to meet people to whom I am deeply indebted, such as Jorge Marcone, Susan Martin-Márquez, and Marcy Schwartz, who generously dedicated many hours of their time to discussing this project with me and reading early drafts of what would eventually become this manuscript. At Rutgers, I was also supported by Carson Cummins, Yeon-Soo Kim, Nelson Maldonado-Torres, Sandra Medina, Ariela Parisi, Roseli Rojo, David Roldán, Carolina Sánchez, Camilla Stevens, Jennifer Vílchez, and Katia Yoza, all of whom were there when the idea I had in Cuzco began to take shape as a manuscript.

It was a privilege to complete the final stages of writing this

ACKNOWLEDGMENTS

book with the support of the University of Pennsylvania, particularly the Wolf Humanities Center, where I found a stimulating intellectual forum and a warm group of friends and colleagues who generously read and commented on excerpts from this book. I would especially like to thank Josué Chávez, Jamal Elias, Huda Fakhreddine, Tim Malone, Jennifer Ponce de León, and Sara Varney.

Another institution with a meaningful presence in this project is the Peruvian-based NGO Servindi, where I worked for seven years. Its advocacy for the Indigenous peoples of the Andes and the Amazon profoundly shaped my political and affective approach to the Indigenous intellectual production examined in this book. I am eternally grateful to Jorge Agurto, Donofré Chuco, Luz Santos, and Roger Tunque, whose words I always listened to carefully during my years at Servindi, which were also the years I spent writing.

This book was also shaped through conversations with many people and colleagues, both in professional settings and informal spaces. I want to thank Diego Baena (Trinity College), Paloma Checa-Gismero (Swarthmore College), Jorge Coronado (Northwestern University), Aníbal González-Pérez (Yale University), Mariana Hernández y Rojas (University of Wisconsin-Green Bay), Priscilla Meléndez (Trinity College), Marco Ramírez Rojas (CUNY-Lehman College), and Camila Torres-Castro (CUNY-Baruch College).

I also wish to acknowledge the institutions that helped fund the various stages of my research and writing, such as the Center for Latin American Studies at Rutgers University, the School of Communications at the Peruvian University of Applied Sciences, the International Work Group for Indigenous Affairs, Trinity College, and the Andrew W. Mellon Foundation, which supported my research stay at the Wolf Humanities Center at the University of Pennsylvania.

Finally, I thank all those who gave me invaluable emotional support over these years. In a sense, this book also belongs to Tatiana, Pepe, Ross, Samantha, and Amarilis, who know the emotional dimension of this manuscript better than anyone.

INSURGENT VEINS

INTRODUCTION
Indigenista Inquiries and the Formation of Cracks

> The development of the indigenista current does not threaten or paralyze other vital elements of our literature. Indigenismo does not aspire to preempt the literary scene by excluding or blocking other impulses and manifestations. It represents the trend and tone of an era because of its sympathy and close association with the spiritual orientation of new generations who, in turn, are sensitive to the imperative needs of our economic and social development.
>
> **José Carlos Mariátegui,**
> *Siete ensayos de interpretación de la realidad peruana,*
> **translated by Marjory Urquidi**

> This polemic of the white and Indian *cholaje* is a mestizo literature. Cholo and neo-Indian writers engender an artful ideology: *indigenismo* and *cholismo*. . . . But the time will come, as it already has, when the authentic and true Indians, Indians of blood and spirit, will irrupt into the "republic of letters," and Indian brains will appear, producing Indian thought. And then, one must be sure of it, that the mourning prayer will be sung for "indigenismo" as well as for "cholismo." Leaving the "vital space" free for *indianista* literature.
>
> **Fausto Reinaga,**
> *El indio y los escritores de América,* **translated by the author**

In the 1920s, *indigenismo* was emerging as a cultural, literary, and political current in reaction to some conservative and racist discourses propagated by the dominant criollo society. Relocating discussions about the challenges of Latin American national projects in the realms of Indigenous societies, Mariátegui's words reflect the sense of novelty, openness, and disruption that this Peruvian *indigenista* gives to his own interpretation of this school of thought in the literary sphere. However, as Bolivian Indigenous intellectual Fausto Reinaga (formerly identified as an indigenista) wrote in the 1960s, indigenismo is presented as a literary trend that eclipses the emergence of purely Indigenous writers who were meant to develop an "indianista literature." Although Reinaga's critique of indigenismo is not consistent, the fact that it embraces several of the revolutionary ideas forged by indigenismo—including some of Mariátegui's—is highly indicative of my intentions in this book: the stimulus which that indigenista critique incarnates for the emergence and consolidation of an *Indigenous decolonial critique* (in the case of Reinaga, *indianismo*).[1] Ultimately, this book is, among many other things, an account of how the decolonizing ideas forged by indigenista writers traveled over time and influenced, were overturned by, or were fermented in the processes of intellectual consolidation that took place in Indigenous literary constructs such as the one posited by Reinaga.

Indigenismo had—and perhaps continues to have—many incarnations in Latin America. Particularly influential in the first half of the twentieth century in the Andean countries (Ecuador, Peru, and Bolivia) and Mesoamerica (Mexico and Guatemala), indigenismo emerges as a discourse that puts Indigenous peoples in the spotlight and questions the marginal role imposed on them by the modernizing national projects led by criollo mestizo elites. Furthermore, there is not much consensus on the definition of indigenismo. Although in this work I refer to the indigenista movement and its porous periodicity as a singular concept (*indigenismo*) in a practical lexical decision, I am fully aware of the variety of indigenismos that unfolded in these countries. Therefore, in this work I use the term "indigenismo" as more than a favorable body of opinion ("corriente de opinion favorable") and a protectionist discourse of Indigenous people as defined by French anthropologist Henri Favre (*El indigenismo*, 7). Indigenismo is a variety of approaches to what Mariátegui defined as the Indian problem ("el problema del indio") embodied by intellectuals, artists, and politicians of criollo mestizo roots who, with different ideological components and institutional commitments, tried to respond to some of the questions raised by Indigenous movements. Along the way, as Jorge Coronado (*Andes Imagined*, 5) points out, the term implied a critical position toward the dominant society and a denunciation of the cultural degradation of Indigenous nations. However, indigenismo is characterized by its amplitude and ambiguity ("amplitud y ambigüedad"), as pointed out by Ángel Rama, who, referring specifically to indigenista literature, defines it as a regionalist movement motivated by a desire for social justice (*Transculturación*, 138–47). We can interpret this definition as a sense of vindication of the Indigenous nations in Latin America. In the end, many indigenismos are formed around this definition.

However, this book is not one more exploration of the ideological and aesthetic diversity of indigenismo. Instead, it is an effort to evaluate and historicize the dialectical bridge that connects indigenismo with the intellectual development that runs through Indigenous literature and Indigenous decolonial movements in two areas where these connections explicitly took place: the Andes and Mesoamerica. In light of the decolonial agenda unfolded by various Indigenous movements on the continent, it is necessary to evaluate the dialectical links that exist in the indigenista essayistic literature of the region (which, quite straightforwardly, defines the programmatic commitment of these intellectuals) and the literary production of the Indigenous writer activists that emerged from the 1960s onward.

In turn, this literary corpus engages with social movements such as the autonomous processes of the zapatista movement of Chiapas in Mexico, the Regional Indigenous Council of Cauca in Colombia, the territorial autonomy of the Wampís Nation in the Peruvian Amazon, and the territorial and cultural resistance of the Mapuche Nation in southern Chile and Argentina, among many other examples. My aim in this book is to establish this symbolic connection between the indigenismo of the early twentieth century and the subsequent development of a distinctly Indigenous decolonial discourse through the study of a large and heterogeneous indigenista and Indigenous literary archive. The argument that structures the successive chapters is that, in spite of its contradictions and limitations (starting with being an essentially criollo mestizo movement), indigenismo contributed directly to the ideological empowerment that Indigenous intellectuals and movements began to develop toward the end of the twentieth century.

In the first half of the twentieth century, Mexico, Peru, and Bolivia experienced periods of social turmoil that coexisted with, and in some cases were fostered by, the intellectual agitation promoted by diverse indigenismos. The Mexican Revolution between 1910 and 1920 and the Bolivian Revolution of the Movimiento Nacionalista Revolucionario (Nationalist Revolutionary Movement, MNR) in 1952 are two historical events in which Indigenous social mobility played a central role, which explains why both revolutions were followed by self-declared indigenista administrations. Without the scope of a national-scale revolution, Indigenous uprisings also took place in Peru during this period, especially in the southern Andes.

At the intellectual level, in the case of Peru, indigenismos created sites of discussion to problematize indigeneity, such as the debates provoked by the rediscovery of Machu Picchu in Cuzco in the 1910s and 1920s, which developed in parallel with the indigenista humanitarian activism of the Peruvian German scholar Dora Mayer who, alongside activists and intellectuals Miguelina Acosta Cárdenas and Pedro Zulen, founded in the 1910s the Asociación Pro Indígena, an entity dedicated to the defense of Indigenous rights. Mayer and Acosta Cárdenas were also regular contributors to the magazine *Amauta*, a key publication in the formation of José Carlos Mariátegui's Indo-Marxist agenda. In the field of literary creation, the major precedent is the work of Clorinda Matto de Turner, and in particular her *Aves sin nido* (*Birds without a nest*, 1889), an emblematic novel that anticipates many of the topics articulated by the indigenista narrative during the twentieth century.

With different ideological approaches and degrees of commitment, Indigenous populations in these countries became indispensable agents of national debate. And yet, it is problematic to claim that the insertion of indigeneity in the national agenda of these three countries meant a form of social and political autonomy for the Indigenous society. Members of that society continued to experience the mediation of criollo mestizo segments who attempted to incorporate them paternalistically into modern national projects.[2]

INTRODUCTION

In this study I concentrate precisely on illuminating this dialectical formation embodied by Indigenous writers, intellectuals, and movements from the second half of the twentieth century onward. Despite the epistemological limitations with which the various indigenismos attempted to include Indigenous peoples of the region, I shed light on how the debates, concerns, and agendas inaugurated by indigenista writers opened—though not always intentionally—paths for the consolidation of Indigenous writers and intellectuals through what I call *indigenista decolonial cracks*, a concept that I anticipate is constituted as a form of symbolic fissure opened from within the hegemonic criollo mestizo structure through the critique of the oppressive trinomial modernity/coloniality/capitalism formulated by indigenista intellectuals.[3]

Turning back to the idea of a symbolic bridge connecting indigenista tradition with Indigenous writer activists, the one who walks through it most explicitly is the Quechua Aymara intellectual Fausto Reinaga (1906–1994) who, at an early stage of his intellectual development, took part in communist indigenista parties, dedicating the first part of his essayistic work to studying figures such as Franz Tamayo and Alcides Arguedas, two mestizo intellectuals and foundational figures in Bolivian indigenismo. Later, disappointed with the indigenista administrations of the 1950s, Reinaga went through a process of ethnic consciousness awareness, embracing his Quechua Aymara identity, and positioned himself as an Indigenous intellectual detached from indigenista schemes. This process modified his political subjectivity, after which he took advantage of some of the insurgent proposals formulated by indigenista intellectuals, mainly the Peruvians Luis E. Valcárcel and José Carlos Mariátegui, to design a dialectically Indigenous alternative in the form of indianismo, a decolonizing school of thought that would influence Bolivian Indigenous mobilizations toward the end of the twentieth century.

Over the last decades throughout Abya Yala, different Indigenous movements, intellectuals, writers, and artists have emerged who, like Reinaga, did not burn bridges with their indigenista intellectual past but, on the contrary, drew inspiration from them or learned from their mistakes to formulate their unique decolonizing agendas.[4] Thus, I consider those criticisms of indigenismo that are limited to pointing it out only as a modernizing, alienating, and homogenizing movement of Indigenous populations (Bonfil Batalla, "Del indigenismo"; Portocarrero, *La urgencia*; Vargas Llosa, *La utopía*) to be exhausted. Undoubtedly, indigenismos had dialectical and teleological limitations in their different approaches and attempts to represent Indigenous societies. These limitations (many of them explored in this book) in some cases serve as lessons for several of the Indigenous writer activists I analyze who capitalize on those limitations so as to design their own strategies of antagonization toward modern national projects. The confluence of some echoes of indigenista ideology and their resonance in the cultural and dialectical creation of Indigenous writer activists justifies the need for a study that shows how these connections significantly sustained the development of the sense of insurgency that nowadays inspires multiple Latin American Indigenous agendas, as well as how said agendas unfolded, mutated, and evolved.

ABOUT THE DECOLONIAL TURN

To work with the history of Indigenous peoples after republican emancipation from the European metropolis is to work with the history of coloniality—that is, with the perpetuation of colonial modalities in the social, economic, political, ecological, and cultural life of Latin American nation-states. In that sense, a decolonial approach (seen as a branch within the broad spectrum of the anti-colonial critical tradition in Latin America) is a crucial instrument in my analyses. The structure of domination, exploitation, and marginalization experienced by Indigenous societies since the establishment of American republics implies an undeniable historical link with the social model implemented during centuries of colonialism. In other words, the problems of Indigenous societies have followed the same historical path since the sixteenth century. Thus, as a theoretical instrument, coloniality refutes the existence of a postcoloniality, or at least the emancipatory extension of the term, insofar as political and economic independence from the European metropolis did not mean cultural and epistemological independence from the habitus imposed during the European occupation of American territory.[5]

In this sense, the discussion established by Aníbal Quijano ("Colonialidad y modernidad") when he points to the coloniality of power as an extension of the colonial modalities of intersubjective domination is a useful perspective not only because it goes beyond the critique of an asymmetrical economic model (capitalist modernity). Rather, this theoretical turn centralizes the modernity/rationality binomial as the dialectical pillar of Eurocentrism, the ideology on which continued colonial oppression is based in spheres that extend beyond materiality, but without leaving economic matters behind. For this reason, in this essay, the decolonial perspective is fundamental in the terms proposed by Quijano ("Coloniality") who, without abandoning his desire to historicize underdevelopment within a dependency theory perspective, sustains decoloniality as the theoretical and practical effort exerted by subalternized subjects to comprehensively escape the model of oppression to which the modernity/coloniality/capitalism trinomial submits them.

These continued colonial practices brought together in this theoretical framework will be responded to by the decoloniality cultivated by activists in their cultural production who antagonize the different forms of existing domination. And this is precisely another reason that a decolonial framework is particularly useful for a thorough exploration of the dialogue between indigenista discourse and Indigenous literature in recent decades, as it highlights how the decolonizing arguments are forged that unite or dissociate both traditions.

In the first stage, which we could attempt to date to the 1990s, decolonial critique pointed to social asymmetries embodied mainly in the economic and political spheres. The focus of the influential essay cowritten by Quijano and Immanuel Wallerstein, "Americanity as a Concept, or the Americas in the Modern World-System" (1992), is on historicizing the subalternity of civilizations of the Western Hemisphere sustained through the economic domination exercised by European empires (e.g., economic dependence and international division of labor). Both authors endeavor to affirm that the insertion of America as a factual and symbolic space—economically dominated through the exploitation of its inhabitants and the extraction of its resources—is itself the inauguration of the modern/capitalist system that, with variations, extends to the present day. Although I consider this interpretation to be quite accurate in historical and economic terms, I must point out that its encompassing impetus eclipses some areas where coloniality also exercised—and still exercises—dominance with colonial characteristics. Quijano ("Coloniality") complements this vision by including *race* as a defining variable of social classification in the peripheries of the world, something for which he takes up some of the ideas of a communist indigenista writer such as José Carlos Mariátegui.

Yet, the evolution traced by decolonial critics describes the versatility of decoloniality as an analytical tool with which I engage in this study. One of the first to expand the theoretical horizons of this corpus was María Lugones, who points out the limitations of the coloniality of power in the terms proposed by Quijano, insofar as it privileges variables such as race and the capital-wage relationship to explain the social asymmetries that constitute the modern/colonial system.[6] In response, Lugones questions whether Quijano's myopia to sexual dissidence implies a tacit biologization of gender and sex. Thus, Lugones posits the "modern/colonial gender system" ("Heterosexualism," 189–200) as an adequate platform of analysis to exhibit these same asymmetries in the spheres of gender and sexuality, where the latter are not only categories of classification as race and salary would be but also instruments of dehumanization of dominated subjects that are embodied in the imposition of heterosexuality and the marginalization of sexual dissidence. This contribution by Lugones not only complements the scope of the decolonial critique opened by Quijano—although not only by him, Enrique Dussel and Walter Mignolo should also be included in this genealogy—but also reaffirms her own theoretical project pointed out years earlier when, in asserting her vision of intersectionality, she argues in favor of the inseparability of race, class, and gender as the central variables of domination for the study of subalternized populations in Latin America ("The Inseparability"). She inaugurates a strong intersectional current in decolonial critique.

A further extension of this theoretical sphere refers to the relationship with nature and the reformulations caused in it by Western perspectives of the *self*. The contribution made by political ecology and the reevaluation of the relationship between humans and nature are worthy of note in a conversation that intersects decolonial philosophical critique with cultural anthropology. A good

INTRODUCTION

illustration of this intersection is the work of Arturo Escobar (*Designs for the Pluriverse, Territories of Difference*) who has been making efforts to theorize the refraction of worlds that emanates from the interaction between Indigenous peoples and nature.

This is a paradigm shift that draws much inspiration from the ideas promoted by French philosopher Bruno Latour (*Politics of Nature*) and the arising of Indigenous philosophies. The shift, which in this work I refer to as an *ontological turn*, transcends the initial debates, which were limited to pointing out and reinterpreting the human-nature relationship with an interest in dismantling the modern Western separatist binarism.[7] The decolonial perspective applied to political ecology allows us to explain teleologically the dialectic that runs through Indigenous ecologist literature as mobilities that, in their links with nonhuman entities, aspire to construct a decolonized space in epistemic and ontological terms within an Indigenous socio-natural framework. In this work I examine this framework in the literatures of Buen Vivir. Therefore, the contributions of Marisol de la Cadena ("Indigenous Cosmopolitics") and Mario Blaser ("Political Ontology") are particularly useful for the purpose of establishing this as an ontological debate in which Indigenous writers articulate decolonizing arguments.

INDIGENISTA DECOLONIAL CRACKS

My conceptual use of the term "crack" is inspired by the multiple definitions that scholar, activist, and theorist of decolonial thought Catherine E. Walsh formulated for it throughout her influential writing:

> To crack coloniality means, for me, to open fissures in this totalizing system or matrix of power, and to widen further the fissures that already exist in coloniality's supposedly impenetrable wall. The fissures and cracks are about the situated and embodied questions and work we need to do with ourselves and about the questions and work to be done with respect to social structures, institutions, and practices. . . . The fissures and cracks evidence actionality, agency, resistance, resurgence, and insurgent forms of subjectivity and struggle; they are the spaces of creation against and despite the

system, of hope against despair, of life living up against coloniality's present-day project of violence-dispossession-war-death all intertwined; of re-existence in times of de-existence. The fissures and cracks are not the solution but the possibility of otherwise, those present, emerging, and persistently taking form and hold. (Walsh, *Rising Up*, 7)

Walsh defines cracks as "fissures" (she sometimes uses both terms as synonyms), which manifest as "spaces of creation against and despite the system." Underlying this sense is a dual notion of spatiality: a factual one (visible in the decolonial praxis she claims) and a symbolic one (rooted in the agency and subjectivity of the crack-maker). What interests me is that she does not define "cracks" as an end but, rather, as a means to a sort of transformation, the tacit recognition of an intolerable present: coloniality and capitalist modernity. The crack opens a fissure in coloniality that can be capitalized upon to activate decoloniality ("The fissures and cracks are not the solution but the possibility of otherwise"). In her theorization, cracks are fissures through which there runs the hope of destabilizing the patterns of domination of the modernity/coloniality/capitalism trinomial. That is why she says: "The crack weakens the structure, weakens the wall; as such, could the crack not also weaken the structure of the wall that sustains the systemic intertwinement of coloniality, capitalism, racism, and heteropatriarchy? Are the cracks not suggestive of decolonial potential and possibility?" (53). The way I understand and employ her conceptual use of "crack" is that of a symbolic construct that creates a sense of insurgency.

A few years earlier, in an interesting text cowritten with Walter Mignolo, Walsh anticipated some of the details of how cracks manifest themselves in praxis. Reflecting on her own intellectual militancy, she notes that her personal vision of crack-making was "to provoke, encourage, construct, generate, and advance, with others, critical questionings, understandings, knowledges, and actionings; other ways of thinking and doing with" (Mignolo and Walsh, *On Decoloniality*, 83). The metaphor of the "crack" as an opening of spaces for political action—and the integral recognition of the subaltern, which antagonizes the inferiorizing colonial contexts in Abya Yala—entails an implicit sense of interiority with respect to the hegemonic structure. Although cracks can be the result of external input, they take place only within a dominant structure, because it is also from within that structure that the pillars of modernity/coloniality/capitalism can be fissured. This is precisely the case of the *decolonial cracks* opened by the indigenista intellectuals whom I explore in this book.

Most of the indigenista writers, artists, intellectuals, and politicians who emerged in the first half of the twentieth century in Latin America, regardless of their ideological commitments, were mesocratic criollo mestizo subjects who enjoyed certain structural privileges within their national projects. Not all of these indigenismos proposed a subversion of the dominant structure. However, the specific corpus of indigenista writers who are studied in Part I is distinguished by offering, from a plurality of approaches, frontal critiques against the model of subjugation implicit in the prevailing national projects of the Andes and Mesoamerica. As a whole, and despite their differences, these authors constitute a type of discourse that I define as *indigenista decolonial cracks* insofar as their arguments from within fissure the apparent solidity of the modern/colonial/capitalist model imposed by the criollo mestizo elites. By centralizing the marginalized subjects of these projects (Indigenous societies), they already destabilize the basic hierarchical pattern of their respective nationalities. But they also go further and construct a frontal critique of the asymmetries of the coloniality of power, something that some of them even tried to modify by working as officials within the state apparatus, finding it impossible to operate from more inner positions.

Thus, indigenista decolonial cracks run through indigenista texts as critical formulations, racial theories, telluric claims, pessimistic and degenerative readings, proposals for inclusion, and revolutionary claims that from different fronts and with different impetuses antagonize the dominant model of colonial features that inferiorized Indigenous societies. These ideas were not solutions but instead they generated possibilities. In that sense, in this book I prove that they were successful decolonial cracks insofar as several of them reappear in the creation process of a *decolonial Indigenous critique* (Part II). However, under the limited objective conditions of the first half of the twentieth century, the indigenista intellectuals who are analyzed here embodied a crucial contribution to Latin American critical thought (and to decolonial discourse) through provocative notions such as an Indigenous-rooted cosmic race, a destabilizing pessimism of the present—historicizing again formulations of peripherality, telluric *andinismo*, and a revolutionary *Indo-Marxism*. In their unique forms, all these tenets opened fissures in a structure of coloniality embodied in national projects that were celebrating their first hundred years of emancipation from the metropolis without having overcome—and in some cases having aggravated—the patterns of social injustice and subjugation of Indigenous societies.

In sum, indigenista decolonial cracks both open and *are* simultaneously symbolic spaces fostered by indigenista writers who express their discomfort with the social injustices articulated by their respective national projects. Hence, conceptually reading the crack in a broad and permeable way, but maintaining Walsh's decolonizing sense, in this study I examine how indigenista writers of the early twentieth century fostered the propagation of these symbolic spaces. They anticipated some of the conceptual frameworks in which decolonial thought developed or inaugurated dialectical trends on which Indigenous writer activists later capitalized.

In this way, I am in conversation not only with decolonial theoretical production but also with existing scholarship in the field of Indigenous literary studies in Latin America—and those who also dialogue with the indigenista tradition—such as the two volumes of *Recovering Lost Footprints* (2018) by Arturo Arias and *Indigenous Cosmolectics* (2018) by Gloria Chacón. In these works both scholars undertake deep philological explorations of a vibrant Indigenous narrative corpus from Mexico and Central America, and in doing so they dialogue in more than a few instances with concerns or arguments raised by the respective indigenista tradition of this region. In a similar vein, the arguments presented here interact with some recent publications that have revisited the indigenista literary tradition, such as *The Andes Imagined* (2009) by Jorge Coronado and *The Impure Imagination* (2006) by Joshua Lund in which the authors explore the alternative forms of modernity re-created by the imaginaries that run through a heterogeneous indigenista corpus in Latin America.

INTRODUCTION

GENEALOGY OF A DISCOURSE

In this work, the use of the term "genealogy" has very little to do with other definitions with which it circulates in the humanities.[8] Here the term refers to the most basic acceptance of the concept: the study of the ancestry and descent of a specific type of discourse in the literature of Latin America. In this book I historicize the emergence of a decolonial discourse through a sequence of texts that are linked progressively throughout the twentieth and early twenty-first centuries.

The book is divided into two parts, in which I explore two specific corpora and describe the periodicity with which the progressive emergence of an Indigenous decolonial discourse is constructed that dialogues with its indigenista decolonial forerunners. In the introductory chapter I describe the theoretical approach that accompanies this study and a base definition of the concept *indigenista decolonial cracks*. The exploration of cracks begins in chapter 1, where I introduce early indigenista discourse as a critique, reimagining and pathologizing the failures perpetrated by criollo national projects in Mexico and Bolivia, and examine the works of Manuel Gamio and Alcides Arguedas, respectively. Through a decolonial reinterpretation of the books *Forjando patria* (Forging fatherland, 1916) and *Pueblo enfermo* (Sick nation/people, 1909), I argue that both indigenista writers open decolonial cracks in their frontal critiques of criollo cultural politics and its failed attempts to incorporate Indigenous societies under homogenizing criteria.

In chapter 2 I move from merely blaming the criollo national project to re-historicizing and revalorizing indigeneity through utopian indigenista constructs such as those formulated by public intellectuals Mexican José Vasconcelos in *La raza cósmica* (*The Cosmic Race*, 1925) and Peruvian Luis E. Valcárcel in *Tempestad en los Andes* (Storm in the Andes, 1927). In their vibrant texts, packaged as racial theories (*raza cósmica*) or telluric invocations of an Inca revitalization (*andinismo*), these writers oppose the positivist readings that minimized the role of Indigenous cultures in the historicization of Latin America. These writers struggle against a one-dimensional sense of modernity by envisioning the emergence or a radical resurgence of an Indigenous-based new race. If

INTRODUCTION

the 1920s is a period in which the indigenista discourse begins to construct features of a political dialectic, taking literature as an instructive device, it is because these are years in which the writers come into contact with the consolidation of socialist structures in the Andes and in Mesoamerica.

Chapter 3 is dedicated to the scrutiny of the Indo-Marxism posited by the Peruvian writer and intellectual José Carlos Mariátegui and its connection with his countryman writer José María Arguedas. Navigating back and forth between the arguments elaborated in Mariátegui's canonical book *Siete ensayos de interpretación de la realidad peruana* (*Seven Interpretive Essays on Peruvian Reality*, 1928 [1952, trans. 1971]) and his controversy with the Communist International, Mariategui's Indo-Marxism ended up opening a pathway for the rethinking of revolutionary dialectics within a Marxist and decolonial perspective. This dialectical intersection was key for an indigenista and socialist writer such as José María Arguedas, whose public interventions in the form of speeches and monographic texts such as "El indigenismo en el Perú" (Indigenismo in Peru, 1965) and "No soy un aculturado" (I have not been acculturated, 1968) not only constitute an attempt to conceptualize indigenismo but also were one of the most clear iterations of the indigenista decolonial cracks as the intersection of decolonial thought and Marxist critique.[9]

Part II begins with a succinct and mainly informative historical passage titled "Interlude," revisiting two relevant historical moments that, although they could be considered "indigenista occurrences," triggered the almost immediate emergence of a decolonial Indigenous discourse between the 1930s and 1960s. I refer to the indigenista administration of former Mexican president Lázaro Cárdenas del Río (1934–1940), crowned with the First Inter-American Indigenista Congress of Pátzcuaro (Michoacán) in 1940, and the Bolivian Revolution of 1952, carried out by the MNR, a socially based Indigenous organization but led by a criollo mestizo elite of intellectuals who governed this country for more than a decade. I illustrate that—more for their failures than their achievements—these historical indigenista milestones generated the material conditions for the consolidation of an Indigenous decolonial critique that would emerge from the cracks anticipated in Part I.

INTRODUCTION

One of those who emerged most explicitly from this scenario was the Bolivian Quechua Aymara writer Fausto Reinaga. I devote chapter 4 to shedding light on how he created, in indianismo, one of the first deliberately decolonizing Indigenous dialectics. By analyzing his books *El indio y los escritores de América* (The Indian and the writers of America, 1968) and more in depth *La revolución india* (The Indian revolution, 1970), I show the dialectical empowerment of Indigenous decolonial thought embodied in the epistemological claims made by Reinaga, which had a direct influence on the Indigenous mobility that, years later, would lead to the triumph of Evo Morales as the first Indigenous president of Bolivia with a straightforwardly decolonizing agenda.

In Chapter 5, I trace how zapatista literature—subjected to the Mayan imperatives of the autonomy-seeking project of the zapatista communities and the Zapatista Army of National Liberation (EZLN) in Chiapas (Mexico)—created through the texts signed by Subcomandante Marcos (now Galeano), the particular form of an author constituted as a decolonizing Indigenous device. Thus, contrasting the limits of author theory and the conventional Eurocentric sense of authorship, I argue that Marcos-author personifies an Indigenous symbolic entity that, through texts such as *Relatos de El Viejo Antonio* (Tales of Old Antonio, 1998), *Cuentos para una soledad desvelada* (Tales for an unveiled solitude, 1998), and *Don Durito de la Lacandona* (1999), conveys an intellectually Indigenous content arguing against what decolonial theory has defined as the colonial matrix of power.

If, by the end of the twentieth century, Indigenous literature in Latin America already vocalizes its decolonial teleology, the emergence of Buen Vivir as an Indigenous eco-social paradigm adds complexity and sophistication to Indigenous decolonial discursive constructs, which in chapter 6 is illuminated in the poetry of Quechua writer activists Ch'aska Anka and Washington Córdova. By a theoretical combination of decolonial critique and political ecology, I close-read books of poetry such as Ninawaman's *Poesía en quechua. Chaskaschay* (Quechua poetry: Chaskaschay, 2004) and Washington Córdova's *Parawayraq chawpinpi / Entre la lluvia y el viento* (Between rain and wind, 2019) to argue that, each from their own worldview, they both interrogate political and ontological conventionalisms such as the society/nature binarism, and they posit alternative forms of political activism through the vibrant intervention of nonhuman *actants* under their respective cosmological commitments.[10]

In the Afterword, I bring together arguments presented in Part II to illuminate how the corpus of Indigenous texts studied here forges a singular Indigenous decolonial critique that resides in the Indigenous enunciation of a decolonizing dialectic that contests the imperatives of modernity/coloniality/capitalism through the refutation of these ideological and epistemological imperatives. In all these chapters as a whole I historicize the various paths of Latin American decolonial discourse. In a way, I illuminate decolonial critique as more than an alternative way of questioning the nation-state but, rather, as a propositional school of thought that expands the old insurgent axiom "destroy to build" by adding other modalities that range from expanding, overturning, questioning, fissuring, to flipping and bypassing, among other possible routes.

PART I

CHAPTER 1

Arguedas and Gamio

Sensing the Criollo Failure

In the first decade of the twentieth century, Bolivia was overwhelmed by what looked like an endless succession of failures. Loss of territory and of an outlet to the sea along with the rupture between the urban criollo societies and the rural Indigenous peoples created a discouraging panorama. Amid this atmosphere of disappointment, one of the founding authors of indigenismo in Latin America, Alcides Arguedas (1879–1946), would make his incursion into the Bolivian cultural and intellectual scene. Three novels portraying different realms of Bolivian social life preceded his essay *Pueblo enfermo* (Sick nation/people 1909), a book dedicated to examining the failures, anxieties, and limitations of Bolivia in its efforts to build a modern and sustainable national project. A pessimistic tone and a tendency to pathologize different components of Bolivian nature and society are the main features of this work. For Edmundo Paz Soldán, Arguedas exaggerates his passion for describing everything, as shown in a degenerative discourse in which he ends up pathologizing society, geography, and both public and private institutions (*Alcides*, 73–94). However, for Paz Soldán, Arguedas's major failure does not lie in the excessive pessimism with which he describes Bolivia but in his tendency to misrepresent the reality of the Indigenous people, mainly Aymaras, under the guise of a seemingly factual narrative.

Paz Soldán's observations could not be more accurate. Arguedas's work is dominated by a tendency to make hasty generalizations from which he deduces Bolivia's national illnesses. In the opening of the second chapter of *Pueblo*, for example, Arguedas analyzes the *indio del altiplano* (high plateau Indian) whom he accuses of not aspiring to progress and of lacking feelings and aesthetic perception. For the author, this "illness" is a result of the close connection between the Indigenous people of the altiplano and the arid nature that surrounds them (*Pueblo*, 44–47). That is to say, the sterility of geography affects the Indigenous spirit.

Although distinct from the Bolivian panorama, in Mexico the national situation was not any calmer when Manuel Gamio (1883–1960) made his literary foray with *Forjando patria* (Forging fatherland, 1916). The Mexican Revolution had entered a terminal stage after the escape of President Victoriano Huerta and the division of contending groups into the revolutionary factions led by Emiliano Zapata and Pancho Villa, on the one hand, and an officialist group led by Venustiano Carranza, on the other. With all these disputes as a backdrop, Gamio became a high-ranking official as the secretary of public education between 1913 and 1916, a period in which he was in charge of the inspection of archaeological monuments in the land surrounding the state of Mexico.

The revolutionary atmosphere and the discovery of new ruins in Teotihuacan, the most important pre-Hispanic city in Mesoamerica, had a significant impact on the formulation of Mexican nationalism as expressed by Gamio in his essay. Aware of the relevance of the Indigenous past in Mexico, in *Forjando* he proposes the incorporation of the different ethnic groups of his country into a single Mexican nation-state project. Inspired by the evolution of anthropology, Gamio points out that the task of the social sciences is to understand the needs, demands, and cultural particularities of different ethnic groups in order to avoid their isolation in small homelands ("pequeñas patrias") and to understand their resistance to assimilating the culture of "European origin" that prevails in the Mexican national project (*Forjando*, 37–41).[1]

The tone with which Gamio in this book refers to Indigenous groups is deliberately paternalistic. For Gamio, Indigenous peoples' inability to partake in Mexico's modern national life is due to the four centuries of humiliation bequeathed to them by the colonial and republican periods. In what could be interpreted as an obliquely self-critical position, this author blames the criollo elites who governed the country during its first century of political sovereignty for failing to integrate Indigenous peoples. According to Luis Villoro's reading of Gamio's work, the realms in which this disharmony between the criollo nation and the multiple Indigenous nations is most visible is in the content of the laws that rule in Mexico, since said legislation is not adapted to the worldview and needs of aboriginal life ("vida aborigen) (*Los grandes momentos*, 228–32). Indeed, Gamio makes a complex critique of the origins and content of the body of laws that shape the institutions of Mexican modern society.

My aim is to reevaluate Arguedas's and Gamio's essays so as to demonstrate how these two seminal figures of Latin American indigenista discourse, while displaying different programmatic intentions in their approaches to Indigenous peoples, exhibit critical components of the scenarios of modernity and coloniality with which the national projects in Bolivia and Mexico were structured. Introducing a decolonial perspective in the analysis of *Pueblo enfermo* and *Forjando patria*, I argue that both essays open up decolonial cracks in their respective assessments of the modern nation projects led by criollo elites, being at the same time books that were written in contexts of social and political instability. On the other hand, I will point out that, either because of a degenerative and pseudoscientific incompatibility among the Indigenous, mestizo, and criollo populations, as Arguedas argues for the Bolivian case, or because of a cultural ignorance of the Mexican multiethnic scenario that can be solved through anthropology, as Gamio points out, both authors seem to detect and collide with a kind of knowledge barrier that prevents the modernization of Indigenous communities. I argue that this inability to integrate/modernize lies in epistemological multiplicity, which will open the possibility of illuminating these essays as early visions that clarify what is nowadays defined as a *pluriversal* perspective applied to the analysis of the Indigenous societies.

SKEPTICISM AND COLONIALITY

Before navigating through the essays of Arguedas and Gamio, however, I suggest we revisit a historical event that paradoxically allows us to historicize the *-isms* that triggers the pessimistic and assimilationist postures of these authors: skepticism about the capacities of the Indigenous population. On the latter, it almost seems commonplace to recall the famous debate of Valladolid in the sixteenth century to discuss the skepticism toward the condition of Indigenous individuals. As is widely known, in the middle of that century, the *encomendero* and Dominican priest Bartolomé de las Casas polemicized with the Catholic priest Juan Ginés de Sepúlveda about the condition that should be attributed to Indigenous people in the recently invaded American colonies. The controversy took place at the Colegio de San Gregorio, one of the main renaissance schools of the Kingdom of Castile. At the core of this discussion, which was held within a theological paradigm, was the definition of whether Indigenous people had souls or not. For Ginés de Sepúlveda they did not and therefore were not part of humankind, thus enabling the colonizers to treat them as beasts of burden during the invasion process, since the suffering inflicted on them could not be considered a sin. For his part, Las Casas postulated that they did have souls, although they were in a state of barbarism because they had not been Christianized, to which he proposed evangelization as a solution. Ginés de Sepúlveda's approach was a barbarizing and beastly enslavement, while for Las Casas it was an evangelizing, benevolent, and paternalistic incorporation. The latter led Las Casas to be considered by some Hispanist and Latin Americanist critics as one of the pioneers of the indigenista discourse, since it was thanks to his position that the Nuevas Leyes de Indias (New Indian Laws) were modified to confer minimum rights, which would prevent the absolute extinction of Indigenous peoples in the viceroyalties of New Spain and Peru.[2]

For Nelson Maldonado-Torres, the theological discussion on the condition of Indigenous individuals as entities with or without souls created a tradition of racism and discrimination that he defines as "misanthropic skepticism," which, despite having emerged during the process of colonization, would be replicated in the former colonies once their political independence was achieved ("On the Coloniality," 243–49). Indeed, the condition of the humanity of Indigenous individuals would not only be questioned in the debate of Valladolid. The skepticism toward the cognitive, physical, and even spiritual capacities of the Indigenous peoples of the American continent would be reproduced in different ways under the projects of modern nationhood led by criollo mestizo elites from the nineteenth century onward. This is the baseline of the decolonial perspective—namely, that administrative emancipation did not entail epistemic emancipation from the colonial conditions of subalternization.

For his part, Walter Mignolo points out that the Valladolid polemic constitutes a historical event that traces the lines of demarcation of the "colonial difference" that underlies the knowledge produced and disseminated through the social sciences, strongly influenced by the epistemologies of the North Atlantic nations ("Geopolitics of Knowledge," 78–80). When Ginés de Sepúlveda was exposed to a social, racial, political, ecological, and theological structure that did not fit into his European knowledge framework—different languages, habitus, beliefs, and sociability between human and nonhuman entities—the Catholic priest found himself with an unknown panorama for his historical structure of thought. This is why literacy policies and the validation of sources of knowledge to a large extent are the playing fields in which the inferiorization of the subaltern is defined. As a result of this cognitive impact, the inhabitants of this new ecosystem sparked in Ginés de Sepúlveda an epistemological skepticism that would motivate the emergence of the components of colonial difference congregated in the arguments he presented in Valladolid.

Las Casas was on the other side of the controversy, but his arguments were not exempt from a discourse of otherness and superiority that corresponded with his lack of knowledge of the sociability to which he was exposed in the colonies. This fact coincides with the reading made by Ramón Grosfoguel, who points to Las Casas as the founder of a "racismo cultural" (a cultural racism) that would be employed by different Western imperialist projects from the sixteenth century onward ("El concepto," 89–92). Hence, the argument given by Las Casas would be an early version of the cultural relativism that would underlie the universalizing multiculturalist discourse—today I would call it a late-capitalist monoculturalism—that dominated in Western societies during the twentieth century and that in recent decades, with special emphasis on Latin America, became institutionalized through the cultural agenda of neoliberalist administrations.

Returning to the sixteenth century, however, for Las Casas humankind appears to be a single universal and global project, albeit contingent on different cultural systems. Under this conception, Las Casas asserts that Indigenous peoples are humans, even if they are in inferior strata because, due to their culture, they practice the wrong religion, language, and lifestyle. They are humans gone wrong, but they can be corrected. Let's remember that, before the colonizing projects began, the main patterns of discrimination within European civilization were social class and religion. From Las Casas's position, we can infer that, regardless of ethnicity, certain values unique to humanity (religion) and certain cultural codes (language) can be transmitted from one social group to another (which is what his evangelizing enterprise intended).[3] In other words, Las Casas apparently advocates a humanitarian process of cultural assimilation whose degree of violence we can identify today in the inherent acculturation involved in such a process.

In different ways, the Valladolid controversy has been interpreted as an event in which colonial difference emerges, underpinned by what Maldonado-Torres calls misanthropic skepticism, a kind of skepticism that is forged as a cognitive gap between the knowledge framework of the colonizers and that of the colonized—one of the reasons that epistemologies, as diverse sources of knowledge, would later become a crucial part of the Indigenous decolonizing agenda. This is how Las Casas constructs an assimilationist discourse in which Indigenous peoples must be incorporated into the Spaniards' imperialist project under the episteme of evangelization, whereas Ginés de Sepúlveda rejects the possibility of such inclusion and reduces Indigenous subjects phenomenologically and ontologically to the category of *animal*, a posture that resembles what would later become more blatant and violent forms of racism.

When confronted with the unknown, colonizers adopted assimilationist patterns to incorporate *others* within the institutions and knowledge frameworks of what is considered a core culture. However, sometimes these formulas deliberately postulated the exclusion of Indigenous people for phenotypical reasons on the basis of pseudoscientific discourses. Either way, these approaches are inexorably elaborated from a monocultural perspective. Likewise, this skepticism highlights the knowledge structures of those groups that assume racial, cultural, and, ultimately, epistemological superiority. The inferiorizing ignorance toward Indigenous peoples will, at the beginning of the twentieth century, explicitly or tacitly agitate indigenista arguments, such as those formulated by Arguedas and Gamio, when confronted with the multiethnicity of Mexico and Bolivia—that is, in the face of the irrefutable reality of an imperfect process of modernization that promotes an impossible homogenization.

ARGUEDAS'S PESSIMISTIC INDIGENISMO

I have suggested that Alcides Arguedas's literature is dominated by hasty generalizations and pessimism. In *Pueblo enfermo* there is no stratum of society, whether racial or socioeconomic, that presents a positive outlook for Bolivia, a country that seems condemned to stagnation or involution. Arguedas affirms that the rural Aymara is ignorant, degraded, miserable ("ignorante, degradado, miserable") (55), but that, when he comes into contact with the white man—that is, with his oppressors—he becomes spiteful, selfish, cruel, vindictive and mistrustful ("rencoroso, egoísta, cruel, vengativo y desconfiado") (47). Likewise, about white people (that is, criollos), he says, in spite of their intelligence, they are lazy, parsimonious, lacking in willpower, and addicted to "empleomanía" (73).[4] He states that the cholo (urbanized Indian), "is active, yet inclined to rapacity; brave, yet lazy; timid, yet haughty" ("es activo, aunque inclinado á la rapiña; valiente, pero holgazán; tímido, a la vez altanero") while the mestizo is described as generous, intelligent, and delicate ("generoso, inteligente y delicado") but fractious, scathing, envious, aggressive, and extremely sensitive ("díscolo, mordaz, envidioso, agresivo y susceptible en extremo") (70).

Arguedas's degenerative discourse is permeated by a racist ideology that attributes certain genotypically rooted intelligence to criollos and mestizos, although he specifies that the latter will not be able to progress as long as they are in contact with the Indigenous strata, who are addicted to the social immobility imposed by the Andean landscape. Unlike other forms of racism such as social Darwinism, which postulates evolutionism on the basis of genetic racial superiority, or the optimistic eugenics that will later appear in Vasconcelos, in the 1910s Arguedas does not see an evolutionary horizon in any part of the heterogeneous Bolivian society.[5] His explanation focuses first on the landscape, which he makes the first step in a sequence of indiscernible elements that constitute the Indigenous Bolivian matter. Speaking about the altiplano, in particular, he points out that the plateau gives the sensation of infinity, of the enormous, of the immeasurable ("la llanura da la sensación del infinito, de lo enorme, de lo inconmensurable") (47). The *llanura*, the habitat of the Aymara societies, becomes for Arguedas a motionless and incomprehensible space that spreads its paralysis to the spirit and psychology of the Indigenous people. Naturalizing Indigenous groups and melting them together with their landscape becomes for Arguedas a rhetorical modality of barbarization, akin to the one used decades earlier by the Argentine writer and politician Domingo Faustino Sarmiento to refer to the native populations of the pampa.

For Paz Soldán (*Alcides*, 84), Arguedas's entire essay is dedicated to enumerating the cholo deviations and their impact on the historical failure of the nation. In the same sense, for Javier Sanjinés C. (*Embers*, 150–51), in Arguedas the "metaphor of disease" (*Pueblo*, 136) ends up being the best formula to explain the dysfunctionality of Bolivian society in its relationship with national geography. Meanwhile, Michael Aronna accuses Arguedas of ignoring the impact international policies and economies had in Bolivia in his eagerness to "biologize national ills" (141). However, it is necessary to note that Arguedas emphatically blames criollos for national failure. His analysis of the *pongueaje* system, in which Indigenous people work for free for landowners who employ them abusively in any type of labor, stresses the oppression that the criollos exerted on the Indigenous population: "When a patron has two or more pongos, he keeps one and leases the rest, simply as if they were horses or dogs, with the small difference that dog and horse are housed in a wooden kennel or in a horse stall and both are fed; the pongo is given the vestibule to sleep in and is fed on scraps."[6]

It is of utmost importance to note that Arguedas presents the oppression, racism, and dehumanization of the Indigenous peoples with a denunciatory quality. In spite of the racism that permeates his discourse, he is aware of the operative structure that creates the conditions of social stagnation in which the Indigenous society is immersed. Decolonially speaking, the Indigenous peoples of Bolivia are burdened with a structure of domination and exploitation inherited from the colonial system that regulates the intersubjective relations between the different social strata (Quijano, "Colonialidad del poder" [2014], 322–25). This rationale defines and poisons the power relations between criollos, mestizos, and Indigenous people, no matter whether they live in rural or urban areas. Furthermore, Indigenous people are categorized as ontologically inferior with respect to criollo patrons, who are entirely placed in the category *humankind*, something that is not done with the Indigenous *pongos*, whose living conditions are worse than those of the livestock. According to the perspective of the racial scheme studied by Grosfoguel, Indigenous people subjected to the pongueaje system live in a "zone of nonbeing" ("El concepto," 94) since in a binary pattern of superiority/inferiority, the *pongo* belongs to the latter, which is below the line of the "human."

Deprived of any humanity, the *pongo* of a Bolivia heading toward its first century of republican life embodies the ontological devaluation that Sepúlveda claimed with respect to the Indigenous population. "But the Indian can not only be leased but also has the obligation to transport the crops at his own expense and risk, from the farm to the patron's urban residence. The transfer is made on the back of a donkey or llama, and 100 or 150 kilometers are covered in this way. Often the part of the harvest that he is responsible for transporting exceeds his means of locomotion."[7] Arguedas stresses their enslaved condition by detailing the dynamics that construct the pongueaje system. Indigenous people epitomized the victims in the social framework sketched by Arguedas, as they are trapped in an exploitative system of labor and barbarizing racism that transforms them into beasts of burden. At this point it is worth asking: Who is guilty of making the Indigenous population "ignorante, degradado y miserable"?

It is clear that the system of exploitation imposed and reproduced by criollo elites, ingrained in the Andes since the colonial administration, debases Indigenous people to the point of stripping them of their humanity—that is, from their ontological values. Arguedas does not blame Indigenous populations for the national failures. Rather, he accuses the oppression inflicted on them by the heirs of the European culture: criollos. In his critique, the criollo national project is a construct that appears to be postcolonial, but to which the prefix "post-" does not do justice, since it reproduces and makes use of the social imbalances forged under the colonial administration of the viceregal state.

Elaborating on this passage from *Pueblo*, Arguedas also questions the fact that, having already built a railroad system, criollos believe that railroads only serve to bring in commodities, carry and bring back and forth persons and packages ("creen que el ferrocarril sólo sirve para introducir mercaderías, llevar y traer personas y bultos") (62), tacitly excluding Indigenous people from the category of *person* who, unable to use trains as a means of transporting crops, move in hazardous and humiliating caravans that force them to cross the implacable Andean geography. Arguedas condemns the fact that criollo elites do not allow Indigenous people to optimize the transportation of crops by using trains, to which he concludes with an eloquent irony: "Of course! They must be a superior race for a reason!" ("¡Claro! ¡Para algo ha de ser raza superior!") (62). This specific topic is later revisited in his novel *Raza de bronce* (Bronze race/breed, 1919), where the tragedies that trigger the main plot occur when a group of Indigenous characters are forced to move across a vast and dangerous extension of land in the Andean altiplano, in the surroundings of Lake Titikaka. From a distant reading, it is possible to infer that, in this work of fiction, Arguedas is portraying in detail how criollos' public policies and the dehumanizing rationale articulated by them violently subdue Indigenous society to a state of barbarism or premodernity.

Despite the fact that the ideological content of his writings does not valorize Indigenous cultures, Arguedas blames the ongoing process of dehumanization on those who followed in the footsteps of a cultural model and ontological domination akin to the one posited by Sepúlveda—that is, Westernized criollo elites. Although it might be correct to assert that the rural geography of the Andean altiplano does not fit with European-based notions of metropolitan modernity, ultimately, it is the fault of criollo groups for not having created the objective conditions for appropriate urbanization of the Indigenous populations, resulting only in an alienated social subject that Arguedas identifies in the cholo, a character he describes as "active, yet inclined to rapacity" ("activo, aunque inclinado á la rapiña")." In short, it is only criollos who benefited from the pongueaje system—that is, from a structure of barbarization of the Indigenous people, a structure that gave criollos economic benefits, a structure with colonial roots. It is graspable that, for Arguedas, in spite of the racist arguments with which he socially constrains Indigenous societies, it is criollos, heirs of the European social privileges, who are the primary culprits of the Bolivian national failure. The criollo failure is evident not only in the loss of territories in the wars with Chile and Brazil but also in the inability to incorporate Indigenous people into the modern national project that criollos were trying to build in urban spaces. It is not only Arguedas's monographic writing that discloses these instances—though it is what is of most interest in this essay—but also his fictional works, which represent similar interrogations.

Among Arguedas's most relevant literary pieces is *Vida criolla* (Criollo life, 1905), which together with *Raza de bronce* (1919) are the second and third entries, respectively, in a trilogy of novels that began with *Watawara* (Month-to-month, 1904). In *Vida criolla*, with the subtitle *novela de la ciudad* (novel of the city), Arguedas presents an indigenista story heavily influenced by the costumbrista style of the nineteenth century, which emphasizes the racial and cultural melting pot taking place in the urban setting of La Paz, portrayed through the life of the journalist Carlos Ramírez, protagonist of the plot. Two aspects of this novel are of interest to this study. On the one hand, the portrait of the Bolivian criollo population is that of a social class lacking in moral virtues, where corruption has contaminated institutional political interactions and romantic relationships in metropolitan settings.

On the other hand, there is the chaotic circulation of subalternized racial groups in urban locations, portrayed as uncomfortable places for the rural migrant population. In these locations, cholos and Indigenous people are portrayed as minor subjects, barely functional for the survival of the corrupt social project led by criollos:

> Down the street, in disorder, came groups of scruffy kids preceding the troupes of Indigenous dancers who advanced slowly blowing on their sad panpipes. The Indians were dressed in their best clothes of gala and the leaders of the groups were making tremble in their hands the flags taken out to show off in the solemn days of the parish feast of any other unforgettable event. Behind the

troupes, several cholos led at a distance of a few meters, two strips of white fabric unfolded across the width of the street and on which, in black letters, the supporters had painted two inscriptions: LONG LIVE THE EGREGIOUS CITIZEN DON COSME ENDARA!!![8]

In this scene, Indigenous people and cholos follow, in a disorderly fashion, an electoral parade in support of Cosme Endara, a criollo character and presidential candidate who projects a haughty superiority ("altiva superioridad," 71) in the face of racialized social classes and, in addition, engages in a set of immoral activities that Arguedas emphasizes throughout the novel. Surrounding Cosme Endara, the epitome of criollo corruption, Indigenous people and cholos move chaotically amid "astrosos chiquillos" (untidy kids), playing their "zampoñas tristes" (sad pan flutes) or carrying "bandas de tela" (fabric strips) with cynical political messages in support of a criollo politician (71). In the social portrait created by Arguedas, Indigenous people and cholos are considered less than human, entities whose subjectivity is erased and who are morphed into useful devices for the model that dominates them. At best, they are functional objects for a corrupt and immoral criollo state project that can only lead to failure. The novel anticipates some topics we have already examined in *Pueblo*: the unfitness of Indigenous people and cholos, as individuals, in the modernizing national project, in this specific case applied to the urban settings, as well as the accountability of the criollo class for this failure, primarily because of what this work illustrates as an ongoing colonial structure of domination whose shortcomings Arguedas congregates in corruption and immorality.

Not long before publishing *Pueblo*, in *Vida criolla* Arguedas anticipated the grounds on which his pessimistic indigenismo is built. Without its being his main intention, the pessimism transmitted in his works seems to open a symbolic crack in the criollo sociopolitical structure. He certainly is not a prescriptive intellectual, but in his critique of the Bolivian heterogeneity it is impossible not to identify a hierarchy of responsibilities unfolded in the idea of failure. Thus, Arguedas's indigenista discourse is paradoxically decolonial, as it points to the fault of the Westernized elites for Bolivian malfunction. The colonial authority bequeathed by criollo sectors forges the precarious power structure that keeps Bolivia and its Indigenous population subjected to social backwardness. In his interpretation, failure is presented as a form of conscious omission in which criollos are morally accountable not for failing to rescue Indigenous societies but, conversely, for having plunged them into a form of social anomie through colonial systems of oppression such as pongueaje. And yet, ironically, Arguedas acknowledges Bolivia as a predominantly Indigenous nation and, therefore, assumes that a social project without a high component of indigeneity is unattainable. Despite his pessimism and racism, he centralizes Indigenous individuals as the Bolivian national subject who gives historical significance and tradition to the modernizing project.

At this point, it is worth mentioning the analysis of the Kichwa scholar Armando Muyolema who intensely questions all aspects of indigenismo, which he defines as a program of incorporation and assimilation of the "Indian" into the cleared path of the national culture created by the criollo mestizo or as a "movement in favor of the Indian" ("una programa de incorporación y asimilación del 'indio' al desbrozado camino de la cultura nacional creada por el criollo mestizo o como 'movimiento a favor del indio'") ("América Latina," 248). Paradoxically, and partially coinciding with the negative outlook provided by Muyolema, Arguedas inaugurates a different indigenista line that—by overemphasizing the failure and anti-progressive status of Bolivian society (a typical stance of pessimistic philosophical tradition)[9]—constructs a singular pessimistic indigenismo that invokes neither the assimilation nor the whitening of Indigenous societies. Throughout his fictional literature, but more explicitly in his essays, Arguedas's indigenismo accepts the malfunction of Bolivian modernization, a tenet that years later in different moments of this country's history will be revisited to foster Indigenous insurgencies. For example, statements like this one would reemerge in the context of the indigenista demands that inspired the nationalist revolution of 1952, the emergence of the indianista discourse in the 1970s, and most notably, in the course of the decolonial activism led by Evo Morales at the start of the twenty-first century.

GAMIO AND THE CHALLENGE OF DIVERSITY

Like Arguedas, Manuel Gamio targets criollos for their inability to incorporate Indigenous people into the national project. In *Forjando patria* (1916), he points to the lack of knowledge about the cultural particularities of the various Indigenous ethnic groups as the major barrier to the construction of a solid Mexican nationalism. In his analysis of the isolation of the Otomi ethnolinguistic communities (one of the largest Indigenous nations in the Mexican highlands), for example, Gamio suggests implementing "scientific observations" in order to gather information on their physical and intellectual needs so that public institutions can supply them with services adapted to their demands (27). Skepticism in Gamio is expressed neither as misanthropy nor as scientific racism but as a skepticism about the suitability of Otomi culture to adapt to modernity. He considers changing Otomi culture in order to modernize their indigeneity, in a manner somewhat similar to that expressed by Las Casas in his doubts about the religious and social practices of Indigenous people. At this stage of his indigenista thought, Gamio proposes modernizing them culturally, as Las Casas once advocated evangelizing them.

Heavily influenced by the evolution of anthropology as a scientific field, specifically by the relativistic methods of Franz Boas, Gamio dissolves the category of *race* as a superiority-defining differential variable. He states that the Indian has equal aptitudes for progress as the white; he is neither superior nor inferior to him ("el indio tiene iguales aptitudes para el progreso que el blanco; no es ni superior ni inferior a él") (38). The reason for the ineptitude of Indigenous people does not have racial or phenotypical explanations but cultural ones. If Indigenous people do not assimilate to European culture, it is only because they have experienced four centuries of oppression and exclusion by purveyors of Eurocentric modalities.

Gamio did not adopt the racist assumptions that circulated in America in those years. According to Ignacio M. Sánchez-Prado, he did not examine Mexico's problems through the dichotomous civilization/barbarism lens, but through the need to use these historical problems in the forging of nationality ("sino en la necesidad de utilizar estas problemáticas históricas en la forja de la nacionalidad") (*Intermitencias*, 386). For his part, Claudio Lomnitz points out that Gamio "developed an indigenismo that dignified Mexican Indian features and blood, thereby paving the way for the mestizo to emerge as the protagonist of national history" (*Deep Mexico*, 54). For Sánchez-Prado and Lomnitz, Gamio was a pioneer of the indigenista discourse for which, with opposing and more radical arguments, José Vasconcelos would later advocate in *La raza cósmica*.[10]

Unlike Arguedas, Gamio is highly prescriptive in his approaches. About *Forjando*, Casey Walsh ("Eugenic Acculturation") points out that it is a manifesto written in the heat of the Mexican Revolution and through which Gamio seeks to convince readers of the racial, cultural, and socioeconomic integration of the country, whereby anthropology played a crucial role in the generation of knowledge about the Indigenous population. For David S. Dalton, the book is also a plea in favor of mestizaje, since "Indigenous Mexico was in dire need of a 'redemption' that would come as it adopted the mixed-race cultural norms of a 'proper' diet, education, and the subsequent eradication of poverty" (*Mestizo Modernity*, 13). Both readings coincide in identifying cultural assimilation as one of the instruments that would facilitate the forging of a postrevolutionary Mexican national project in which Indigenous peoples would inevitably play a preponderant role.

To pave the way for cultural assimilation, Indigenous people need to be understood by the criollos and mestizos who marginalized them so much. Such understanding can only be reached through the use/work of the social sciences. The Mesoamerican native people, then, are humans—not inert, cultureless objects but active subjects with an incorrect culture, which also converts them into subjects of study. Under the paradigm categorization of *strata of humanity* designed by Osamu Nishitani, Gamio positions himself at the top of a knowledge regime by practicing anthropology, assuming the status of civilized subject (Nishitani, "Anthropos," 259–62), and thus assigning himself the status of a "modern Mexican citizen."[11] In the Valladolid controversy, Gamio would be standing on the side of Las Casas advocating with the benevolence of an ethnographer the need to incorporate Indigenous peoples into a project of modernity unrelated to their own historical circumstances.

The backdrop as Gamio formulates this proposal is a revolutionary panorama in which different ethnic groups claim their political autonomy from the Mexican state that had excluded them for a century. His greatest fear is the fragmentation of Mexico into multiple small homelands epitomized by each ethnicity—that is, he fears a Mexican balkanization. For Gamio, it is imperative to anthropologically systematize Indigenous knowledge for the use and benefit of a modern nationalism driven by the Mexican nation-state. For him, politicians must pay attention to anthropologists. Besides this, he is aware that a modern national project is a social recipe imported from Europe. Its creators were European cultural heirs who never tried to understand the ethnic plurality of Mesoamerica, and in this unfamiliarity lies the failure of Mexican nationalism. "Contemporary European civilization has not been able to infiltrate our Indigenous population for two main reasons: first, because of the natural resistance that this population opposes to the change of culture; second, because we do not know the reasons for this resistance, we do not know how the Indian thinks, we ignore his true aspirations, we prejudge him with our criteria, when we should permeate ourselves with his criteria in order to understand him and make him understand us."[12]

As a social scientist, Gamio notes an Indigenous resistance to assimilation to the European culture indexed in Mexican nationalism and unfolded within a criollo sociopolitical endeavor. He ascribes this resistance to criollos' lack of awareness of the internal demands of the Indigenous population. He, therefore, postulates a paternalistic solution: to approach Indigenous cultures in order to get to know them, understand, and persuade them to join the Mexican nation-state—that is, to engage them in a seemingly friendly process of modernization. To achieve this, he emphasizes, along with other things, the need to disseminate Spanish as a lingua franca among criollos, mestizos, and Indigenous people. However, he also defends embracing the dialectal variants of this language, which are reflected in Mexican regionalist literature: "we must demand that no attempt be put in the way . . . to regional literature, the cultivation of Spanish as it is naturally spoken and written in each region of the country and not as a few people want it to be spoken and written in all of them" ("debemos exigir que no se intente poner trabas [. . .] a la literatura regional, al cultivo del español como naturalmente se habla y se escribe en cada región del país y no como unos pocos quieren que se hable y escriba en todas ellas") (*Forjando*, 195). This part of his essay is interesting as this quote corresponds with the section dedicated to the national language, in which Gamio foreshadows his main argument about literature and the role of the Indigenous tradition.

In the following section of *Forjando*, entitled "Literatura nacional" (National literature), Gamio challenges the arguments of those claiming that the Mexican literary tradition begins with the alphabetic and Castilian texts produced during the colonial period. For him, these texts only represent the literary tradition of a reduced mesocratic, metropolitan, and lettered elite—that is, a *lettered city* that is not a representative sample of the vast Mexican cultural tradition. Instead, he suggests granting legitimate national character ("legítimo carácter nacional") to the Mayan and Aztec literary tradition, recommending that his readers explore the work of the pre-Hispanic Indigenous poet and intellectual Netzahualcoyotl. Being a promoter of the social sciences as an instrument of nation-building processes, Gamio criticizes philologists who have not paid enough attention to Indigenous literary tradition: "The majority that in our present population is represented by the Indigenous race, suggests the temptation to confer to its literature nationalist filiation. Actually, a limited number of people are aware of the amazing number of relations, songs, poems . . . that our Indigenous people cherished, but, precisely, for being almost ignored by those who do not belong to the Indigenous race or are not investigators of our Indigenous populations, it cannot be called national literature."[13]

Although his main argument is based on the diffusion of Spanish as a lingua franca, Gamio asserts that Mexico will achieve a solid national literature when it incorporates the Indigenous literary tradition in all its formal diversity. For him, this is a pending task of the Mexican academy. Once the incorporation of Indigenous literary production has been achieved, it will be possible to discuss national literature—albeit, of course, in Spanish—since in this way it "will present diverse origins but a single body of exposition" ("presentará diversos orígenes pero un solo cuerpo de exposición") (*Forjando*, 205).

The integrationist telos that he centralizes in the instrumentalization of a lingua franca is constantly reiterated in his discourse, although not necessarily as a monocultural homogeneity. The development of Mesoamerican literature ended up proving Gamio somewhat right. Decades after his death, toward the end of the twentieth century, there emerged in this area a robust cohort of Indigenous writers and activists such as Irma Pineda, Natalia Paz Toledo, Nefi Fernández Acosta, among others, who assumed the editorial strategy of either writing their works in Spanish or self-translating them into bilingual publications to facilitate their circulation among non-Indigenous audiences. What I cannot say about these authors is that, as a body, they all aspired to a Mexican literary nationalism. On the contrary, they may reflect an impulse of intellectual and cultural sovereignty from and for their respective Indigenous nationalities.[14]

Shortly after his death, the reception of Gamio's work in the 1960s and 1970s generated some resistance to his vision of Indigenous people, especially from scholars of critical anthropology. For example, Guillermo Bonfil Batalla, one of the most prominent Mexican anthropologists during the second half of the twentieth century, questioned Gamio's indigenista agenda because it consisted of the de-indianization of Indigenous communities. "The ideal of the redemption of the Indian is translated, as in Gamio, into the negation of the Indian. The goal of indigenism, brutally put, is to achieve the disappearance of the Indian" ("El ideal de la redención del indio se traduce, como en Gamio, en la negación del indio. La meta del indigenismo, dicho brutalmente, consiste en lograr la desaparición del indio") ("Del indigenismo," 144). While apparently aware of how essentializing his critique is, Bonfil Batalla is probably right if we pay attention to one part of Gamio's approach: the urgency to include the Indigenous population in the Mexican national culture at all costs—an urgency that Gamio expresses in that vein only in *Forjando*, a book permeated with the warlike atmosphere of the Mexican Revolution.

However, over time, Gamio slightly readjusts his ideals, without displacing Indigenous societies from the axis of his intellectual concerns. Toward the end of his life, while serving as director of the Instituto Nacional Indigenista (INI), Gamio said: "Indigenous art should never be systematically transformed and modified [by Westerners] with regard to its production by Indigenous people, because it would lose the high values which distinguish it" ("el arte indígena nunca debe ser sistemáticamente transformado y modificado [por los occidentales] en lo que se refiere a su producción por los indígenas, porque perdería los altos valores que lo distinguen") (Gamio, *Arqueología*, 115). Remarkably, in the final stage of his career, after having held public office and having led archaeological expeditions, Gamio seems to reconceptualize his understanding of indigeneity with a notion that yearns for purity. Far from his old claim to modernize and incorporate Indigenous societies into a monocultural nationalism, including their literary traditions under the umbrella of a common language, in his intellectual maturity Gamio pleads for the least possible alteration of Indigenous cultural authenticity. In that authenticity, which seems to allude to a formal and aesthetic sovereignty, lies its significance ("los altos valores que lo distinguen").

Am I trying to say with this that Gamio's late arguments in the fields of art and literature presented a seminal demand for Indigenous autonomy? Not at all. Gamio always advocated for a modern Mexican national unity, but certainly, the monocultural character of his claims was tempered, at least with respect to those he presented in *Forjando*. Gamio's sense of homogeneity, after all, is that of a cracked homogeneity, where the symbolic interstitial spaces—some kind of fissures—must be occupied by the emergence of the pure Indigenous cultures that constitute the bedrock of what he considered proper Mexican nationalism. Quite contrary to Bonfil Batalla's interpretation, it is difficult to assume that Gamio's indigenismo (if there was only one) proposes the negation or de-indianization of Indigenous societies.

In *Forjando*, Gamio points to cultural gaps between different ethnic groups that impede the homogenization of Mexico into a single nation. A few years after, he would radicalize his pro-Indigenous views by pointing out, during a speech given as director of INI, that Indigenous cultures are the ethical and aesthetic basis of every American national project (*Consideraciones*, 8).[15] As the history of the Indigenous movements in Mesoamerica has shown, the gaps highlighted by Gamio at the dawn of the twentieth century remained unresolved in following decades. Despite the indigenista policies assumed by postrevolutionary Mexico, inequalities, racism, and marginalization would continue and would motivate a number of Indigenous uprisings all around the country over the course of a century, among them the zapatista uprising of Chiapas.

In his approach to the Indigenous population, Gamio is strongly constrained by a Eurocentric matrix of knowledge, despite being aware and partially critical of it. The European nature of Mexican legislation will be the ground on which Gamio discovers the limits of Eurocentrism as a paradigm for regulating the social life of Indigenous peoples. For Quijano, Eurocentrism is not only a perspective of knowledge globalized by Western Europe through its colonies. It is also the ideology that anchors and systematizes the modern/colonial structure that inferiorizes or primitivizes non-European social habits ("Coloniality," 549–53). Despite Gamio's benevolence when speaking of Indigenous cultures and their relevance in the creation of Mexican nationalism, this anthropologist rationalizes from a regime of knowledge whereby the historical development of the Indigenous population does not make sense if it is not integrated into a modern project. He tacitly situates Indigenous culture as a premodern, outdated, or even primitive form of society. Indigenous Mexicans must join the linear and progressive history as constructed by European social projects. Gamio assumes that the Mexican nation-state is already a part of this history—a telling fact of the influence of historicism on his arguments.

A PROTO-PLURIVERSALITY?

Notwithstanding the different tonalities in their approaches to Indigenous cultures, Arguedas and Gamio are advocates for the consolidation of modern and liberal nationalisms. Both authors denounce the fact that the system of oppression imposed by the holders of power—that is, criollos—has suppressed any chance for social mobility or incorporation of Indigenous peoples into modernity. Decolonial critics have argued that what these authors are denouncing, either directly or figuratively, are the denigratory dynamics suffered by Indigenous societies dating from the viceregal period. In other words, both writers address one of the key axes of what Quijano calls the "coloniality of power," which, through social classification and configuration of institutions, makes the intercultural development of Bolivia and Mexico impossible and frustrates indigenistas' aspirations to construct modern nations in harmony with Indigenous societies.

However, neither author suggests the need for an Indigenous uprising, either because they do not consider Indigenous groups suitable for such a thing or because they do not find it necessary. After all, they both had experienced warlike periods in their respective countries, so it would be natural to presume that neither would see an armed uprising as a plausible solution. Similarly, the discourse of mestizaje does not appear in their essays from a harmonious or coincidental point of view, unlike what was postulated by other indigenista authors such as José Vasconcelos or José Carlos Mariátegui. For Arguedas, mestizaje would only congregate the negative aspects of the contributing races; Gamio disregards mestizaje in racial or phenotypical terms and identifies potential outlets in cultural mestizaje—that is, in the adoption of social codes and cultural signs between one group and another. Gamio's programmatic framework discards racial supremacism in favor of an integrationism, albeit one that was not entirely free of basic notions of social and racial engineering.

Nonetheless, a common key concept is graspable in their essays, and that is *knowledge*. For these intellectuals, Indigenous individuals compose a social entity that has not been entirely decoded by ruling criollo mestizo elites. Arguedas denounces the fact that the humanity of Aymaras has not been fully recognized, while he himself describes the *indio del altiplano* as an enigmatic subject because of their close relationship with the immeasurable geography of the Andes and their apparent unsuitability to urban settings. On the other hand, Gamio asserts that criollos are unfamiliar with the specificities of the Mesoamerican multiethnic panorama, and although he never claims to have succeeded in understanding Indigenous groups in an epistemological sense, he at least posits the social sciences as the instrument to bridge that gap and assist politicians in a process of assimilation that, somehow, could also be interpreted as a method of acculturation—at least in the initial stage of his approach, what I would call an early Gamio.

Pueblo enfermo and *Forjando patria* point to the scorn caused by criollos' ignorance about Indigenous societies as the principal obstacle to their incorporation into modern nationalisms. From a decolonial perspective, in this study I argue that the failure observed by Gamio and Arguedas—that is, the inability of criollos and mestizos to understand the Indigenous societies of their countries—lies in the fact that their analyses are framed in a Eurocentric locus that defines their knowledge frameworks and their geohistorical coordinates. For both indigenista authors, the history of their societies is imagined as a linear and progressive course. By default, this path should lead Bolivia and Mexico to live under a nation-state project that, despite their cultural diversity, standardizes the daily life of their population: all governed by the same institutions, speaking the same language, and being ruled by common law—a dream republic for criollos. The historic trajectory of Indigenous social groups per se does not seem to offer these writers a perspective for modernizing development.

For Arguedas and Gamio, modernity is not possible without Indigenous people, but given the configuration of Bolivian and Mexican populations as well as their geographies and multiethnic cultural singularities, the dream of a modern nation is not possible without their racial and cultural integration. In view of these problematic crossroads, Arguedas adopts a pessimistic approach and affirms that Bolivia will never be modern, attributing the national failure mainly to the social asymmetries provoked by the criollo ruling class. For his part, Gamio argues that Mexico can achieve this goal, but only to the extent that criollo politicians learn the cultural singularities and social signs of the various Mexican ethnic groups and integrate them into their project of modernity. Thus, Gamio proposes that criollos assimilate Indigenous peoples into the national social apparatus, not necessarily altering their Indigenous cultural roots, which, as has been seen, is an idea that he makes clearer when he was directing INI. Will it be possible to make Bolivia and Mexico modern and homogeneous nations? Arguedas's and Gamio's concerns allow us to sense that, in those Latin American countries with a high proportion of Indigenous populations, a notion of homogeneous modern nationalism will be problematic or impossible because of the scenario of Indigenous ethnic and cultural diversity as well as the troubled legacy between this multiethnicity and the criollo class.

In recent years, part of the decolonial critique applied to Latin American intercultural scenarios has shifted toward a pluriversal gaze, primarily inspired by a series of Indigenous and Afro-descendant uprisings and by claims for autonomy made by various marginalized groups in the last three decades. Among the many components that constitute pluriversality is the acknowledgment of the failure of nation-state models and the global interstate system as an adequate ruling structure for multiethnic contexts (Mignolo, "On Pluriversality," 92–105) or the coexistence of different cosmopolitical designs (De la Cadena and Blaser, *A World*, 3–6). Considering its flexibility and porousness, pluriversality as an analytical framework helps us understand the incompatibility between the modernizing model of the multicultural nation-state and the plural demands of the various subalternized social groups (Indigenous peoples, Afro-descendants, sexual dissidents, etc.). Indigenous mobilizations in pursuit of autonomy—such as the zapatista project in Chiapas (Mexico), the Mapuche resistance in La Araucanía (Chile), or the tempered sovereignty of the Wampís Nation in the Amazon (Peru)—are visible examples of the incapacity of nation-state models to consolidate their projects in multiethnic settings. To put it another way, Indigenous mobilizations exemplify the failure of modern national projects to operate as homogeneous social schemes. A pluriversal perspective not only requires acknowledging that what was called ethnic diversity in reality also responds to an ontologically and epistemologically heterogeneous stage of action, it also involves the acceptance that each of these stages constitutes autonomous political and social realms that are impossible to homogenize under a unitary project such as a modern nationalism.[16]

Pluriversality is a theoretical approach born in the twenty-first century and inspired by Indigenous social movements in the late twentieth century, but in the arguments of Arguedas and Gamio one can perceive a similar concern for the possibility that modern nation-state models are not the suitable system to achieve a coexistence among criollos, mestizos, and Indigenous peoples. Are both authors pluriversal? Not necessarily, but their failures, their argumentative frustrations, and the blatant epistemological limitation in their approaches to Indigenous societies make it possible to identify the decolonial cracks that paved the way for what would later be a turn to pluriversality. Understanding cracks as symbolic interstices that capture the lack of solidity in indigenista arguments, Gamio's and Arguedas's frustrations reinterpreted through a decolonial lens serve to highlight the fact that the pluriversal scenario is the main reason for their constrained indigenista programs.

Failure is not the norm that historically guides all indigenista arguments. In fact, in the following chapters, I will analyze how some ideals forged under the broad umbrella of indigenismo evolved throughout the twentieth century and how the arguments of some indigenista writers connected with the ideologies of some contemporary Indigenous movements. However, for Arguedas and Gamio, failure does seem like a fair description for the approaches they formulated in *Pueblo* and *Forjando*. The area in which the epistemological divorce between the modern nation-state formula and Indigenous ethnic multiplicity becomes most evident is in the elaboration of legislation that constitutes the ruling principles of the failed modernity in Bolivia and Mexico, respectively:

> The Indian has no remote idea of what the law is. According to his simplistic criteria, good is what satisfies his needs and bad is what opposes their satisfaction; and in order to impose a sanction, it is necessary that the one who is the object of it has at least an idea of what is bad or good, fair or unfair in its current meaning. To speak the language of law to the illiterate and bewildered Indian is to incur a serious lack of logic, because when faced with this curious language, not well understood even by literates, for the many interpretations to which it is susceptible, he remains mute, and if he possesses any conscience at all, it is at the last, when, loaded with shackles, stiffened at the bottom of a filthy dungeon, he is hungry and thinks that he must have committed a bad action for being treated this way and men are so angry.[17]

> That the Constitutions and laws of almost all Latin American countries are more or less faithful copies of the European or North American Constitutions and laws, and, therefore, exclusively appropriate to the social element that by origin, culture or language, or by all three characteristics, is similar to European or North American social elements. . . . It is suggested to the Latin American republics, in which the Indigenous population predominates, the convenience of revising the current Constitutions, so that they respond to the nature and needs of all the constituent

elements of the population and the harmonious and integral development of the same can be achieved, thus strengthening, positively, what is the basis of the true pan-Americanism.[18]

Still with a racist tone, Arguedas indicates that, as a modern nation, Bolivia has failed in its integrative program because Aymara people do not understand the functionality of national legislation, and therefore, it is a mistake to punish them for noncompliance with the laws. For his part, Gamio proposes the modification of the constitution as a mechanism for the incorporation of Indigenous peoples into the state apparatus.[19]

Both authors implicitly consider that the legislation that grounded modern nationalism as a homogenizing project of multiethnicity in Mexico and Bolivia is an inadequate model for achieving coexistence between the different Indigenous groups and the Westernized populations of criollos and mestizos. For Gamio, the divorce between Indigenous peoples and national legislation can be resolved in cultural terms, because the shortcoming resides in the fact that laws were copied from national projects without an Indigenous population—that is, European/Europeanized contexts. Gamio's indigenista telos aims to intervene in the configuration of the state project—"the convenience of revising the current Constitutions, so that they respond to the nature and needs of all the constituent elements of the population" ("revisar las Constituciones vigentes, a fin de que respondan a la naturaleza y necesidades de todos los elementos constitutivos de la población")—which interestingly seems to suggest the state institutions' adapting to the Indigenous population and not the other way around. On this specific point, the effort of assimilation is to some extent reciprocal, as the main burden of responsibility falls into the hands of the criollo technocracy. After all, it is the criollo elite who are mostly responsible for not having included the needs of Indigenous societies in their constitutive texts.

On the other hand, to Arguedas the knowledge gap seems irreparable because the Aymaras do not understand the legal procedures of the national state. The divergence that he highlights and that he explains with precarious arguments can be theoretically approached today from arguments that connect epistemological or ontological variations, depending on each particular case. According to Arguedas, a knowledge gap in Indigenous societies provides a form of cultural immunity, as it results in a significant lack of logical coherence: "to incur a serious lack of logic" ("incurrir en grave falta de lógica"). As in the arguments of the Mexican anthropologist, for the Bolivian writer, the principal liability lies in the criollo technocracy, which has failed to identify such a gap and only adopts a punitive perspective in the face of the dissociation between Indigenous societies and the body of laws.

In one way or another, the constitutions of both countries do not function as guiding principles for Indigenous peoples. For liberal indigenistas such as Gamio and Arguedas, modern nationalism cannot be developed without the Indigenous population, though they do not claim their incorporation as key stakeholders in the nation-state project. Likewise, the legal literature of national institutions is not designed to include Indigenous peoples as subjects of law, in the same way that the Indigenous people do not conceive laws within their regulatory social framework. In the midst of this multidimensional disconnection, according to these authors, the implementation of a modern nation-state apparatus would be destined for failure. The central axis of the anxiety that runs through both essays is the incompatibility between Indigenous diversity and the knowledge regime of the criollo mestizo project. This enables me to interpret *Pueblo enfermo* and *Forjando patria* as incipient versions of a preoccupation with grasping the diverse social and political arrangements embodied by Indigenous peoples, a preoccupation that decolonial scholars are currently striving to explain.

The interrogations that both authors conduct in various ways against the criollo mestizo national project—whether to denounce the inadequacy of national landscapes (cities or rural areas) or the unfitness of the legal bodies that constitute a modern nation—are instances that open up decolonial cracks within a Latin American critical tradition of modernity. As I defined in the introduction, in conversation with some ideas of decolonial theorist Catherine E. Walsh, decolonial cracks are critical symbolic venues that highlight or deliberately expose the internal and structural contradictions of the trinomial modernity/coloniality/capitalism in Latin America. These cracks—as abstract metaphors, just as in their physical versions—open spaces for analysis and contestation that are not always seized upon by the crack-makers, but which provide the opportunity to discuss ideas or to leak thought forms that aspire to overturn the pillars of the colonial structure on which several Latin American national projects were founded. In the specific cases of Bolivia and Mexico, Arguedas and Gamio have offered us a seminal and visible example of how these cracks were formed through the forging of an epistemologically limited indigenista critique—limited, yet solid enough to fissure the foundations of their precarious modern nationalisms.

CHAPTER 2

Vasconcelos and Valcárcel

Historicizing Peripheral Cultures

One of the most significant aspects of the indigenista discourse is its determination to recognize and revalue Indigenous societies, either because they are perceived as essential components of nationalist projects or because their resurgence permits cultural independence from Europe. In different ways, the cultural and racial revindication of Indigenous societies was promoted by the indigenista discourse in its various modalities. Unlike Arguedas and Gamio, for whom Indigenous societies of the Andes and Mesoamerica represented a challenge that complicated national modernization, for Mexican writer José Vasconcelos (1882–1959) and Peruvian intellectual Luis Eduardo Valcárcel (1891–1987), Indigenous issues represented the ethnopolitical possibility of creating a future horizon.

For these writers, advocating for Indigenous societies in their texts is a form of intervention in the present that makes it possible to forge a post-European future. In both authors, any future without Indigenous societies as protagonists will be fated to fail. To support their arguments, Vasconcelos and Valcárcel make radical intellectual efforts to provide interpretations to counteract the positivist historicism that labels the history of humanity as a one-dimensional sequence of events and individuals. Both authors challenge the time-space premises of Eurocentric thought, intending to enhance the historical value of Latin America and, more emphatically, the valorization of Indigenous societies. In the search for an alternative to the linear interpretation of historical time in which Indigenous societies only seem to be destined to fail (namely, to reject the linearity of European historicism), both writers elaborate radical indigenista proposals aimed at forging a *transmodernist indigenismo*.

Valcárcel posits the messianic notion of Inca resurgence as a formula that allows Andean society to favorably vindicate Indigenous peoples and to channel them into revolutionary rhetoric that would justify the time-space rupture with historical positivism, which I read through the conceptual lens of *nayrapacha* (past-as-future). Vasconcelos on the other hand suggests the imminent triumphant emergence of a new race phenotypically and culturally dependent on Indigenous societies—a vision that, although not exclusively "aboriginal," allows this Mexican intellectual to envision social projects with future aspirations to recentralize Indigenous people and, in parallel, counteract Anglo-European imperialist domination. In response to the intrinsic peripheralization to which European modernity subjected Indigenous societies, Vasconcelos and Valcárcel in different ways re-historicize the role of indigenousness in the Americas. Both counter Eurocentric notions of temporality and spatiality, and despite the contradictions or limitations with which they formulate their approaches, they provide ideas that act in opposition to the positivist thinking that downplayed the role of indigeneity in the historicization of Latin America.

Despite his numerous literary productions, Vasconcelos is renowned in Mexico also for his role in reconstructing the national educational system in the postrevolutionary period. He stood out as rector of the Universidad Nacional de México (now UNAM) and then as secretary of public education under the reformist government of Álvaro Obregón, occupying both positions from 1920 to 1924. During this period, he wrote his polemic book *La raza cósmica* (1997), initially published in Barcelona in 1925. The central thesis of this work is the claim of the emergence of a fifth race embodied in the Ibero-American race, which would be the merging of white Iberians and Indigenous. For Juan E. de Castro, this book is plagued with contradictions. On the one hand, Vasconcelos proposes a utopian discourse in which post-national and post-racial notions encounter each other, while on the other hand, he covers with universalist rhetoric what is a mere Latin American nationalism (*Mestizo Nations*, 107–8). For de Castro, the cosmic race is the expression of a supposed Ibero-American race utopically intended to integrate other racial groups and flourish in the American continent. It is impossible to deny the utopian tone with which Vasconcelos conceives of a universal racial integrationism that would be fated historically to be developed in the geography of Latin America, an argument that he uses to, for instance, contradictorily posit a sort of racial superiority of the Ibero-American population over the Anglo-European people of the United States, who are also derived from a colonial experience. The radical mestizaje he proposes in *La raza* is clearly aimed to exalt the racial mixture of Iberian and Indigenous ethnic groups and to condemn European positivist discourses through a racially messianic proposal.

Valcárcel is perhaps the most relevant intellectual figure in the city of Cuzco in the twentieth century. Although he was not born in this city, he completed his college education there and wrote his famous essay *Tempestad en los Andes* (1927), one of the most influential books in the formation of indigenista philosophy in Peru. Valcárcel's intellectual role acquired relevance in this city in the 1920s when a group of artists and intellectuals congregated in what was later called the cuzqueño indigenista school, formed as a response to the indigenista discourse propagated by authors based on the Peruvian coast such as José Carlos Mariátegui and Víctor Raúl Haya de la Torre.[1] Like Vasconcelos, Valcárcel also stood out as a statesman for his role as minister of education between 1945 and 1947 and, where he perhaps had his greatest institutional impact, as founder and director of a series of museums dedicated to the study of Peruvian culture, among which the Cuzco Anthropological Museum and the National Museum of Culture deserve special mention.

Taking advantage of the privilege conferred by his role as a public intellectual, Valcárcel promoted the study of Andean culture with a special emphasis on Inca civilization and the space occupied by Cuzco, which for him was not only a metropolitan place but an *anthropological place*.[2] For Marisol de la Cadena, the indigenismo cuzqueño capitalized on the ideological potential of regionalist discourse, based on the Inca cultural legacy, as a response to the centralist and pro-mestizaje indigenismo limeño (*Indigenous Mestizos*, 62–65). Likewise, Coronado argues in his analysis of Valcárcel and José Uriel García, the other intellectual leader of the city, that the indigenistas cuzqueños constitute a nationalist discourse that is regulated by the desire to construct a regional subjectivity (*The Andes Imagined*, 155). It is impossible to question the relevance of the historical and symbolic weight of Cuzco in the formulation of Valcárcel's indigenista discourse and his consequent approach to concepts such as *nation* and *ethnicity* in the search for an authentic intellectual project.

Vasconcelos and Valcárcel not only re-historicize Indigenous societies in the face of the oppressive peripheralization that centralizes terms such as "history" and "civilization" in Western European societies. They also re-historicize how they both perceive the emergence of a *transmodern subject* in their respective ethnic reclamations. Critics of their work do not agree on whether they succeeded in disassociating themselves from the historical interpretations imported by the positivist Eurocentric perspective, even if their intentions were to counter it. However, it is irrefutable that, although perhaps utopian, messianic, or unrealistic, from a decolonial perspective their arguments should be valued as remarkable attempts to (re)construct the history of Indigenous societies from a post-European humanism—or, at least, a humanism exogenous to modernity.

My understanding is that, despite their apparent ideological aloofness, Vasconcelos and Valcárcel represent pioneering efforts of what decades later would be consolidated within decolonial critique as *transmodernity*, as understood by Enrique Dussel. This means a philosophy that antagonizes Europeanizing modernization and claims its liberation from Western subjective constraints in the formulation of historical and social perspectives from and on cultures peripheral to modernity. In this sense, in *La raza* and *Tempestad* these authors attempt to take Indigenous societies out of the oppressive and linear track of European modernity in order to provide them with an authentic historical trajectory strongly connected to the territoriality of Latin America. With this aim, they also seek to reinsert Indigenous cultures into a new universal historical stream, either rehabilitated from the humiliations of colonialism or enhanced by philosophical interpretations that seek to create an aura of exceptionality over their new social subjects.

READING INDIGENOUS HISTORY FROM A TRANSMODERN PERSPECTIVE

In her analysis of the circumstances that motivated Aymaras to rebel against the Spanish colonial system in the uprisings of Túpac Katari in La Paz in 1781 and the differences concerning the rebellion of Túpac Amaru II in Cuzco, which occurred simultaneously, Silvia Rivera Cusicanqui reflects on a possible perception of the historical time that would have inspired the Indigenous Andean people to unleash such revolts:[3]

> The restoration of a cosmic order—which the idea of a linear and progressive historical time refuses to understand, other than as a "turning back the wheel of history"—can also be apprehended with the concept of *nayrapacha*, which serves as an epigraph: past, but not just any vision of the past; rather, "past-as-future," that is, as a renovation of time-space. A past capable of renewing the future, of reversing the situation experienced: is this not the aspiration currently shared by many Indigenous movements of all latitudes that postulate the full validity of the culture of their ancestors in the contemporary world?[4]

Some deductions can be made from Rivera Cusicanqui's elaboration. On the one hand, the relevance of the resurgence or return of the past in the historical design of the future, which is condensed in the Andean philosophical principle *nayrapacha*, translated by her in this essay as "past-as-future." A complimentary reading of this concept is that of the Aymara intellectual María Eugenia Choque Quispe who suggests that, in the context of Indigenous activism, the concept refers to the fact that "the future of the Indigenous collectivity resides in its past" ("el futuro de la colectividad indígena se encuentra en su pasado")—not in a return to it but, rather, in its interrogation ("Principios," 274). In any case, in this principle, the resurgence or revisiting of the past allows the spatial and temporal reframing of the present, which articulates the insurgent motivations of the Indigenous uprisings that occurred in the eighteenth century, and which constituted foundational events within a decolonial—and transmodern—reading of Bolivian history. The other deduction, perhaps less explicit, is the historical relevance that Rivera Cusicanqui gives to the Indigenous uprisings of the eighteenth century as events that allow her to explain the political and ideological motivations of the Indigenous insurrections that occurred in Bolivia in the mid-twentieth century.

Throughout Rivera Cusicanqui's essay, another major rebellion that occurred in the eighteenth century, and which for the Eurocentric historical design is one of the foundational events of later European nationalisms, is noticeably absent: the French Revolution. In her historical analysis, Rivera Cusicanqui anticipates the motives for Katari's Indigenous anti-colonial uprising—"the restoration of a cosmic order" ("la restauración del orden cósmico")—which are diametrically opposed to the motives for said European uprising. The French Revolution, as is well-known, far from seeking the resurgence of the past to design the future, sought and achieved the abolition of a past system (absolutist monarchy affiliated with the Catholic Church), in order to progress in the social evolutionary line toward a new formula that triggered the development of a European bourgeoisie intellectually nurtured by the Enlightenment. For Rivera Cusicanqui, the eighteenth century is the century of the Indigenous uprisings instigated by *nayrapacha*, not the century of the enlightened French Revolution. Thus, in a singular way of historicizing the eighteenth century, Rivera Cusicanqui decentralizes Europe and centralizes Indigenous societies along with its philosophical principles, which a modern Eurocentric view would peripheralize.

What is the implication that Silvia Rivera Cusicanqui, a Bolivian mestiza intellectual familiar with Quechua Aymara groups in her sociological approach, omits revolutions such as the French or the Anglo-American when speaking of the eighteenth century? None, upon making a superficial analysis of the text's goals. After all, she is talking about an uprising in La Paz, not in Paris or Philadelphia. But apart from that, we cannot ignore that she is analyzing a local history, the history of an event that is liberated from the modernizing global design, and that from her historical readings the eighteenth-century revolutions were aimed at the construction of modern nation-states. In that sense, Mignolo (*Local Histories*, 127–71) argues that the emphasis placed on historical events such as the French Revolution and the Enlightenment as occurrences that originate the creation of the modern nation-state design, created a local history that would become a global design as it spread geopolitically through the process of modernization of territories located on the peripheries of Europe and the North Atlantic.

In her explanation of the ideological connections among Katari's uprising in 1781, the nationalist revolution of 1952, and the subsequent Indigenous insurrections in the late twentieth century, Rivera Cusicanqui is recounting the political history of Quechua Aymara society. But she is doing so from the historical periphery of the modern European project created, propagated, and imposed through the colonization of intersubjective relations by which knowledge is transmitted to and across peripheries. In 1781 and in the late twentieth century, the Aymara and indianista-katarista insurgent groups, respectively, struggled for their economic, political, and mainly epistemological emancipation—that is, for a revitalization of their sources of knowledge—as opposed to the group led by Túpac Amaru in Cuzco.

For this reason, under a decolonizing historicization, the constant revindication of the social, political, and historical principles of local Aymara cosmovision becomes crucial. What should be highlighted in Rivera Cusicanqui's essay is that she explicitly and skillfully circumvents the influence of what Quijano calls "cultural coloniality," which implies the reproduction of certain founding events of European rationality as useful paradigms for analyzing, examining, and explaining the sociocultural reality of Latin American societies ("Colonialidad y modernidad," 12–16).[5] In short, decolonizing the way Indigenous societies have been historicized by the universalizing Eurocentric narrative becomes an intellectual imperative for a decolonial theorist such as Rivera Cusicanqui, just as it was for Vasconcelos and Valcárcel in the early twentieth century.

Now, if Rivera Cusicanqui does not historicize from a symbolic and ideological modern perspective, then where does she do so from? As a response to the notion of postmodernity, Dussel ("Transmodernity," 41–43) raises the concept of *transmodernity* as a confrontation to European centrality that emerges from exteriority with respect to modernity and responds to cultural perspectives situated in peripheral locations and developments concerning modern cultures. In *The Invention of the Americas* (1995), Dussel argues that the invasion initiated in 1492 constitutes the foundational moment of the Eurocentric modernity project because it permitted Europe to form its subjectivity in relation to the analysis of its peripheries—until then restricted to the Asian and Arab worlds. With the emergence of a "new world," Europe was able to consolidate the sense of otherness required for the prototypical design of what is non-European, asserting the continent's centrality in this new design (*Invention*, 23–26). In historical terms, European colonialism re-historicizes the globe by expanding the global narrative under a centrifugal design that marginalized and, in many cases, made invisible the development of local histories in the global periphery.

But Dussel goes further in his challenge to modernity and argues that, in 1492, Europe not only placed itself at the center vis-à-vis other civilizations but also turned the inhabitants of these—that is, the *othered individuals*—into objects and instruments of civilization and Europeanization who would be attuned to the modernizing purposes of Western empires (*Invention*, 88–90). As such, transmodernity occurs in spatial, cultural, and historical frameworks unrelated to the homogenizing criteria of modernity. It is along these lines that transmodernity is inscribed within the framework of the philosophy of liberation, with all the structural detachments that this implies concerning Eurocentrism (theological, political, cultural, social, economic, and so on). Or, as Dussel himself expresses it, transmodernity points to "all of those aspects that are situated 'beyond' (and also 'prior to') the structures valorized by modern European/North American culture, and which are present in the great non-European cultures and have begun to move toward a pluriversal utopia" ("Transmodernity," 43). In this sense, I understand that geohistorical referents play a crucial role in the perception of knowledge produced outside modernity, and in the locus of enunciation of the knowledge producers themselves which inevitably influences the construction of a transmodern historical narrative.

In the various indigenismos and the criticism of some of their authors, matters related to the geohistorical referents that structure indigenista cultural production are often addressed. This is why some authors question the fact that A. Arguedas and Vasconcelos published the first editions of their books in Barcelona. Meanwhile, others appreciate that Valcárcel wrote and published in Cuzco, a geohistorically marginalized physical and symbolic space. Ultimately, all of these criollo mestizo and mesocratic authors wrote from Latin America, and it is within this periphery that they benefited from structural privileges. Now, these privileges not only positioned them as influential public intellectuals but also created around them the objective conditions to forge an intellectual proposal that, more or less with success, managed to bypass the overwhelming weight of cultural coloniality whose historical narrative overshadows the role of Indigenous societies.

My interest in employing transmodernity as a decolonial theoretical approach is not to discuss the authors' locus to infer their legitimacy as public intellectuals but, rather, to explore the vindicatory or revolutionary ideas that run through their writings. After all, it is unquestionable that *La raza* and *Tempestad* are parts of a literary corpus that influenced the formation of such a broad and heterogeneous notion as the Latin American indigenista thought in the twentieth century. Nevertheless, transmodernity as an anti/post/exo-Eurocentric point of view, which rejects the forced secularization of peripheral societies and is based on an anti-positivist principle, would provide a lens through which to examine some of Vasconcelos's and Valcárcel's proposals that have been widely questioned for both their utopian and messianic character, but which are illuminated here as alternative forms of historicizing Indigenous cultures.

VASCONCELOS AND A NEW RACE IN HISTORY

In the opening pages of *La raza*, Vasconcelos eloquently expresses his intention: to find a new historical purpose for America. "If we are, then, geologically ancient as well as, in respect, the tradition, how can we still continue to accept the fiction, invented by our European fathers, of the novelty of a continent that existed before the appearance of the land from where the discoverers and conquerors came?" (Vasconcelos, *Cosmic Race*, 8).[6] Belittled by some and respected by others, after a hundred years of its publication *La raza* remains a fundamental text in the discussion of the notion of mestizaje in Latin America. Still, the historical and political intentionality that underlies this text continues to be a less examined line of analysis. Vasconcelos's arguments are interwoven, since the emergence of a cosmic race is subordinated to a reinterpretation of the historical progression of time in America, an interpretation that relocates Indigenous societies and grants them a telos that antagonizes the Eurocentric historical narrative. As inferred from the variety of racial approaches suggested by indigenismos, mestizaje was anything but a homogeneous proposition in the corpus of indigenista works. In particular, the mestizaje proposed by Vasconcelos in this essay leads to the emergence of a fifth race, the product of the confluence, development, apogee, and fall of a set of color-codified races: red (Indigenous), white (Europeans), black (Africans), and yellow (Asians), although he notes that each of these races has several branches.

Right from the beginning of the essay, he emphasizes the leading role of Indigenous peoples in forging the cosmic race, since he argues that the European invasion of America "has set the moral and material basis for the union of all men into a fifth universal race, the fruit of all the previous ones and amelioration of everything past" (*Cosmic Race*, 9). The cosmic race is intended to develop superiority and lead the future of society, carrying with it the attributes of the preceding races and thus achieving a status of phenotypical, cultural, political, and historical exceptionality. Vasconcelos points out that, throughout history, the cultures embodying each of these races enjoyed a cyclical civilizational zenith and subsequent decline until they created the imminent scenario of the emergence of a fifth race, aimed at settling a civilizational project in the tropical zone of America because of the peculiarities of its geography; the travel chronicles of Brazil and Argentina that follow the essay seek to support this argument.

In *La raza* Vasconcelos concentrates on predicting the decline of the white races of Europe. "The days of the pure whites, the victors of today, are as numbered as were the days of their predecessors" (*Cosmic Race*, 16). He then claims that the invasion of America created "the basis for a new period: The period of the fusion and mixing of all peoples" (16). However, he prioritizes the racial mixture between Indigenous peoples and white Iberians to the detriment of white Anglos of North America, whom he accuses of replicating imperialist methods in their policies of extermination of Indigenous peoples and in their dissemination of discourses of selectivity such as social Darwinism. For Vasconcelos, the Ibero-American race is aimed mainly at racial, ethical, and social superiority, which would make it the dominator of a world whose capital city he calls "Universópolis" and which would flourish in the Amazonian rainforest, suggesting an environmental theoretical implication that Jorge Quintana-Navarrete ("José") reads as a particular form of plant theory inherent in Vasconcelos's thesis. However, this antagonistic stance toward the Anglo-European imperial project in America with its genocidal policy toward Indigenous peoples anticipates the underlying political intention of the essay.

The reception of such an all-encompassing sociohistorical approach could not be homogeneous. In her now canonical *Borderlands/La Frontera*, Gloria Anzaldúa relies on Vasconcelos to construct a pro-mestizaje legacy that she uses as a baseline for the formulation of a "mestizo consciousness" inherent in Chicano culture (99–100). For de Castro, the cosmic race is the utopian extension of a discourse of mestizaje that emerges from other authors with the intention of founding projects of nationhood, but which, in Vasconcelos, would be presented as a post-national notion (*Mestizo Nations*, 107). In an opposite reading, Ignacio Sánchez-Prado points out that it is insufficient to read *La raza* only as a "utopian essay" that prophesizes mestizaje, but rather, it should be read as a political gesture that had repercussions on state policies (*Intermitencias*, 169–75). For his part, Joshua Lund accuses Vasconcelos of two things: replicating racist patterns (despite being critical of imperialism) and inserting Latin America into the universal flow of history, thereby fulfilling Europe's universalist pretensions (*Impure Imagination*, 110–13). For Lund, with these contradictions and inconsistencies, instead of distancing himself from positivism, as explicitly expressed in *La raza*, Vasconcelos ends up copying how positivist discourses use the notions of *race* and *nation*. Emphasizing a utopian reading of this essay, Juan Carlos Grijalva argues that Vasconcelos ambiguously uses categories such as *race*, *culture*, and *civilization* to construct a discourse of mestizaje that de-indianizes and forces the incorporation of ethnic sectors into an emerging national culture ("Vasconcelos," 341–43).

It is undeniable that Vasconcelos's anti-imperialist impetus fails when he formulates the imminence of a "Universópolis" dominated by a superior race, which is an imperialist proposal with a rhetorical packaging that attempts to project an anti-Eurocentrism. In *La raza*, Vasconcelos directs his holistic mestizaje toward the predominance of the Ibero-American mixture (Iberians with Indigenous peoples) and tacitly downplays the historical evolution of the other mixtures, which are also subalternized (for instance, Indigenous peoples mixed with Africans). Vasconcelos's racial program, seen only as a phenotypical scheme, is untenable; however, I consider that reading *La raza* only as Vasconcelos's interest in creating a particular racial theory is insufficient. As Sánchez-Prado points out, it is also a political program with the aim not only to intervene in the politics of the nation-state but, more importantly for this study, to formulate a political response to the historical Eurocentric annulment of Indigenous societies. Thus, he states that the emergence of a cosmic race entails a "question [that] has paramount importance to those who insist in looking for a plan in History" (*Cosmic Race*, 8). In his argument, History—with a capital H—becomes a symbolic battlefield on which the cosmic race figures as a desirable transmodern identity, an identity that contends with the historical narrative of modernity and is figured as an alternative to peripheralizing discourses. Therefore, rather than viewing it as a mere racial and utopian discourse, in this work I advocate understanding *La raza* as a dialectical response that runs through the political program inherent in the emergence of a cosmic race.

A DEFINITIVE RACE OR A TRANSMODERN IDENTITY

Dussel formulates transmodernity as a theoretical framework of analysis that allows for the countering of historical and political rationalist assumptions adhering to modernity. In short, he sees rationalism as an instrument that justifies European imperial centrality. Rivera Cusicanqui's analysis of the eighteenth century, for example, can be considered a transmodern interpretation that, in its selective exploration of historical events, overshadows Eurocentric narratives. The Uruguayan philosopher Yamandú Acosta builds on Dussel's ideas to affirm that transmodernity implies not only a detachment from modern rationality but also a liberation from "the anti-emancipatory and anti-universalist effects of the conceptual meaning of modernity, which result from its Eurocentric self-centering, excluding any alterity" ("los efectos antiemancipatorios y antiuniversalistas del sentido conceptual de la modernidad, que resultan de su autocentramiento eurocéntrico, excluyente de toda alteridad") (*Sujeto*, 44). In other words, Acosta asserts the need to avoid the centripetal forces that stem from the conceptual analysis framed by rational modernity. Furthermore, and particularly interesting for my analytical intentions, he claims that all forms of transmodernity require a transmodern subject—that is, an individual who transcends the emancipatory logic intrinsic to modern reason. He states, "The transmodern subject, by overcoming its modern alienated condition in its transmodern liberating activation that has its center in alterity, transcends the subject centered in its own selfhood, the subject of modernity" ("El sujeto transmoderno, al superar su condición enajenada moderna en su activación liberadora transmoderna que tiene su centro en la alteridad, trasciende al sujeto centrado en su mismidad, el sujeto de la modernidad") (45).

In what follows, I propose understanding the figuration of the cosmic race and its historical and political intervention as a dialectical effort that anticipates the forging of a transmodern subject as it implies the construction of an identity that re-historicizes Indigenous societies. Thus, in sociopolitical terms, the telos of the cosmic race can be interpreted as an incipient effort to imagine a transmodern identity, although conditioned by certain epistemic limitations.

> There is no going back in History, for it is all transformation and novelty. No race returns. Each one states its mission, accomplishes it, and passes away.... The days of the pure whites, the victors of today, are as numbered as were the days of their predecessors. Having fulfilled their destiny of mechanizing the world, they themselves have set, without knowing it, the basis for a new period: The period of the fusion and mixing of all peoples. The Indian has no other door to the future but the door of modern culture, nor any other road but the road already cleared by Latin civilization. (Vasconcelos, *Cosmic Race*, 16)

The reframing of historical time in *La raza* is one aspect that makes this essay a disruptive work. This approach not only dissociates itself from the notion of time as a linear construct that justifies the "progressivist fallacy" (to use Dussel's terminology) but also proposes an alternative design. It has typically been read as a cyclical conception of history, but this would imply recognizing some point of return, which Vasconcelos explicitly denies ("There is no going back in History").

Beyond the conventional linearity and circularity, the trajectory with which he configures historical time is a progressive spiral, where supremacies are superposed and transformed. In this layout, the last transforming milestone is brought by the racial, cultural, and political contribution of Indigenous societies, which will succeed and complement Iberians in the forging of the cosmic race: after all, "the Indian is a good bridge for racial mixing" (*Cosmic Race*, 26). It is noteworthy that this edition translates *mestizaje* as racial mixing, which reduces the conceptual meaning with which Vasconcelos uses this word, which, in reality, has connotations that touch on values that go beyond the phenotypical (culture, politics, subjectivity, etc.). That said, the telos of American indigeneity is that of a more-than-racial and sine-qua-non-conductive vessel for the success of the cosmic race as a definitive race.

The ambiguous use of some concepts can lead to essentialist readings of Vasconcelos's thesis. For example, when he points out that "the Indian has no other door to the future but the door of modern culture," the connotation given to the word "modern" acquires both a temporal and a qualitative dimension simultaneously. Temporally speaking, modernity is an interval of time within the spiraling historical trajectory that leads humanity toward the cosmic race. Qualitatively, modernity is an inevitable stage that must be crossed—that is to say, transcended—and the metaphor of the door thus correctly describes Vasconcelos's intentionality. He does not suggest that the cosmic race will flourish in modernity but, rather, that going through modernity is a preexisting scenario for its flourishing. Recalling Acosta's ideas, the cosmic race will emerge as the result of a process in which it manages to overcome its modern alienated condition ("superar su condición enajenada moderna"), and it becomes a subject that transcends modernity and, therefore, constitutes itself as transmodern. After all, as Acosta states, "the transmodern subject is a transcendentality immanent to the modern subject" ("el sujeto transmoderno es una trascendentalidad inmanente al sujeto moderno") (*Sujeto*, 45). Initially, modernity is an inevitable stage but it is "transcendible," and the result of this is the cosmic race, a form of transmodern identity that derives from the spiral interpretation of historical time.

As a sociopolitical proposal, the cosmic race, because of its strong Indigenous influence and the historical disruption that comes with it, constitutes a type of transmodern subject. Insofar as having been subjected to the modern rational structure, the cosmic race transcends that structure. I have opted to describe it as the desire for a transmodern identity inasmuch as *La raza* argues for the ultimate race not only as a racial convergence but as a set of moral values, cultural symbols, traditions, and political purposes joined around a range of social codes that are amalgamated into the cosmic race. The forging of the cosmic race adheres to quite traditional senses of identity formation as it calls for social identification and is constituted as a communitarian dialectic through which individuals are destined (at least in Vasconcelos's illusions) to be identified with the race, tradition, and geography of America.

Regardless of how outlandish the configuration of a definitive race may be for some critics, the exercise of historical interpretation carried out by Vasconcelos to liberate Indigenous societies from the ostracism in which they were enclosed by Eurocentric historical paradigms is remarkable. The revindication of Indigenous people becomes notable since the need for their asymmetrical acculturation is discarded as Gamio proposed in *Forjando*, and they become a central entity in the correct functioning of a historical assemblage that subverts the progressive linearity of events as a path to the future. Vasconcelos does not dispense with progress, but he does alter its trajectory and reduce the contribution of modernity, which is described only as an interim stage. At the same time, this approach discards the spatial references of Western civilization and locates the future in the Amazon and tropical areas.

For Vasconcelos "there will come a period when all of humanity will establish itself in the warm regions of the planet" (*Cosmic Race*, 24). Besides the prophetic tone, with this statement, Vasconcelos challenges one of the foundational milestones of European historicism, which since ancient Greek culture's heyday conceived the "torrid zones" as inhospitable. By advocating for the "warm regions of the planet," he is unfolding a political dialectic to counter the historicizing method that marginalizes the societies of these regions—that is, Indigenous peoples. But, in doing so, he overturns the civilizing paradigm by discrediting Anglo-European geography as the ideal space for human settlement or, even more politically, for whatever comes after modernity.

His confrontational stance against European positivism does not stop here, since in his critique of natural selection and social Darwinism he ends up blaming science (mainly the natural sciences) for being a mere reproduction of the arrogance of Anglo-European societies. Through this critique of positivism and its inherent scientism, his discourse reenters into the realm of transmodernity as he argues, in this spiraling succession of races that follow one another in domination, that each ascending race needs to constitute its own philosophy, *"the deux ex machina* of its own success" (*Cosmic Race*, 36). At this point, the category of *race* in Vasconcelos's work loses the color-coded rigidity of the early pages of his essay and assumes a connotation closer to cultural, moral, and epistemic singularity. In that sense, he defends the emergence and succession of these societies from the creation of their own philosophies—that is, the valorization of their sources of knowledge. He tacitly refers to a form of empowerment that is rooted in local histories, though we need not forget that for Vasconcelos everything leads to a universalizing mestizaje. The use of the Greco-Latin expression "deus ex machina" reveals the disruptive perspective with which he envisions the emergence of the cosmic race, with its elevated Indigenous component and its sovereign structures of knowledge.[7] In short, the cosmic race is an identity of universal aspirations that, with the inevitable influence of Indigenous society, will constitute a transmodern subject capable of building a sovereign civilizing process.

VALCÁRCEL, ANDINISMO, AND INCA RESURGENCE

"Cuzco and Lima are, by the nature of things, two opposite focuses of nationality. Cuzco represents the mother culture, the inheritance of the millenary Inkas. Lima is the yearning for adaptation to European culture. And the fact is that Cuzco preexisted when the conquistador arrived and Lima was created by him, ex-nihilo. . . . Only Cuzco is reserved to redeem the Indian."[8] Luis E. Valcárcel condenses two of the main ideas formulated in *Tempestad en los Andes*: the privileged political symbolism of Cuzco and, tied to this, the *incaismo* expressed as a form of redemption or resurgence of the Inca culture. This book was of utmost importance in the forging of the Cuzco indigenista school and, likewise, it is difficult to label in terms of genre. Although it is mostly a monographic text, it is interrupted by narrative passages in which Valcárcel provides stories that emphasize the arguments set forth in the essayistic sections. The passionate tone of the book reflects a context of the proliferation of indigenista discourses in different parts of Peru, which occurred simultaneously with a series of Indigenous rebellions in several Andean provinces. The book was printed in 1927 by Editorial Minerva, a publishing house founded in 1925 by his intellectual counterpart in Lima, José Carlos Mariátegui. As a whole it is written with a tone of historical reclamation of Inca culture, with some prophetic passages. Its monographic sections are intercalated with social analyses of the Andean reality and historical revisions of the influence and survival of the Inca culture in the Andes.

Present throughout is the idea of a foreseen resurgence of Inca dominance, which would occur alongside the return of the values of Inca society in a project to be centralized in Cuzco. Valcárcel calls the philosophical perspective that should guide this project *andinismo*, which he defines as a "doctrine full of mystical unction" ("una doctrina plena de mística unción") that "will emerge to enclose in its orbit all that the Andes dominate from their majestic altitude" ("surgirá para encerrar en su órbita todo lo que los Andes dominan desde su altitud majestuosa") (*Tempestad*, 201). Within andinismo, a telluric philosophical doctrine, incaismo operates as a political rhetorical instrument that allows Valcárcel to give his ideas a non-European historical dimension and a spatial ubiquity—that is, to promote a cuzqueño regionalism attached to Inca legacy. Valcárcel's indigenismo can be figured as a concentric scheme in which Cuzco operates as the central axis from which all dialectical forces that constitute his political program spread out.

Like most indigenista essays, *Tempestad* also denounces the dynamics of colonial oppression that have kept Indigenous peoples marginalized within national projects. However, for Valcárcel, the Andean Indians, pure subjects closely linked to their landscape and their Inca origins, should not be incorporated into the Peruvian national project, but rather rebuild their own national enterprise inspired by the political, ethical, and racial appreciation of the Inca culture. *Tempestad* is an incisive call to dismantle the criollo national project built in Lima, the Westernized capital city of Peru. Valcárcel proposes Cuzco as the historical site in which the Andean renaissance will take place, as he considers it the only genuinely Inca city. His indigenista discourse is characterized by a strong regionalism, which is invigorated by the intellectual agitation caused by the rediscovery of Machu Picchu and the social tensions provoked around the first political and aesthetic interpretations of the citadel.[9]

The first reaction to *Tempestad* is incorporated in its first edition, in the prologue written by Mariátegui in which he highlights the figure of Valcárcel as a passionate evangelist ("apasionado evangelista") of Indigenous resurgence and, therefore, of the emergence of the *nuevo indio* (*Tempestad*, 40). Mariátegui notes that the book offers a mythical and prophetic interpretation of an Indigenous resurgence that for him is inexorably linked to socialism. For de la Cadena, the main proposal of *Tempestad* is that of a national redemption that can happen only through the resuscitation of the "soul of the Inca race" ("alma de la raza inca") where Inca spirituality not only assumes moral connotations but is portrayed as a spirituality that has not been altered over time (*Indigenous Mestizos*, 65–66). Gonzalo Portocarrero is more incredulous about Valcárcel's ideas, and he affirms that if Valcárcel uses that prophetic and persuasive rhetoric to affirm the Inca resurgence, it is because the dimensions of the change he promises seem improbable, insisting on the miraculous character of his approach (*La urgencia*, 230). From a liberal perspective, Mario Vargas Llosa offers a political critique of Valcárcel, discrediting his incaismo by accusing the Inca state of paralyzing the Andean people and by suggesting that the indigenista writer falsifies history by providing an "ideological" and "mythical" reading (*La utopía*, 170–71). It is undeniable that, for the exaltation of Andean people and their Inca past, Valcárcel relies on premonitory statements that lead to the construction of a regionalist and prophetic indigenista discourse at the same time.

But every indigenista prophecy requires a spatial reference to ground its prognosis as a viable social project. In the same way that for Vasconcelos that space would be the Amazonian rainforest for Valcárcel it is Cuzco. In his regionalist indigenismo, this city operates as a symbolic site, a device that allows him to fracture the modernizing temporal linearity by indexing the past in the present, since it is the birthplace of the Indigenous society ("El Cusco representa la cultura madre, la herencia de los inkas milenarios"). And, as such, it is the space reserved to redeem the Indian ("reservado para redimir al indio") and to turn him into the *nuevo indio*, a revolutionary social subject freed from the peripheralizing European historical arbitrariness, a subject to whose qualities Valcárcel dedicates a whole chapter of *Tempestad*. For him, as a symbolic and physical site, Cuzco is a place of action and enunciation in which "the Andean peoples who feel the profound trembling of a World to come" ("los pueblos andinos que sienten el estremecimiento grávido de un Mundo por venir") (167) will be empowered. The future is still the horizon toward which Valcárcel's rhetoric of resurgence moves.

It is worth recalling the Andean principle *nayrapacha* formulated by Rivera Cusicanqui and adapted in her terms as a notion of "past-as-future." On this point, Valcárcel's idea concurs with the restoration of a cosmic order as elaborated by the Bolivian sociologist in her analysis of the Aymara uprisings, as he calls for the restoration of an authentically Indigenous social order with the aim of building a bridge to the future, an order that reinstates Inca values and worldviews as regulating principles of the present. The temporal and spatial matrix of *Tempestad*'s main thesis lies in a local history emerging from the historical and political peripheries of modernity (Inca culture and Cuzco). Thus, in Valcárcel's early texts—and in the other exponents of the Grupo Resurgimiento—Cuzco is inscribed as a *locus amoenus* propitious for the literary re-creation of incaismo. Because of its geohistorical symbolism, this city becomes the perfect place for the reflourishing of Andean civilization.

Such a resurgence (which here I read through the lens of *nayrapacha*) does not imply a return to an extinct sociopolitical model nor a return to the past but, rather, the confluence of the values of the past in a project that aspires to intervene in the present in order to build a genuinely Andean future. In Valcárcel's book, the concept of *nayrapacha* serves to index the valuable Inca past in the unsustainable modern/colonial republican present without forgetting about the future. This dialectical phenomenon can only occur in Cuzco, in its physical and symbolic dimensions. In other words, Cuzco is the only two-dimensional space that is capable of opposing Lima, since "the modern virus of elegant parasitism penetrates Peru through the open door of its Europeanized capital" ("el virus moderno del parasitismo elegante penetra al Perú por la puerta abierta de su capital europeizada") (*Tempestad*, 202). Thus, the regionalist aspect of Valcárcel's indigenismo runs through a dialectic that counteracts the overwhelming criollo national project expanding from Lima. "The day that all consciences feel the pride of being born of this sublime mother—the race—that awaits for long centuries the hour of its rehabilitation, the Indigenous problem will have disappeared. . . . Only a great fraternal love, sympathetic, one of those loves that originate in the genesis of the species and are the outcry of the blood, will have the power to save Peru by dignifying the Indian."[10]

Valcárcel prescribes dignifying Indigenous people—that is, enhancing their subjective qualities—to achieve the decolonization of the Peruvian national project. The political force aimed for such a resurgence lies in a national consciousness that recognizes in Andean society—and in Inca culture more specifically—the origin of a civilization exogenous from Europe since the Andes is pictured as the "birthplace of species" ("génesis de la especie"). The use of the category of *race*, as in Vasconcelos, is ambiguous because it refers not only to the specific phenotypical traits of an ethnic group but also to the cultural, moral, and epistemic singularity of a given community. For Valcárcel, this understanding of race allows him to illustrate what he considers to be the objective conditions for the revolutionary Andean resurgence. "The 'white man,' after all, has not replaced the Indigenous but an Inkaic social class. . . . But the essence of Peru, the invariable Peru was never, could never be anything but Indian" ("El 'hombre blanco', en buena cuenta, no ha sustituido al indígena sino a una clase social inkaica. [. . .] Mas, el Perú esencial, el Perú invariable no fue, no pudo ser nunca sino indio") (*Tempestad*, 215–16). This is why I argue that Valcárcel envisions the contemporary Andean Indian as a transmodern subject who transcends the constraining forces of modernity to constitute a disruptive subjectivity—in this case, the redeemed *nuevo indio*. For Valcárcel, it is important to portray this transmodern subject as an unalterable entity intent on overcoming the imposing European social paradigm inherited from colonialism and which, within the criollo national project, has as its main focus of diffusion the Westernized city of Lima.

ANTI-MESTIZAJE AND TELLURISM, CORNERSTONES OF ANDINISMO

Unlike Vasconcelos, who is a well-known apologist of mestizaje as a process of forging the transmodern subject (cosmic race), for Valcárcel, mestizaje implies the decomposition of the Indigenous people or, if anything, a perverse adaptation to colonial modernity. For Valcárcel, the mestizo only yearns "to procure money to pay for his dipsomania" ("procurarse dinero para pagar su dipsomanía") (*Tempestad*, 86) and "does not inherit ancestral virtues but instead vices and defects" ("no hereda las virtudes ancestrales sino los vicios y las taras") (208). Partially, this diatribe against mestizos is somewhat reminiscent of the pathologizing descriptions of A. Arguedas we saw before. However, for Valcárcel, the only way to construct a sovereign national project that is not subject to the colonial-rooted arbitrariness of criollos would be to privilege an Indigenous social, political, ethical, and cultural structure that includes a certain degree of racial purity, if such a thing is possible.

We cannot forget that beneath this approach is a self-criticism of class and race. After all, Valcárcel was not Indigenous but a mestizo mesocratic intellectual. In this political and historical anti-mestizaje construct that is part of his andinista approach, incaismo operates as an instrument that re-historicizes Indigenous peoples, endowing them with sovereign genealogies and epistemologies (at least rhetorically) and counteracting the denigrating peripheralization introduced by the modernity/coloniality binomial. Indigeneity in Valcárcel's work functions as a generator of a national imaginary that, with the Inca resurgence, aspires to become an empirical reality.

Opposition to mestizaje is the mode through which Valcárcel constructs a pro-autochthonist discourse where the origin is located in Inca civilization, and more specifically, in Cuzco. Hence, Valcárcel antagonizes those indigenismos that celebrate mestizaje such as those of Vasconcelos, Mariátegui, young José María Arguedas, and Franz Tamayo—whom Javier C. Sanjinés (*Mestizaje Upside-Down*) argues was a pioneer among the indigenistas who perceive mestizaje as a contribution to Western civilization.[11] However, Valcárcel's anti-mestizaje stance also does not fit with the philosophical pessimism of A. Arguedas, who does not see a civilizing horizon in any of the social groups that compose the Bolivian national project. This stance helps Valcárcel delineate the sociocultural singularity of Andean indigeneity, which, once redeemed and re-historicized, must undertake a national project to achieve its epistemic autonomy by transcending European sociohistorical influence. In andinista philosophy, mestizaje is neither an end nor a means but, rather, an obstacle to be avoided and, in a worst-case scenario, a stage to overcome.

It is worth examining a vital aspect of Valcárcel's andinismo: the ecological balance inherent in his tellurism (or animal magnetism).[12] In defining the philosophy that was to trigger the Inca resurgence, Valcárcel says: "Andinismo is the love of the land, of the sun, of the river, of the mountain. It is the pure feeling of nature. . . . It is the community in the richness and well-being" ("El andinismo es el amor a la tierra, al sol, al río, a la montaña. Es el puro sentimiento de la naturaleza. [. . .] Es la comunidad en la riqueza y el bienestar") (*Tempestad*, 203). In a context of cruel *gamonalismo* (a species of bossism) that subjected Indigenous people and peasants to an oppressive system of land exploitation, Valcárcel prescribes the harmonious reconciliation between nature and the Andean community. The subtext of his description presumes the overcoming of gamonalismo—that is, putting an end to the domination that criollo landowners exercised over farmland, a system inherited from the colonial administration and that in the early twentieth century was manifest in the form of capitalist primitive accumulation.

Valcárcel points against gamonalismo, as do almost all indigenistas regardless of their ideological affiliations. He argues that "andinismo is agrarianism" ("andinismo es agrarismo") (*Tempestad*, 203), a collective social model that requires the abolition of the principle of accumulative landownership and privatization of the means of production. The return of the ayllu—the communal system of collective property and reciprocal distribution of labor—becomes an urgency to materialize an Inca resurgence, which had already been anticipated in his book *Del ayllu al imperio* (From the ayllu to empire, 1925), where he warns of the need to stop the regression of the ayllu. In *Del ayllu* and *Tempestad*, Valcárcel celebrates the survival of this collective social form because, although its condition is precarious, he (like Mariátegui) believes that this form of collectivity is empirical evidence of an Inca communist model that predated the capitalist one imported from Europe. The ayllu empirically confirms the Andean "past-as-future" principle, not because it reverses the control of the means of production but because, in this collectivity, the love for nature that defines the Andean identity remains alive—that is, a sense of belonging to the land that is constituted as the backbone of tellurism in the philosophy promoted by Valcárcel.

About the Andean people of the past and present, he asserts that "they coexist with the mountain and the river, they extend their sociability to the infrahuman and mingle, in a pantheistic haze, with all that surrounds them" ("conviven con la montaña y con el río, prolongan su sociabilidad a lo infrahumano y se confunden, en la nebulosa panteísta, con cuanto les rodea") (*Tempestad*, 205). Although this seemingly bucolic description of Andean Indians appears to be a paternalistic and indulgent portrait made by an urban intellectual, some terms of this description anticipate concerns that would later emerge in the work of Indigenous writer activists. On the one hand, Valcárcel senses in the harmonious bond with nature a degree of engagement that transcends the conventional socialization among humans ("prolongan su sociabilidad a lo infrahumano" (106). The fact that he opts for the word "infrahuman" is telling of the limited nomenclature he had to describe what in reality is a more-than-human collectivity in which humans, mountains, spirits, and rivers coexist. On the other hand, the religious attribution he gives to this harmonious human-nature relationship ("nebulosa panteísta") is the result of his limited ontological perspective of the more-than-human sociabilities inherent in Indigenous communitarian life—or to put it another way, in the Indigenous socio-natural assemblage.

Many years after the flourishing of indigenista discourses, the discussion on human-nature sociability will be reopened by Indigenous writer activists who convey through their texts part of the agenda of Buen Vivir as a diverse Indigenous philosophical and eco-social construct. It is remarkable that, with the theoretical and dialectical limitations constraining him in the 1920s, Valcárcel subtly sensed the existence of a more-than-human sociability derived from Andean cosmology that structured the life of Indigenous communities. Moreover, this indigenista writer anticipated the inadequacy of the conventional sense of the category *human* to explain the energy that permeates the harmonious relationship between Indigenous peoples and nature.

Tellurism was the most effective analytical instrument at the time to explain the earthly bond that Valcárcel wants to illuminate in his attempt to delineate the uniqueness of Andean individuals. Toward the end of the twentieth century and the beginning of the twenty-first, objective conditions in the Andes changed significantly, and Indigenous intellectuals would build their political and cultural agenda on the basis of some early decolonial indigenista arguments such as those of Valcárcel. Although limited, his reading of the Indigenous socio-natural context is a good illustration of this emerging dialectical genealogy.

TRANSMODERNIST INDIGENISMOS

The works of Vasconcelos and Valcárcel extend beyond *La raza* and *Tempestad*, and their ideas changed over time. Their most emblematic books, as devices that convey indigenista discourses, re-historicize Indigenous societies and, in doing so, can be read as seminal versions of debates on transmodernity. Hand in hand with the contributions of Dussel, Rivera Cusicanqui, and Acosta, I believe transmodernity is a decolonial theoretical framework that delineates Indigenous singularity through the reinterpretation and revalorization of geohistorical referents peripheralized by Eurocentrism. Transmodernism suggests the dialectical construction of identities, genealogies, and subjectivities that antagonize the objective conditions derived from the modernizing European imperial projects in Latin America. In this framework, the books analyzed here reveal to us that the *raza cósmica* and the *nuevo indio* are transmodern entities insofar as they transcend the Eurocentric peripheralizing process; their emancipations imply a re-historicization and re-politicization of Indigenous societies. After all, this is the political telos of transmodernist indigenismos and not the arbitrary speculation of a messianic Indigenous entity providentially fated to (re)emerge with vengeful intentions.

To constrain these texts to the idea of sterile utopianisms would entail depoliticizing them and stripping them of the dialectics that run through their argumentative constructs. This is why, for Vasconcelos, it is important to imagine, without much empirical basis, that the great Ibero-American civilization will settle and develop its transmodern project in the Amazon. In the same way, for Valcárcel it is the claim of an Inca resurgence that, embracing an andinista philosophy, will dominate the Andean geography based on collective agriculturism. The historical distance allows us to perceive that both predictions were not fulfilled, which encourages some critics to read and reread these works as discourses loaded with improbabilities. However, a teleological interpretation allows me to infer that, within the efforts of historical reframing made by both indigenista intellectuals, there is a decolonial intent that contends with an unsustainable present. In the end, a *raza cósmica* and a *nuevo indio* are needed because the present conditions of Indigenous societies in Latin America are not tolerable. It would be insufficient to point again to the criollo sector as the culprit of this situation. Still, the temporal disruption and political significance that both intellectuals attribute to categories such as *race*, *history*, and *territoriality* highlight a structural epistemological framework that thoroughly addresses the system rooted in colonialism, beyond merely critiquing class hegemony.

Thus, *transmodernist indigenismo* is not a homogeneous pro-Indigenous construct that appeals to the incorporation of Indigenous peoples into a Latin American mode of modernity. Rather, it is the formulation of a social project—regionalist or post-national—that transcends modernity as an ultimate goal and rewrites Latin America's political and cultural genealogy by centralizing Indigenous subjectivity. I argue that two approaches to Indigenous societies as different as Vasconcelos's with his selective universalizing mestizaje versus Valcárcel's with his regionalist anti-mestizaje are equally transmodernist. What they both agree on, and this is illustrative of the decolonial intention I highlight, is that for them the future is to be found in traditionally peripheralized geographical spaces: the Andean corridor and the Amazonian rainforests. Both writers imagine the emergence and empowerment of transmodern identities in areas that have been marginalized even within their respective national projects. We cannot discard from a decolonial analysis the anti-Eurocentric intentionality underlying these visions.

Despite their being contemporaries, little is known about any possible intellectual exchange between Vasconcelos and Valcárcel. Regarding the Mexican philosopher's links with Peruvian intellectuals, there is information about his animosity toward the modernista poet José Santos Chocano and his friendship with the writer and politician Víctor Raúl Haya de la Torre, with whom he established a relationship while Haya de la Torre lived exiled in Mexico in the 1920s. It is possible to find an ideological resonance in the types of indigenismos that both advocated, since some concomitants can be detected between the ideas of Vasconcelos and those of the internationalist indigenismo propounded by Haya de la Torre in *Por la emancipación de América Latina* (For the emancipation of Latin America, 1927).

Valcárcel, however, does allude repeatedly to the Mexican author in his writings, where he sets out his disagreements on Vasconcelos's racial theory. For example, in one of the essays compiled in the second volume of *Mirador indio* (Indian lookout, 1941), Valcárcel criticizes Vasconcelos for being "a generous publicist, who observing these mixtures, has thought of the 'cosmic race' on which the existing ones would be founded" ("generoso publicista,-que- observando estas mezclas, ha pensado en la 'raza cósmica,' en que quedarían fundadas las existentes") (*Mirador indio*, 2:241), a loose reference that illustrates Valcárcel's consistent anti-mestizaje ideas. And yet, as I have shown, both writers follow the same dialectical path with the main motive of antagonizing the Eurocentric interpretations and prejudices that subjected Indigenous societies to what I have here called peripheralization, a form of marginalization that segregates non-European cultures from national projects. In doing so, both authors end up advancing arguments in favor of a critical transmodernist debate such as the one that has proliferated in recent years under the large umbrella of Latin American decolonial critique.

CHAPTER 3
Mariátegui's Indo-Marxism and Arguedas's Cultural Program

The critical literature on José Carlos Mariátegui (1894–1930) is abundant in analyses and reinterpretations of his work and later influence. Beyond his *Siete ensayos de interpretación de la realidad peruana* (1928), his body of work is crucial for an understanding of Peruvian politics throughout the twentieth century and the amalgamation of Marxism with Latin American reality.[1] Despite a brief but decisive stay in Europe, Mariátegui spent most of his short life in Lima, where he became one of the most recognized intellectual personalities in the 1920s, when he published his main essays and founded both the Peruvian Socialist Party and the iconic indigenista magazine *Amauta*. Between the indigenistas of Cuzco and Lima there was a fluid exchange of ideas that is reflected not only in the editorial interaction between their members but also in the coincidences, which are larger than the divergences, between the two main indigenista exponents: Valcárcel and Mariátegui.

Some authors have highlighted the disagreements between them, pointing to Valcárcel as the promoter of a regionalist and andinista discourse and to Mariátegui as the propagator of an alternative form of cosmopolitanism that sought only to respond to criollo exceptionalism. However, with different ideological sediments (after all, Valcárcel never explicitly embraced Marxism), both authors advocated a national refounding of Peru as a predominantly Indigenous national project. Mariátegui and Valcárcel embodied a frontal denunciation against the failure of the republican state administered by criollo elites who, by reproducing patterns of marginalization inherited from the colonial system, prolonged a scenario of coloniality structurally linked to the process of modernization in Peru.

This critical perspective was continued by the Peruvian indigenista writer and anthropologist José María Arguedas (1911–1969). He not only was a follower of Mariátegui's ideas but also expanded Mariátegui's cultural program through a social and historical interpretation of indigenismo. This interpretation emphasizes the framework of coloniality as the structure of domination to which Indigenous peoples are subjected. The extension of this dialectical bridge can be seen by revisiting two monographic works that are part of Arguedas's public interventions. These works include his speeches "El indigenismo en el Perú," presented at the Writers' Colloquium in Genoa in 1965, and "No soy un aculturado," presented at the ceremony of acceptance of the Inca Garcilaso de la Vega Award in recognition of his career in 1968. Although I situate Arguedas's reflections within this periodization as a late manifestation, considering that by the 1960s, Indigenous political subjectivity was already articulating an independent intellectual production with no mestizo mediation, I am interested in illuminating his ideas as the latest iteration of a type of *indigenista decolonial crack*, which had been opened by Mariátegui and which traces an inescapable influence on later developments of Indigenous decolonial discourse.

My main purpose here is to illuminate how Mariátegui's Indo-Marxism emerged as a pioneering dialectic in the identification of the colonialist continuum that many decades later would be theoretically articulated as coloniality. I examine the decolonial cracks opened by Mariátegui in his *Siete ensayos*, such as the need to revitalize Inca communism as a revolutionary formula that decolonially adapts Marxist dialectics into the historical and cultural conditions of the Andes, as well as the repercussion that this adaptation caused in what can be considered an orthodox Marxism. I refer specifically to the impasse that the historian Alberto Flores Galindo labeled "the polemic with the Comintern" ("La polémica con la Komintern").

I explore two specific spheres of the ideas and influence of the singular dialectic created by Mariátegui. On the one hand, I review his exercise of historical interpretation made by him to substantiate the viability of an Indo-Marxism rooted in Inca communism with which he proposes an epistemic bypass of the historical-economic linearity imposed by orthodox Marxism. In theory, this bypass is visible in his interpretation of the historical validity of the ayllu and the use of the notion of myth as a driving force of the Indigenous revolutionary potential, while, in praxis, it is grounded in his dissociation from the Marxist orthodoxy of the Comintern, a critical line that inspires the theoretical formulation of decoloniality in the sociologist Aníbal Quijano. On the other hand, I explore how Indo-Marxism runs through Mariátegui's definition of indigenista literature in his essay "El proceso de la literatura" (The process of literature), which forms part of *Siete ensayos*, in order to present his thoughts on literature and arts as a dialectical program that aspired to contend with the coloniality of culture.

Finally, the critical monographs of J. M. Arguedas, particularly his evaluations of indigenismo and the role of indigenous literatures—especially Quechua—constitute both a continuation of the Indo-Marxist cultural program initiated by Mariátegui and open a series of productive lines of inquiry that would be taken up by Quechua writers years later. I argue that Arguedas accomplishes this by shifting Mariátegui's Indo-Marxist dialectic from a focus on the political-economic dimension to one centered on the political-cultural dimension. From this perspective, I emphasize his role as a creative writer and, more significantly, as a cultural promoter.

MARIÁTEGUI'S NATIONAL REASSESSMENT

Throughout his *Siete ensayos*, Mariátegui challenges different aspects of the criollo national project in Peru. In his denunciation of the dispossession of Indigenous land under gamonalismo, a model of feudal latifundia (*latifundismo*) that was consolidated after independence from the metropolis, he sheds light on different aspects of the coloniality of power, insofar as under this system the subjugation and epistemological devaluation of the Indigenous peoples and knowledges is reproduced through and with a system of production. He accuses the criollo emancipation process that took place between 1821 and 1824 of having been hypocritically Jacobin because its republican promise of equality under the law never included Indigenous society, since it was a "bourgeois and liberal" revolution (*Interpretive Essays*, 52).

For Mariátegui, Indigenous peoples are less protected under the republican system than during the viceregal system. What he defines as the Indian problem, to which he devotes an entire essay ("El problema del indio"), is a matter of dispossession of the land (primitive accumulation), an issue of material conditions, since it is a model of economic subjugation—with ontological implications: "The problem of the Indian is rooted in the land tenure system of our economy" (*Interpretive Essays*, 43). This idea allows him to vindicate the figure of the ayllu, a form of community social organization inherited from the pre-Inca Andean civilizations, where the work and the use of the land are carried out collectively—that is, a noncapitalist organization, to phrase it in Marxist terms. This is how he introduces the foundations of Inca communism that he will vindicate in different ways throughout his monographic literature.

Mariátegui calls for the revitalization and expansion of pre-Hispanic communism, which is in reality an agrarian communism rather than an industrial or postindustrial one, since Andean society naturally tends to organize itself under principles of agro-culturalism, an idea in which one can already see his deproletarianized vision of the revolution. Pages later, he completes the presentation of his sociopolitical program by proposing Marxism as a catalyst for the aspirations of the Indigenous population, which is why I call the dialectic that runs through this approach Indo-Marxism. From this, it can be deduced that, for Mariátegui, socialism is not an end but, rather, a means of restructuring national reality through an Inca communism much older than the conventional European socialist endeavors and which did not need the emergence or apogee of capitalism and an oppressed urban labor class in order to exist. In bypassing capitalist consolidation, Mariátegui disengaged himself from the orthodox sense of Stalinist historicity with which orthodox Marxists interpreted the history of class struggle, thereby engaging himself in a polemic on which Alberto Flores Galindo has written extensively (*La agonía*, 21–53).

I must specify that I do not necessarily concur with the notion of a precapitalist Peru, as described by Mariátegui, since the insertion of the Andes in the global economic world system through the extraction of natural resources and the circulation of enslaved people dates from the sixteenth century, which in itself is already a form of capitalism—albeit an incipient version of this model. Nevertheless, it is true that in the early twentieth century, Peru was in fact a preindustrial capitalist country, although its economic forces, concentrated on the coast, were already defining the political direction of the national project. I will return to this point in the following sections.

Mariátegui's Inca communism, as a revolutionary, cultural, and social project, had diverse receptions. For Antonio Cornejo Polar, the idea of what Mariátegui describes as a "primitive communism" in the Inca civilization is historically unsustainable and its postulation is the result of an effort by Mariátegui to create an alloy between indigenismo and communism (*Escribir*, 187–90). Slightly similar readings have been made by de Castro (*Mestizo Nations*, 76–81) and Coronado (*The Andes Imagined*, 43–49), who point out that Mariátegui sees a revolutionary potential in the Andean subject, as well as a proto-communism in the ayllu, as a formula oriented to an alternative modernity instead of the liberal criollo project. Coronado, likewise, points out as one of Mariátegui's failures the fact that his design of a "revolutionary Indian" is addressed to a literate audience, which reveals the poor contact between the *Siete ensayos* author and the illiterate Indigenous population (47–48). For his part, Gerardo Leibner identifies Mariátegui's analysis as an "attitude" that forges a uniquely Latin American Marxism (*El mito*, 22). For Juan Carlos Grijalva, Inca communism is a mere figment of Mariátegui's imagination because it lacks archaeological and historical support, and only seeks to provide his socialist interpretation of Peruvian reality with a link to Andean nativism ("Paradoxes," 319). More essentialist in his criticism is Gonzalo Portocarrero, who argues that "Indo-American socialism" is Mariátegui's response to the liberal exclusivism of the criollo aristocracy that had marginalized him in his condition of "mestizo acriollado" (mestizo pretending to be criollo) which ended up making him resentful ("mestizo resentido") (*La urgencia*, 270–73).

Some of these criticisms are irrefutable. As Coronado states, Mariátegui miscalculates the impact of his essay if he expects it to become an instrument of agitation within illiterate Indigenous groups. Similarly, there is no doubt that underlying *Siete ensayos* is a proposal for the modernization of the Peruvian national project as an alternative to the liberal process of criollo aristocracy. Does Inca communism have no historical backing? This is a perspective that I find more arguable, and it is on this basis that I construct an argument about the decolonial potential in the dialectics articulated by Mariátegui.

Efraín Kristal (*Una visión*, 15–33) and Thomas Ward (*La resistencia*, 204–5) are more moderate in their criticisms. They highlight Mariátegui's accuracy in drawing a distinction between the incompatibility of the Inca economy and Peruvian incipient capitalism (the latifundista regime). Ward even acknowledges that Mariátegui's effort to synchronize Tahuantinsuyo with Marx's sense of a communist society makes him "an epistemological border thinker" ("un pensador epistemológico de bordes") (213), a clear and insufficiently developed reference to Mignolo's "border thinking."[2] Precisely, Mignolo (*Local Histories*, 140–41) defines Mariátegui as an intellectual writing from the margins of the modern colonial system who is strongly influenced by his local history although, to be precise, it is undeniable that Mariátegui is also dialectically instructed by what today could be considered an incipient version of Western Marxism to which he was exposed during his stay in Europe.[3] Thus, the conventional baselines of historical materialism were adapted by Mariátegui to the Peruvian legacy of racism and dehumanization of Indigenous peoples to make this conflation central in his critique of capitalism as a critique of colonialism under the label of gamonalismo.[4] According to Javier Sanjinés (*Embers*, 76–83), Mariátegui stops analyzing Latin America by mimicking a Eurocentric view but, rather, adapts a European social theory such as Marxism to the historical and social conditions of Andean Indigenous people, which led him to break with the inevitable imperative of proletarianizing Indigenous communities in order to achieve revolutionary subjective conditions in his identification of the perdurability of ayllus.

THE AYLLU AS SOCIAL UNITY FOR AN INDIGENOUS REVOLUTION

Mariátegui lays the foundations of his critique of the deterministic approach to history of what could be called orthodox Marxism in a crucial and extensive footnote in *Siete ensayos*. "Modern communism is different from Inca communism. This is the first thing that must be learned and understood by the scholar who delves into Tawantinsuyo. The two communisms are products of different human experiences. They belong to different historical epochs. They were evolved by dissimilar civilizations. The Inca civilizations was agrarian; the civilization of Marx and Sorel is industrial" (*Interpretive Essays*, 74).

The Andean social reality, without advanced industrial development, could not assume that a capitalist bourgeoisie would put an end to the feudal economic model but, rather, that Indigenous social mobility would have to do so. In other words, the Indigenous campesino population (an agrarian civilization) had to undertake its revolution in the absence of what in the European context was conceptualized as *proletarian* (an industrial civilization). The reason for this situation is the difference in the historical development of Europe with respect to the Andes ("They belong to different historical epochs") (74). This idea inspired many decades later what Aníbal Quijano, one of the founding voices of what is known as the *decolonial turn*, defined as "historical-structural heterogeneity," a term that describes the asymmetrical process whereby power relations are regulated not only by economic variables but also by racial, historical, and cultural factors; a sense of heterogeneity that is expressed in discontinuous, inconsistent, and conflicting ("discontinuos, inconsistentes y conflictivos") fields of relations ("Colonialidad del poder" [2014], 295).

These inconsistencies, asymmetrical power relations, and historical developments are what delineate the differences between modern communism and the Inca communism described by Mariátegui. According to Quijano, "Mariátegui was, without a doubt, the first to begin to see (and not just in Latin America) that in his space/time, the social relations of power, whatever their previous character, existed and acted simultaneously and together in a single and whole structure of power. He perceived that there could not be a homogeneous unity, with continuous relations among its elements, moving itself in a continuous and systematic history" ("Coloniality," 573). The possibility of a socialist revolution based on Inca communism is inspired by an interpretation in which Andean society derives from a singular historical-structural current that is different from progressive Western industrialization. Mariátegui explicitly opens a crack that bypasses the expansive and deterministic Marxist revolutionary orthodoxy as it was imposed institutionally by Comintern (dialectical materialism in a Leninist sense). If Inca communism were to have reemerged, it would have been because of the survival of the ayllu, which he identifies as a social cell that grounds Andean agrarian communism and collectivism and that predates Inca society.[5]

To build his argument, Mariátegui cites a study by sociologist Hildebrando Castro Pozo that he embraces as empirical truth: "The ayllu has conserved in natural peculiarity, its character as an almost family institution that continued to harbor, after the conquest, its main constituents" (*Interpretive Essays*, 56). These words of Castro Pozo are used by Mariátegui to articulate the peculiar historicity of the Indigenous collective and the potentiality of economic independence based on agrarian collectivism and aimed at abolishing the persistent feudal system (latifundismo). This allows Leibner to mythologize under the conceptual umbrella of *community* the idea of an Indigenous communism ideologically rooted in a form of Indo-Marxism: "The supposedly obvious direct relation between the contemporary Indigenous community and the Inca past, mediated by the collectivist spirit of the Andean Indigenous people, became one of the most frequent and most important arguments for the configuration of Mariátegui's myth of Indigenous socialism" ("La supuestamente obvia relación directa entre la comunidad indígena contemporánea y el pasado incaico, mediada por el espíritu colectivista de los indígenas andinos, se fue convirtiendo en uno de los argumentos más frecuentes y más importantes para la configuración del mito del socialismo indígena de Mariátegui") (*El mito*, 120). With this reading, Leibner suggests that the ayllu—which was then a subject of discussions about the intangibility of its survival—was capitalized on and forcibly adapted by leftist indigenistas to fit into the prospect of a socialist construct that would agitate and modernize Indigenous societies.[6]

Coronado is of an opinion similar to Leibner's, writing that "the interpretation of the ayllu as inherently Marxist relied more on a purposeful misconstruction of this traditional Indigenous social formation than on reality" (*The Andes Imagined*, 65). Certainly, Mariátegui's conceptual use of the *ayllu* seems to manipulate an

Indigenous sociocultural reference into a Marxist revolutionary construct. The political intention that runs through this forced association is his interest in re-historicizing the Andes through a refractory lens that would allow him to set the pillars of what nowadays decolonial approaches imbedded in materialist critique label as historical-structural heterogeneity. For this purpose, the ayllu has a double functionality. On the one hand, it offers a sort of historical empirical evidence that justifies and mythologizes Indigenous communism (ideologically structured by him as an Indo-Marxism) on which it would be possible to trigger an agrarian revolution. On the other hand, the ayllu operates as a symbolic device to vindicate Indigenous society's social, political, and economic autonomy and to integrate this vindication into insurgent rhetoric. Thus, at the political-rhetorical level, the ayllu fissures the constrained and inflexible understanding that the criollo national project elaborated about Andean society as a demobilized group.

The ayllu, as a symbolic device, opens a decolonial crack that encourages the revalorization—or in a way, the capitalization—of Indigenous sociocultural referents. This expanded and even permeable understanding of this notion reappears in several parts of *Siete ensayos*. In the famous essay titled "El proceso de la literatura," the ayllu returns in the section dedicated to the definition of indigenista literature where Mariátegui says: "Indian life has a style. Notwithstanding the conquest, the latifundium, and the gamonal, the Indians of the sierra still follow their own tradition. The ayllu is a social structure deeply rooted in environment and race. The Indians continue their old rural life. To this day, they keep their native dress, their customs, and their handicrafts. The Indigenous social community has not disappeared under the harshest feudalism. The Indigenous society may appear to be primitive and retarded, but it is an organic type of society and culture" (*Interpretive Essays*, 283).

At that time, there were many epistemic limitations that constricted the knowledge Mariátegui could have of the *ayllu*, so it does not seem fair to ask for a compelling use of this concept.[7] In addition, physical difficulties precluded him from traveling to the Andean area to do fieldwork, so his main sources for theorizing about Indigenous communities were the studies of Castro Pozo and Valcárcel and, as Leibner suggests, also fictional indigenista literature such as that of Enrique López Albújar, which was adopted by Mariátegui as empirical evidence. However, the symbolic use of the *ayllu* as a rhetorical device oriented toward the construction of what these days we can consider a decolonizing claim is quite remarkable.

Putting aside possible sociological readings, the ayllu is a crucial tool in what I argue is one of Mariátegui's main contributions to Latin American decolonial genealogy—a decolonial and indigenized adaptation of Marxist dialects. J. M. Arguedas is among those who adopted this method and adapted Marxism to the Andes. For Irina Alexandra Feldman, Mariátegui's economic problem of the latifundio is transformed into a cultural problem through Arguedas's fictional narrative. She addresses connection more specifically in the prophetic death of the *patrón* in the short story "La agonía del Rasu Ñiti" (*Rethinking*, 114). However, as I show later, this transformation made by Arguedas is also present in the monographic writing where he defines his cultural program and provides a definition of the social and political role of indigenismo within the framework of Indo-Marxism.

Mariátegui's Indo-Marxism is rooted in the historical reframing of the material conditions and subjectivity of the revolutionary social base: Indigenous campesinos. This variable allows him to delineate the dialectical singularity of the Andes, despite certain concomitances with other agrarian-centered revolutionary processes such as the Russian experience: "Feudalism similarly let rural communes continue in Russia, a country that offers an interesting parallel because in its historical process it is much closer to these agricultural and semi-feudal countries than are the capitalist countries of the West" (*Interpretive Essays*, 44). With an evident selectivity in his indirect allusion to what the Soviet kolkhoz was, Mariátegui tries to justify the harmony between the Andean precapitalist status and the possibility of a triumphant socialist revolution whose insurgent force would emerge from the peasant population.[8] After all, he knew better than anyone the reluctance of the domestic bourgeoisie to abolish feudalism, since it was the social sector with which he had dealt the most. And, based on his experience building the Peruvian Socialist Party in urban areas, he had learned the limitations of the incipient Peruvian proletarian class, which had not yet been developed enough to antagonize the agrarian-dependent bourgeoisie.

For Leibner, who re-created Marxism in Mariátegui as an "attitude," Mariátegui's dialectic is articulated in the form of a revolutionary myth that solidifies in the confluence of two factors: "his incorporation into the cultural and ideological current of indigenismo and his analysis of the Indigenous question as a socioeconomic problem" ("su incorporación a la corriente cultural e ideológica del indigenismo y su análisis de la cuestión indígena como un problema socio-económico") (*El mito*, 27). Although I concur with this reading, and it would be interesting to nuance what type of indigenismo Mariátegui adheres to, it is necessary to contextualize the role occupied by the ayllu in the revolutionary mythological construct. Mariátegui is strongly influenced by the ideas of the French philosopher Georges Sorel who reconceptualizes the notions of *myth* in the socialist revolutionary context as follows: "men who are participating in great social movements always picture their coming action in the form of images of battle in which their cause is certain to triumph. I proposed to give the name of 'myths' to these constructions, knowledge of which is so important for historians" (*Reflections*, 20).

The symbolic notion with which Mariátegui reframes the *ayllu* in his Indo-Marxist dialectic precisely occupies the place of those images Sorel refers to and which inspire the political and ideological praxis of the revolutionary social base. Without a consolidated urban proletarian class, only the ayllu contains the necessary symbolic force and the subjective conditions compelling enough to create the image of a possible revolutionary triumph rooted in the Andean historical structure. Agrarian collectivism, proclaimed as surviving from pre-Hispanic times, offered Indo-Marxism a ground for political action and provided Indigenous communities with inspiration for social mobility, contrary to other demobilizing sociological readings such as that of Alcides Arguedas.[9]

POLEMICS AND DIALECTICAL DECOLONIZATION

In June 1929, a year after the publication of *Siete ensayos* and a few months before Mariátegui's death, the first Latin American Communist Conference took place in Buenos Aires, where communist delegations from different countries of the region met and a small delegation led by Julio Portocarrero and Hugo Pesce, friends and co-partisans of Mariátegui in the recently formed Peruvian Socialist Party, arrived in representation of Peru.[10] They brought to this event lectures and texts by Mariátegui, who was unable to travel because of his precarious health. Among the works that circulated at this meeting were the book *Siete ensayos* and other articles that condensed the programmatic content of his Indo-Marxism. The aim of the conference was to make a collective balance of the situation of the communist organizations in Latin America, with the purpose of evaluating if the objective conditions were present for the triumph of a communist revolution in this region and what those conditions should be like. The person in charge of leading the organization and the sessions at the event was the Italian Argentine communist activist Victorio Codovilla who had already participated in Communist International (Comintern) meetings in Moscow and who had contributed to the creation of the Argentine Communist Party.

In an atmosphere of considerable programmatic affinity among the various Latin American delegations who presented their reports and ideas in Buenos Aires, the delegation that generated the most discomfort was the Peruvian one whose Indo-Marxist ideas did not fit comfortably with the orthodox Marxism (in the Lukácsian sense) and the Stalinist line advocated by the Comintern. Discrepancies between the Peruvian delegation and others had several causes, such as tension with the Chilean delegation because of the open debate on a border problem reminiscent of the Pacific War or the fact that the Peruvian communists created a Socialist Party and not one called "Communist."[11] But, what I am interested in highlighting here is the discomfort generated by the historical-structural scheme with which the Indigenous factor entered Mariátegui's Indo-Marxist program. For Codovilla, the main representative of Stalinist line of orthodox Marxism in this event, it was problematic that the Indigenous campesinos were not historically situated in the *proletarian* category and that they, in turn, were not primarily organized under the scheme of a communist party.

The Italian Argentine intellectual also rejected the singularity with which Pesce and Portocarrero referred to the Peruvian reality as a scenario determined by particular objective conditions and still rooted in colonial influence. For Flores Galindo, this impasse was because the Comintern representatives were "thinking of Marxism as a closed body of doctrine or as a theory with universal validity" ("pensando al marxismo como un cuerpo cerrado de doctrina o como una teoría con validez universal") (*La agonía*, 29). To this position, the Peruvian delegation—commissioned by Mariátegui—responded that "as was the case with the workmen, the important thing is looking for the peculiarities of these peasants, who in the Andean area were born of a special union between their class condition and their ethnic situation, that is, they were peasants but also Indians" ("como ocurría con los obreros, lo importante es buscar las peculiaridades de esos campesinos, que en el área andina nacían de una especial unión entre la condición de clase y la situación étnica, es decir, eran campesinos pero también indios") (quoted in Flores Galindo, *La agonía*, 30). Andean indigeneity and its historical-structural singularity, which I have previously illuminated as a theoretical pillar of decolonial critique in the Andean corridor, provoked a sort of programmatic fracture between orthodox Marxism and Indo-Marxism insofar as both sides disagreed on the sociopolitical and historical condition of the revolutionary subject.

Mariátegui problematizes something that seemed to be a blind spot in the agenda of the Comintern: the problem of race and indigeneity. The revolutionary subject of Indo-Marxism was not only a subject exclusively oppressed by the material and economic conditions under a feudal system but also a racialized subject as a consequence of the sociocultural experience of colonialism. He exposes this in the Buenos Aires congress through an article entitled "El problema de las razas en América Latina" (The problem of races in Latin America), the second part of which was cowritten with Pesce.[12] In this article, Indo-Marxism establishes the race struggle as a necessary dialectical pillar in a struggle that ran through the racial symbolic construct imposed by the colonial matrix of power. "The interest of the exploiting class—first Spaniards, then criollo—has invariably tended, under various disguises, to explain the condition of the Indigenous races with the argument of their inferiority or primitivism" ("El interés de la clase explotadora,—española primero, criolla después—ha tendido invariablemente, bajo diversos disfraces, a explicar la condición de las razas indígenas con el argumento de su inferioridad o primitivismo") (*Ideología*,

22). Here, Mariátegui directly articulates racism as a determining factor for the subalternized status of Indigenous peasants and at the same time describes the colonialist continuum upon which the decolonial critique is built. For de Castro, in this work Mariátegui "presents Indigenous culture in a manner that emphasises the difference between its practical socialism, including the commune, and modern socialism" (*Bread and Beauty*, 65). This difference resides in the historical articulation of the revolutionary subject (Indigenous campesinos) and its singular historicity (colonialization and racialization). Thus, Mariátegui incorporates race as a driving axis of revolutionary action, which, I argue, is decidedly decolonizing, since it points to the historical-structural pillars of the coloniality of power that encompasses an anti-capitalist stance. "An Indigenous revolutionary consciousness will perhaps take time to form; but once the Indian has made the socialist idea his own, he will serve it with a discipline, a tenacity, and a strength in which few proletarians of other milieus will be able to surpass him."[13]

One might sense that such a statement would be interpreted by orthodox Marxists (at this point, it must be reemphasized that Mariategui is dealing with a Stalinist-driven Comintern) as a provocation or a displacement of the proletarians from the historical linearity of Leninist dialectical materialism. Moreover, a Eurocentric Marxist reading might infer that Indo-Marxism suggests a revolution embodied in the mobility of declassed sectors because of its myopic view of Indigenous societies as racialized segments.[14] However, in the discomfort triggered by Indo-Marxism lies one of the main arguments of this chapter: Mariátegui dialectically decolonizes the import of Marxism in Latin America by introducing a radical indigenista vision that not only reframes the historical-structural conditions of revolution (the myth of ayllu or the ayllu as a myth) but also problematizes the racial conditions of the present by centralizing the race of Indigenous societies as a crucial factor in the revolutionary agenda of the Andes.

Decolonially speaking, one of the major lessons of what Flores Galindo popularly labeled "La polémica con la Komintern" resides in that it exposed, early on in Latin America and perhaps in other sectors of the Global South as well, the limitation of Western revolutionary dialectics in dealing with the historical-structural heterogeneity of diverse forms of coloniality. In other words, the influence that indigenismo had on Mariátegui is exhibited in the way he demonstrated that the international division of labor produced by European colonialism (whether one calls it preindustrial capitalism or latifundismo) is intrinsically attached to racial/ethnic division and hierarchization in the former colonies. This is the reason the revolutionary subject in Indo-Marxism must emerge from this intersection of class and race derived from the economic and ethnic asymmetries forged by colonialism. Thus, it is important to highlight the figure of Mariátegui as a pioneer of the variables that, years later, reappear in the decolonial discursive genealogy as that of Reinaga and Quijano.

I read Mariátegui's adaptation of Marxism to the Andean reality as a decolonizing praxis because of its incorporation of the variable of race, which, due to the colonial experience of the social sector about which he theorizes (Indigenous campesinos) is central to his dialectical construct. In that sense, he anticipates several of the terms used by decolonial critics to define the decolonial turn; for example, factors such as race and the power dynamics derived from colonialism constitute a nondeterministic vision of history that allows him to centralize Indigenous peoples as revolutionary subjects within an Indo-Marxist proposal.[15] The type of indigenismo he articulates is one that is inscribed as the epitome of what has been called here a decolonial crack, insofar as it opens new interpretative lines within a current of insurgent thought and, in its very unique form, is both anti-colonial and anti-imperialist. Another way of defining Mariátegui's interpretative approach is as a dialectical bypass based on the negation of the historical determinism advocated by orthodox Marxism, skipping the industrial phase of capitalism, which in his analysis had no immediate material basis in Peruvian reality. As the disagreement with Comintern suggests, the fusion of Marxism with indigenismo articulated by Mariátegui destabilizes positivist interpretations of history as a linear construct (which was problematic for most indigenista intellectuals) and monocultural readings of subaltern subjects that constrained their social and political development to the Western working-class experience.

The recognition of historical-structural heterogeneity, whose roots Quijano identifies in Mariátegui, has inspired in the academic and activist decolonial critical tradition the appreciation of the varied, asymmetrical, discontinuous, and even old-fashioned forms of oppression by the dominant classes. Each oppressed legacy required its own unique forms of insurgency and race, particularly the race of Andean Indigenous subalternized peoples since the beginning of colonization, forcing a reformulation of dialectical materialism. After all, as Mariátegui states, when referring to the situation of the Quechua and Aymara societies in Peru and Bolivia in the exposition he submitted to Buenos Aires, in these countries it is necessary "to transform the race factor into a revolutionary factor" ("convertir al factor raza en factor revolucionario") (*Ideología*, 33). These ideas, repudiated by orthodox Marxists, anticipate the dialectical limitation of unproblematic adaptations of dialectical materialism and inspire the search for other anti-colonial alternatives such as those embodied by the indianismo of the Quechua Aymara intellectual Reinaga (Aimé Cesáire does the same with *négritude* in the Caribbean context), whose ideological particularities trace a dialectical bridge with the Indo-Marxist formulations of Mariátegui. From a world-system perspective, where a central symbolic space is assumed for the formation of ideologies and dialectics, Mariátegui occupies a peripheral space despite his European journey before writing *Siete ensayos* and the national centrality of having lived most of his life in Lima.

INDIGENISMO AS A CULTURAL PROGRAM

The Indo-Marxism that runs through the more sociopolitical essays of *Siete ensayos* is also part of Mariátegui's cultural program. In a famous essay entitled "El proceso de la literatura," he explores various literary currents as well as authors and trends. The first sections of this essay are devoted to a fustigation of what today we can call the coloniality of culture, which Mariátegui identifies in the continuing Hispanist trope embodied by the criollo literary tradition articulated under the currents of classicism, romanticism, and modernism (*Interpetive Essays*, 165–67). Antagonizing this tradition, he defends indigenismo as a literary and artistic current that is reparative of the cultural injustices to which Indigenous society was subjected. "Indigenism in our literature, as may be gathered from my earlier statements, is basically aimed at repairing the injustices done to the Indian. Its role is not the purely sentimental one of, for example, criollo-ism. It would therefore be a mistake to judge indigenism as the equivalent of criollo-ism, which it neither replaces nor supplants. The Indian is prominent in Peruvian literature and art, not because he is an interesting subject for a novel or a painting, but because the new forces and vital impulses of the nation are directed toward redeeming him" (*Interpetive Essays*, 225).

After all, as Grosfoguel points out, the expansion of Eurocentrism is not only a geographical construct but a geo-cultural expansion of the modern imaginary that hierarchizes the production of knowledge and thus lays the foundations for cultural racism ("Colonial Difference," 212–17). Mariátegui identifies these asymmetries and approaches the field of cultural production through the Indo-Marxist dialectical lens that Melisa Moore interprets as "an attempt to rethink politically and culturally the seemingly irreconcilable duality of the nation" ("un intento por repensar política y culturalmente la dualidad aparentemente irreconciliable de la nación") ("Rompiendo fronteras," 92). This is how it can be explained that, in his conceptualization of indigenismo as a literary and artistic movement, Mariátegui has to clarify that it is not an "equivalent of criollo-ism, which it neither replaces nor supplants." His historical-structural vision illuminates a particular genealogy embodied in the indigenista movement, in the same way that Indigenous communism is part of an original historical-political construct materialized in the mythologized survival of the ayllu.

However, despite his exaltation of the indigenista literary movement, Mariátegui is well aware of its epistemic limitations and therefore says: "Indigenist literature cannot give us a strictly authentic version of the Indian, for it must idealize and stylize him. Nor can it give us his soul. It is still a mestizo literature and as such is called indigenist rather than Indigenous. If an Indigenous literature finally appears, it will be when the Indians themselves are able to produce it" (*Interpretive Essays*, 226). He is straightforwardly highlighting the epistemological delimitation—grounded on identification and sources of knowledge—under which mestizo writers became the main producers of the indigenista literary movement (in his time, López Albújar, César Vallejo, Valcárcel, and in his own way, Ventura García Calderón, and with the striking exclusion of Clorinda Matto). In addition, Mariátegui identifies the political teleology that justifies the representative traits of this literature inasmuch as it should idealize and stylize Indigenous societies, not aspire to re-create their "soul."

Interestingly, in what Mariátegui essentializes as "soul," there seems to hover in a sort of inaccessible positionality in the world a symbolic space unbreakable even for mestizo intellectuals who approach Indigenous culture sympathetically. In order to understand the operativity that he confers upon indigenista literature, we must return to the title of the essay "El proceso de la literatura." As an integral part of a process that addresses the asymmetries derived from colonial dynamics in the cultural field, indigenista literature is itself a process through which Indigenous symbolic devices contend with criollo cultural production while generating the objective conditions so that "Indians themselves are able to produce" their own literature. Mariátegui overlooks—perhaps purposefully—that there was already an ongoing Indigenous literary tradition in the Andes even before colonization. What is interesting is that, despite the skepticism with which he phrases it, Mariátegui hopes for the advent of an empowered production and circulation of Indigenous literary works that would allow the subalternized to speak for themselves, and indeed, these hopes would materialize in the form he expected many years after his death.

In an interesting study of Mariátegui as cultural critic, Álvaro Campuzano Arteta synthesizes that art and literature in his vision are influenced by the mobility of the debates on "lo indígena" in his time. "The search for a tradition rooted in the historical and sociocultural particularity from which he thinks and writes, led Mariátegui to territories located outside the walls of Latinism and Hispanism" ("La búsqueda de una tradición arraigada en la particularidad histórica y sociocultural desde la que piensa y escribe, condujo a Mariátegui hacia territorios situados en los extramuros del latinismo y del hispanismo") (*La modernidad*, 256). Campuzano Arteta adds that this is noticeable in his "hunting for living roots" ("acecho de raíces vivas") (256) in a pre-Hispanic world. It is also identifiable in his reception of Indigenous pictorial works such as those of the Peruvian painter José Sabogal or the Mexican muralist Diego Rivera whose work for Mariátegui owes its content to the agrarian insurrection ("insurrección agrarista") of the Mexican Revolution (261). The search to which Campuzano Arteta refers is certainly true and can also be identified in the editorial profile that Mariátegui created for the magazine *Amauta*, but that symbolic extramural space intrinsically implies a bypassing of the hegemonic criollo literary tradition that reproduced the coloniality of culture.

It was not easy for Mariátegui to ground his ideas about the role of literature in the Indo-Marxist cultural construct. In an interview published in *Perricholi* magazine in 1926, he was asked who he considered to be the greatest figure of Peruvian literature. As expected, he began by problematizing the axis of periodicity, when, where, and who starts Peruvian literature? He says: "The literature of the Spaniards of the colony is not Peruvian literature. There are, undoubtedly, exceptions. [Inca] Garcilaso de la Vega is one of them. In him, the Indigenous sense is in his blood" ("La literatura de los españoles de la colonia no es literatura peruana. Hay, sin duda, excepciones. [Inca] Garcilaso de la Vega es una de ellas. En éste el sentido indígena está en la sangre") (*La novela*, 149). As he consistently articulates throughout his work, for Mariátegui, Andean indigeneity is an inescapable factor in the construction of a Peruvian national consciousness. Inca Garcilaso, as a mestizo, fits into this singular genealogy that Mariátegui constructs, although Garcilaso does not transmit the Indigenous soul that Mariátegui requires for an authentically Indigenous literature. Who does seem to achieve this, at least relatively, is the poet and martyr of emancipation Mariano Melgar, who cultivated the *yaraví*, a literary genre with Andean roots. For Mariátegui, Melgar did translate the true Indigenous sentiment ("tradujo el verdadero sentimiento indígena") (152) although without the potential he identified in César Vallejo. Ultimately, as a thematic corpus and a discursive telos, indigenista literature for Mariátegui is a process that is mobilized in tune with the revolutionary and redemptive purposes of Indo-Marxism and whose symbolic forces seem to be oriented toward the creation of the historical conditions for the emergence of an Indigenous literature that would "peruvianize" the Peruvian cultural field.

It could be asserted that this cultural program was adopted quite explicitly by J. M. Arguedas, who assumed as his own the search for literature containing the "soul" of the Andean Indigenous. An initial approach to this can be seen in the monographic section of his collection and translation of *Canto quechua. Con un ensayo sobre la capacidad de creación artística del pueblo indio y mestizo* (Quechua chant: With an essay on the capacity for artistic creation of the Indian and mestizo people, 1938). Through a self-referential approach, Arguedas justifies the editorial project contained in this publication by pointing out that the poetry of these songs "demonstrates that Indians know how to express their feelings in poetic language; demonstrates their capacity for artistic creation, and shows that what the people create for their own expression is essential art" ("demostrar que el indio sabe expresar sus sentimientos en lenguaje poético; demostrar su capacidad de creación artística y hacer ver que lo que el pueblo crea para su propia expresión, es arte esencial") (*Canto quechua*, 26). For Arguedas as for Mariátegui, literature seems to be a process oriented toward identifying a culturally productive agency of the Indigenous people. This explains why Mariátegui highlights the *yaraví* and Arguedas, at this stage, the Quechua chants. Though still early in his career, Arguedas does not yet clearly define categories such as *indios* or *mestizos*. I am interested in illuminating this text as an initial gesture of the Indo-Marxist orientation that articulates his later monographic production. Arguedas transforms the economic problem of Indigenous communities into a cultural problem that Quechua poets will address decades later.

ARGUEDAS AND THE CHALLENGE TO CULTURAL COLONIALITY

Peruvian writer and anthropologist José María Arguedas is probably one of the most notable adherents of the political and cultural program inaugurated by Mariátegui in the 1920s. Arguedas is the author of remarkable narrative works and a vast monographic literature, a significant portion of which is methodologically influenced by his anthropological instruction. He is a crucial figure in the development of Latin American indigenismo and in understanding the dialectical link that this work illuminates through the connection of indigenismo with indigenous cultural production in the late twentieth century.

There are political connections that define the link between Arguedas and Mariátegui as a link that anticipates some of the terms that years later describe the indigenous decolonial agenda. In one of his last public interventions, Arguedas delivered the famous speech entitled "No soy un aculturado" in which he explicitly describes his adoption of what has been defined here as Indo-Marxism—that is, the interpretation through which Mariátegui adapts Marx's revolutionary thesis to the Andean reality. "It was while reading Mariátegui and then Lenin that I found a permanent order in things; the socialist theory not only gave a course to the whole future but to all the energy that was in me, it gave it a destiny and charged it even more with force by the very fact of channeling it" ("Fue leyendo a Mariátegui y después a Lenin que encontré un orden permanente en las cosas; la teoría socialista no sólo dio un cauce a todo el porvenir sino a lo que había en mí de energía, le dio un destino y lo cargó aun más de fuerza por el mismo hecho de encauzarlo") (*El zorro*, 14).[16]

Arguedas defines in this way the ideological course that organizes his cultural agenda within the framework of Mariateguian Indo-Marxism. For Javier García Liendo (*El intelectual*, 100–104), Arguedas identifies in Mariátegui's work and, in particular, the project embodied in the magazine *Amauta* a possibility for consolidating a social space through cultural communication promoted by the circulation of cultural material devices. For Mabel Moraña, "Arguedas's intellectual mission is informed by the need to contribute to the project of refounding identity without renouncing the vernacular aspects and without betraying the utopia of egalitarian progress" ("[la] misión intelectual de Arguedas está informada por la necesidad de contribuir al proyecto de refundación identitaria sin renunciar a las vertientes vernáculas y sin traicionar la utopía de un progreso igualitario") (*Arguedas-Vargas Llosa*, 160). Arguedas's activity as a compiler and disseminator of Andean culture, which he combines in his different roles as creative writer, college professor, and public officer is ideologically articulated by the decolonizing spirit that defines Indo-Marxism.

However, Arguedas is also a thinker who reflects on and through indigenismo, despite a certain reluctance to self-identify as such. For cultural critic Mirko Lauer, Arguedas is part of a second wave of indigenista intellectuals that Lauer labels *indigenismo-2* and which he distinguishes from a first wave because of its sociopolitical and more technocratic character. This second wave deals with areas such as the literary, plastic, architectural, or musical ("[lo] literario, plástico, arquitectónico, o musical") (*Andes Imaginarios*, 12). Nevertheless, Arguedas is an intellectual whose work is informed by social and political realities, and this is largely explained through his connection with Mariátegui. This connection makes it difficult to read his cultural agenda in a depoliticized way since Arguedas deeply identifies with Mariátegui's political and cultural project: "*Amauta* becomes a tribune for the dissemination of Marxist socialist ideology, and as it reaches a vast circulation in the country and in Latin America, it becomes, at the same time, a means of expression for rebellious provincial writers who denounce, through narrative or essay, the state of servitude in which the Indigenous population is situated."[17]

This appraisal of Mariátegui's cultural program, presented by Arguedas at the Genoa Writers' Colloquium as "El indigenismo en el Perú" (Indigenismo in Peru) (*Indios*, 9–20), expresses his adherence to Mariátegui's ideas and reveals that Indo-Marxism is the critical foundation of his indigenista framework. For Arguedas, *Amauta* is valuable because it integrates class struggle into a cultural discussion that positions the Indigenous population within a defined political structure (socialism). From this perspective, Arguedas's own project can be interpreted as the continuation and expansion—epistemologically radicalized—of a cultural production that defines what Mariátegui attempted to describe as a literature with an Indigenous soul. In other words, a literature that reflects the political and cultural subjectivization of actors who, until the early twentieth century, were primarily objects of interpretation and representation.

Unlike other indigenista authors, Arguedas's quest is characterized by a kind of obsession with what could also be described as a process of achieving political agency through literature. Although he retains his appreciation for the denunciatory nature of indigenismo, Arguedas seeks a more comprehensive approach. In that same conference, he says: "The indigenista narrative achieves the value not only of accusatory documents but of revelations about the integrity of the human possibilities of native peoples" ("La narrativa indigenista alcanza a tener el valor no sólo de documentos acusatorios sino de revelaciones acerca de la integridad de las posibilidades humanas de la población nativa") (*Indios*, 15). This explains interpretations like that of William Rowe ("Arguedas,"

98) for whom Arguedas sees in Indigenous communities not only a cultural source but also a means to transcend the limited idea of resistance to achieve a form of revolutionary social transformation.

This is how I interpret Arguedas's work of cultural promotion as an extension of Mariátegui's program, inextricably connected to the decolonizing character that defines Indo-Marxism as a unique ideological formulation rooted in Andean social and historical conditions. In short, I argue that for Arguedas, the integrality of the "human possibilities" of Indigenous peoples positions them, their art, and their culture as revolutionary tools—agents destined to bring about social change that is both anti-capitalist and decolonial.

This radical transformation is transferred by Arguedas to a fundamentally cultural sphere, without implying any depoliticization. Through this particularly dialectical lens, I suggest understanding his perspective on the role of native cultures as presented in the essay "La cultura. Un patrimonio difícil de colonizar" (Culture: A heritage difficult to colonize, 1966), where he responds to anthropological approaches that obscure the contribution of Indigenous societies in America in light of homogenizing and Westernizing visions.[18] Within a discussion evaluating literary and artistic production, Arguedas distinguishes the cultural formation of some countries characterized by their mimicry of Western cultures. He includes Argentina, Chile, and (surprisingly) Brazil in this category. For Arguedas, writers and artists in these countries are no longer "colonizable" because their works embrace the contemporary and Western conditions, severing ties from their pre-Hispanic roots. In opposition, he highlights the literary and artistic production of those "Latin American countries sustained by a millenary *indigenous* tradition" ("países latinoamericanos sustentados en una tradición *indígena* milenaria") (*Formación*, 187), where he includes Mexico, Peru, and Bolivia. Their insertion into modernity has resulted in an original cultural formation—likely, indigenista manifestations fit this description—that has resisted the colonial imperative of displacement.

Thus, Arguedas translates Mariátegui's primarily political-economic notion of resistance (the survival of the ayllu as a pre-capitalist productive model) into a political-cultural pattern with transformative potential (the search for a Quechua cultural revitalization). However, for Arguedas, resistance is only one aspect that defines the revolutionary potential of the cultural formations articulated by Indigenous subjectivity. Another aspect of this potential lies in its material circulation and its capacity to challenge what this work defines as cultural coloniality—the forced learning and inevitable acculturative process of merging with Western forms and knowledges. In other words, its opposition to the colonization of culture is always guided by epistemological arguments.

It is in this setting that I interpret the political significance of projects such as the translation of the manuscript known as *Huarochirí Manuscript* or the publication of his own poetry in Quechua, both projects that curiously materialized in 1966, the same year he published "La cultura."[19] Both projects embody Quechua language as a symbolic space that counters the imperatives of cultural coloniality. Although this political stance explains projects such as the compilation and translation of *Canto quechua* (1938), it also illustrates an Andean project that transcends Arguedas himself and describes a productive line that extends to contemporary Quechua poets such as Ch'aska Anka Ninawaman and Washington Córdova.

Even though Indo-Marxism ideologically inspired Arguedas, his cultural program modifies some of the principles proposed by Mariátegui, who considers the mestizo as the subject destined to reproduce the "Indigenous soul" in arts and literature, highlighting César Vallejo as an emblematic figure. In contrast, throughout his career Arguedas was an advocate for the revitalization of Quechua, acting as a necessary counterbalance in what we can define today as a culturally decolonizing praxis. This relentless pursuit explains the link that developed between Arguedas and many Indigenous movements in the Andes in later decades.[20] However, I'm most interested in illuminating how this project is continued by Quechua writers who define their language and its content as a fundamentally decolonizing source of expression.

For Arguedas, indigenismo, focused primarily on narrative production, offers a political contribution that goes beyond simple social denouncement. He attempts to capture in his creations the humanistic and universal potential of Indigenous peoples. Yet he remains profoundly aware of the representational limitations of this current in its literary and cultural sphere. The dialectical bypass initiated by Mariátegui as he sought to adapt Marx's revolutionary thesis to the Andean context is continued by Arguedas through fundamentally epistemological considerations. These are formulations where access to and the generation of knowledge—or material cultural production (poems, music, dance)—becomes a symbolic battlefield.

Here, Arguedas aspires to champion Indigenous modes of subjectivization. Nevertheless, his critique of colonialism doesn't abandon a materialist perspective. He consistently points to the servitude endured by Indigenous peoples under the hacendados, which is essentially a critique of their role in social relations of production. With varying degrees of explicitness, Indo-Marxism navigates through his creative and monographic work. Yet, cultural coloniality, the sphere where knowledge about Andean society is defined and valorized, remains one of his main concerns. It's a symbolic struggle where the creation of enunciative spaces—for example, the ability to produce literature in Quechua—becomes a key political target.

INTERLUDE

The Indigenous Turn of the Mid-Twentieth Century

It is problematic to claim that indigenismo had a zenith and a decline from the early to the mid-twentieth century. The periodicity we have studied so far correlates with critical moments in the three main countries explored (Mexico, Peru, and Bolivia). Revolutions, coups d'état, military defeats, loss of territory, Indigenous uprisings, dictatorships, and the culturally influential discovery and appreciation of pre-Hispanic archaeological sites such as Machu Picchu, Kalasasaya, and Teotihuacán, all provided political content and historical significance to debates on the role of Indigenous societies in the asymmetrical processes of Latin American modernization. Regardless of their ideological commitments, indigenista arguments ran through the reactions generated by each of these events between 1910 and 1940, and the group of intellectuals we have explored is a testament to this.

What happened next, in both the Andes and Mesoamerica, is the recognition of the need to transcend rhetorical inclusivism and to generate the material conditions for the incorporation of Indigenous societies into national projects. Since the 1940s, these conditions developed without much simultaneity, mainly through public policies.[1] The concatenation of two historical events—where indigenista inclusivist pretensions and the increasingly ideologized mobility converge—triggered the objective and subjective conditions for what would later become the Indigenous turn embodied in the intellectuals, activists, and writers that we are about to study in Part II.

INTERLUDE

The first of these events was the administration of Lázaro Cárdenas, president of Mexico between 1934 and 1940, whose social policies were characterized by promoting the organization of Indigenous people and peasants through a number of measures fostering the expansion of education and strengthening the agrarian system. This period was crowned with the First Inter-American Indigenous Congress in the city of Pátzcuaro in Michoacán (1940), where a set of principles and recommendations were established for the incorporation of Indigenous societies in almost all the countries of the Americas. In this meeting, the Mexican delegation was the largest, including Indigenous participants from the Mayan, Zapotec, and Mixteco Nations. There was also participation from Peruvian indigenista intellectuals who would later occupy political positions in the state apparatus, such as José Ángel Escalante and José Uriel García, who had been part of the Grupo Resurgimiento that promoted the cuzqueño indigenista school. Another important figure in the Peruvian delegation to Pátzcuaro was the writer and anthropologist José María Arguedas, whose ideas would be especially influential decades later.

The other key event in this period occurred in the Andes. It was the Bolivian Revolution of 1952, carried out by the MNR led by a group of criollo mestizo intellectuals of indigenista inclinations who were backed by multiple Indigenous popular organizations of campesino and mining segments. After defeating the conservative civilian and military criollo elite, who had ruled Bolivia since its independence, the MNR administrations implemented a set of indigenista policies that promoted the organization of Indigenous peoples and their inclusion in the educational system.

By spotlighting this period, which loosely stretches from 1940 to 1964, I show that there is a logical and genealogical link between the consequences of the indigenista ideas formulated at the beginning of the twentieth century—plus their correlation with the material conditions generated in the Andes and Mesoamerica—and the emergence of an insurgent discourse embodied in an Indigenous decolonial critique.[2] However, it is not my intention to assert that these indigenista administrations were the main drivers of the emergence of Indigenous intellectuals, since the latter have existed throughout Latin America for centuries.[3] But they do, sometimes accidentally, foster a space in which decolonizing ideas—anticipated as cracks in the pool of indigenista intellectuals studied in Part I—are empowered from said moment onward. Indigenista ideas, with their decolonizing cracks, travel over land and time in the ideological construction of a variety of Indigenous intellectuals to either resume, expand, or revoke them.

CÁRDENAS'S INDIGENISMO AND THE SPIRIT OF PÁTZCUARO

The administration of Lázaro Cárdenas del Río was characterized by an effort to materialize the aspirations of the Mexican Revolution. Promises such as the distribution of land for agrarian work and the recognition of the right of Indigenous peoples to organization, incorporated in the 1917 Constitution as part of popular demands in the context of revolution, were resumed by the Cárdenas administration. The agrarian reform was one of the most interesting policies, because it involved the expropriation and redistribution of land in several regions with a high Indigenous population, for which a new agrarian code was enacted in 1937.[4] The ejidatario system, which had already begun in the first postrevolutionary administrations, was promoted, thus constituting the ejido (collectively owned agricultural land) as the symbol of popular economy and a way for the inclusion of Indigenous peoples through a process that aspired to their *campesinización* (conversion into organized peasants).[5] These redistributive measures were accompanied by a policy promoting the agricultural industry through the Banco Nacional de Crédito Ejidal (National Ejido Credit Bank), with the aim of providing credit for campesinos who owned ejidos.[6]

In this context, the Confederación Nacional Campesina (National Campesino Confederation) was created and expanded—thanks to its being sponsored by Cárdenas's administration—throughout almost all rural areas of Mexico through local units that could either be agrarian communities or campesino unions, which were developed in parallel with an educational program that sought to bring schools closer to the Mexican campesino population. In the area of agrarian reform, Cárdenas touched on an old indigenista demand, targeting the feudal structure of land distribution. The ejidatario system would sooner or later be co-opted by the political interests of the Partido Revolucionario Institucional (Institutional Revolutionary Party, PRI), which would distort the vindictive spirit of land redistribution.

As Ben Fallaw describes, these policies were implemented through "public ceremonies [that] exemplified the new order of rural society envisioned by Cardenistas" (*Cárdenas Compromised*, 89). Thus, it can be said that this administration was concerned with creating the material conditions for the incorporation of Indigenous people, mainly through the agricultural industry, and re-creating an image of close ties with the Indigenous population, principally through public performances that adopted Mayan symbols.[7] It can be said that Cárdenas had a binary vision of Mexican social classes: Indigenous and criollo mestizos, eclipsing under this perspective other sectors such as Afro-Mexicans.

Focusing on the impact of Cárdenas's policies in the state of Michoacán, Marjorie Becker points out that the indigenista discourse of this administration misused rhetorical devices such as *purity* and *redemption* that were oriented toward the "reinvention of the Indians" (*Setting the Virgin on Fire*, 72–76) through the promotion of their cultural values. Precisely in Michoacán is the small city of Pátzcuaro, a place where Cárdenas's indigenista spirit converged with the realization of the First Inter-American Indigenista Congress in 1940, which was initially meant to be held in La Paz. Because of the instability experienced in Bolivia after its failure in the Chaco War, the congress was postponed, and Mexico, which was already involved in the promotion and organization of said summit, took over as host.[8] This event was chaired by Cárdenas himself and is a key event in Latin American indigenista historiography, with the participation of multiple delegations from countries such as Bolivia, Peru, Guatemala, Ecuador, Colombia, Panama, Brazil, and the United States, since delegates agreed upon a series of international treaties for the cooperation and integration of Indigenous societies.

The declarations and commitments made by participating countries show a desire for rapprochement and the inclusion of Indigenous societies. Commitments were made on issues such as health, education, politics, and linguistic embracement. In addition, it is interesting that one of the first recommendations dictated in the final resolution of the congress states: "We recommend to the American nations that in planning and administering their respective programs for the welfare of the Indians, they explore and use what applied anthropology can teach them on the matter" ("Se recomienda a las naciones americanas que al plantear y administrar sus respectivos programas para el bienestar del Indio, exploren y utilicen lo que sobre la materia pueda enseñarle la Antropología Aplicada") ("Acta Final del Primer Congreso," 10). This influx of social sciences very much resembles the indigenista arguments of Manuel Gamio, who was part of the large Mexican delegation at this event. Another interesting section of the Pátzcuaro agreements is the one dedicated to education, which was to be inspired by the principles of the Mexican Revolution and which, to a large extent, anticipated many of the terms with which some intercultural pedagogical programs were implemented in decolonizing administrations such as those of Evo Morales and Rafael Correa at the beginning of the twenty-first century.

The inclusive political telos of this summit, which included the participation of several Mexican Indigenous activists, can be labeled the Spirit of Pátzcuaro, in the sense that several ground rules were set outlining state policies that would allow for the inclusion and the political organization of Indigenous movements years later.[9] Of course, the approach advocated at this congress had several limitations in terms of intermediacy that hindered Indigenous political agency. After all, the protagonists of this meeting were criollo mestizo politicians and intellectuals who embodied a humanitarian approach to Indigenous societies. Likewise, Pátzcuaro was not an accidental location; in this city, populated mainly by the Purépecha ethnic group, Cárdenas made institutional efforts to reconstruct a postrevolutionary national image of Mexico through a project strongly connected to its pre-Hispanic cultural roots. As Jennifer Jolly argues, Cárdenas turned Pátzcuaro into a "microcosm of cultural power" by fostering a kind of "touristic *indigenismo*" with which he aspired to reshape the Mexican nation-building process by politically, culturally, and aesthetically reinventing the Indigenous imaginary (*Creating Pátzcuaro*, 70–75).[10] Thus, Pátzcuaro during *cardenismo* was a political site that contained a particularly influential symbolic weight in the formation of an official indigenista discourse in Mexico.

With its epistemic limitations, the spirit that ran through this meeting was later evoked in other key moments of indigenista historiography in the Andes and Mesoamerica. Although the congress in Pátzcuaro was the first and most significant, it was not the only Inter-American Indigenista congress. It was initially going to be held in La Paz, but the Bolivian context did not allow the event to take place in 1939; this would happen in 1954, two years after the triumph of the most important indigenista revolution in Andean history during the twentieth century.

THE MNR, CAMPESINIZACIÓN, AND DISENCHANTMENT

The rise to power of the MNR after the Bolivian Revolution of 1952 marked a milestone in indigenista historiography. The popular movement was composed mainly of Indigenous people, peasants, mining workers, and nationalist military members, led by a criollo mestizo elite among whom Víctor Paz Estenssoro and Hernán Siles Zuazo stood out as leaders. They would take turns in the Bolivian presidency during a stage known as the "period of national revolution." War failures such as the loss of territory in the Chaco War and the economic crisis of the Great Depression generated a sense of pessimism toward conservative criollo administrations.[11] Part of this inspired, for example, pessimistic indigenista discourses such as that of Alcides Arguedas.

Capitalizing on popular unrest, the leaders of the MNR, traditional intellectuals in the Gramscian sense, led the 1951 elections that would end in their victory. However, the resistance of a military junta allied with the conservative elite meant they had to trigger a national popular uprising that would take power by means of revolution in April 1952. As Guillermo Lora describes it (*History*), in forming its revolutionary popular base the MNR brought together diverse ideological sectors ranging from dissatisfied liberals, orthodox communists, and Trotskyist socialists, as well as loosely organized Indigenous campesinos and mining workers.[12] With the paradoxical invocation of the Mexican Revolution and support from the United States at the same time, MNR administrations continued until the military coup d'état of 1964.

These governments introduced several measures that resembled the inclusivist indigenismo that had been outlined in Pátzcuaro. Until 1952, it is estimated that only 10 percent of the Bolivian population had the right to vote, so they declared universal suffrage as one of their first measures. Like Cárdenas's administrations, MNR administrations promoted the organization of the Indigenous segments through the creation of the Central Obrera Boliviana (Bolivian Workers' Central Union, COB), which to this day brings together Indigenous and mestizo workers in mining and agricultural sectors. In fact, it is quite illustrative of this book's articulated genealogy that the COB was one of the main labor union allies of Evo Morales before and throughout his government in the early twentieth-first century.

Other relevant measures were the expropriation and nationalization of Bolivia's main mining sites as well as the complex and overbureaucratized agrarian reform, in which Fausto Reinaga participated, at that time a young Quechua Aymara activist who a few years later would formulate one of the most directly decolonizing Indigenous discourses: indianismo. Education was also subject to MNR reform since the coverage of schools in rural sectors was expanded, which raised the enrollment rate in the Indigenous population by 40 percent, according to Manuel E. Contreras who adds that education was of low quality ("de baja calidad") because the pedagogical program was under the charge of the Ministry of Peasant Affairs, which only reproduced a model of memorization and recitation ("memorización y recitación") of Castillian Spanish ("Comparative Perspective," 265). It is possible to interpret this policy as part of the *campesinización* of Indigenous people, a model through which they sought to modernize Indigenous society by making the category *campesino* into a sort of social class that could be articulated by the state apparatus, akin to the case in Mexico. This is reflected in the organizational alliance between the MNR and the COB, which copied the Russian revolutionary model by proletarianizing Indigenous people in a preindustrial country where the category *obrero* (laborer) did not have the same identification as campesino.

Bolivian philosopher and sociologist René Zavaleta Mercado has pointed out that the MNR triumph did not mean the end of the system of dependence of Indigenous people and campesino groups on the political and intellectual class of La Paz (*Lo nacional-*

popular, 11–20). After all, the MNR administrations ended up creating a national indigenista bourgeoisie that promoted the discourse of mestizaje as a form of modernization of Indigenous societies. Here it can be said that the indigenismo of the MNR failed in its inclusive policies because it employed them with a representational ideology (mestizaje) that oxymoronically reproduced the patterns of exclusion and relegation against which they themselves had fought before 1952. Bolivian sociologist Silvia Rivera Cusicanqui has identified this failure in the visual policies within MNR discourse, where the figure of the mestizo intellectual is heroized, submitting Indigenous representation to a subordinate and colonial role (*Sociología*, 145–49). In fact, she uses "colonial Andean mestizaje" ("mestizaje colonial andino") (94) to describe the indigenista discourse that structured the policies of the MNR. Ultimately, these administrations never proposed the reinstallation of an Indigenous epistemology in the Bolivian republican project.

It was in this context that the Third Inter-American Indigenista Congress was held in La Paz between August 2 and 13, 1954. By this time, official Latin American indigenismo was mainly a declarative platform with no major correlation with the Indigenous social mobility, which was starting to build intellectual autonomy in the form of miners' unions, campesino associations, territorial defense committees, and political parties. The final act of this congress declared the need for the following: "Literacy of the Indians in their native languages and in the official national language, leaving the form of doing so up to pedagogical criteria" ("Alfabetizar a los Indios en sus lenguas autóctonas y en la lengua oficial nacional, dejando al criterio pedagógico la forma de hacerlo") ("Acta Final del Tercer Congreso," 12). This was not reflected in the reality of the MNR's educational program, however, where castillianization was privileged as a literacy method. Thus, the MNR's indigenismo reproduced colonial patterns of subalternization. As described by Zavaleta Mercado in a Marxist reading of this period, the project ended up reduced to "its ideology, its liberal dream, developmentalism, the game in which all are fulfilled and classes are in struggle" ("su ideología, su sueño liberal, el desarrollismo, el juego en el que todos se colman y las clases son lucha") (*La caída*, 57). This sort of demobilization placed the MNR in a vulnerable position, and some Indigenous groups, once organized, became disillusioned and left the project.

THE INDIGENOUS TURN

Under this decolonial critique, it is difficult to say that two indigenista administrations led by criollo mestizo elites fostered what I have come to call the "Indigenous turn," but this is indeed what happened albeit perhaps unintentionally. In their respective ways, both official forms of indigenismo failed, as they were co-opted by the political expansionism of the PRI in Mexico and by the implosive internal distortion of the MNR in Bolivia. However, these administrations did promote the educational inclusion of Indigenous sectors (with clear programmatic and material limitations), which generated the emergence of an Indigenous political class that transcended criollo mestizo intermediacy.

Incidentally, these two experiments proved the need to radicalize Indigenous dialectics and transcend the inclusivist mechanics of the various indigenismos. Perhaps the most eloquent case is that of Reinaga, who initially identified himself as a communist indigenista (one of the various ideological currents that formed the social base of the MNR) and turned toward an ideological detachment and dialectical reframing that proclaimed to be genuinely Indigenous (indianismo). Similarly, the ejidatario system in Mexico, strengthened by Cárdenas, was later distorted by small mestizo elites who reproduced the colonial patterns of subordination against which *cardenismo* was rebelling. This inspired the zapatista Indigenous uprising in Chiapas at the end of the twentieth century.

Although there were other, later, Indigenous uprisings in Mexico (for example, those in Oaxaca in 1990s), the interesting thing about the zapatista decolonizing project is that one of its first measures was the implementation of a Mayan Indigenous agrarian reform. Indigenismo, which is not a homogeneous school of thought, contributed to the ongoing discussion on the situation of Indigenous societies in Latin America. By creating a genealogy that connects indigenismos with the Indigenous mobility described in the following chapters, my aim is to establish a contrapuntal reading illuminating a dialectical bridge that progressively builds a decolonial critique of Indigenous roots, whether directly promoted by revolutionary indigenista discourses (e.g., Mariátegui, Valcárcel) or accidentally favored by the material conditions for Indigenous groups under the indigenista administrations themselves (e.g., Cárdenas or MNR).

PART II

PART II

CHAPTER 4

Indianismo

Reinaga's Indianization of Revolutionary Dialectics

Although Fausto Reinaga (1906–1994) is almost unanimously recognized as the founding intellectual of indianismo, he was not always an indianista. By "indianismo," I mean a current of political thought with Indigenous roots, which is totally opposed to the criollo indianista literary movement that expanded from the end of the nineteenth century to the beginning of the twentieth century. A writer and philosopher with dual Quechua Aymara roots, Reinaga was born in Colquechanca, a small Indigenous mining town located near the city of Potosí in Bolivia. In his early adult life he was a member of several leftist parties, belonging for a long time to the Partido Comunista de Bolivia (Communist Party of Bolivia) from which he supported the 1952 revolution carried out by the MNR. At that time, Reinaga was a radical allied with indigenistas who promoted the immediate incorporation of Indigenous people into Bolivian social and political life. However, as an Indigenous ally within a broad coalition, his identity wasn't simply submitted to voluntarist factors through the later political construction of indianismo. In 1952, he also published *Tierra y libertad* (Land and freedom), a book in which he proposed the nationalization of farming lands and their redistribution to Indigenous collectives under the formula of the ayllu. Interestingly, in this demand for agrarian reform in the Andes, Reinaga concurs with a hypothesis also formulated by Mariátegui: the problem of Indigenous people is the dispossession of their land and the concentration of the capital generated by their agriculture into the criollo sector.

INDIANISMO

As the MNR administrations proceeded, Reinaga became disappointed with the revolutionary nationalist project and its paternalistic indigenista discourse, showing an initial sign of the forging of an indianista philosophy in his critique of indigenistas formulated in the book *El indio y los escritores de América* (The Indian and the writers of America, 1968).[1]

In this essayistic text, he evaluates the work of various Latin American writers from the nineteenth century onward. About Vasconcelos, Reinaga says that he prophesizes a utopia that would have no major impact on the life of the Mexican Indigenous people and ascribes his proposal to "the Indianness that wants to come out of the depths of his being" ("lo indio que quiere salir de lo profundo de su ser"), which leads Vasconcelos to oppose the Indigenous spirit of America with the spirit of the West ("oponer el espíritu autóctono de América al espíritu de Occidente") (*El indio*, 124). However, he still considers Vasconcelos a Europeanizer seeking to assimilate Indigenous people into Western culture (117).

Reinaga has a more ambiguous position on Valcárcel, highlighting the historical veracity of *Tempestad en los Andes*, although he questions how the cuzqueño intellectual promulgates an indigenista evangelism ("evangelio indigenista") by using terms such as "indígena" and "nuevo indio" instead of just calling them "indios," to announce their imminent revolution (66). Reinaga seems to especially lament that Valcárcel does not emphasize the colonial origin of the racial and social conditions embedded in the category *indio*, preferring instead other terms that for Reinaga de-indianize the Andean subject, such as "mestizo," "cholo," or "nuevo indio." In this way, this Bolivian writer activist began to delineate the cornerstones of indianista thought.

In the late 1960s, Reinaga went through what Carlos Macusaya Cruz (*Del indianismo*, 101–4) has defined as a crisis of conscience ("crisis de consciencia") in which he transitioned away from his commitment to indigenistas. Macusaya labels it a "pre-indianista" phase where Reinaga adhered to the values of the MNR instead of his indianista consciousness. Despite having worked in the MNR administrations, where he served in positions of trust in the agrarian reform process, Reinaga was disappointed by the marginal role played by Indigenous societies in this project. For Esteban Ticona Alejo ("La producción," 41–43), this moment of rupture with the MNR represents the dawn of the "decolonizing praxis" that indianismo articulates—in other words, the moment in which Reinaga embraces the centrality of Indigenous peoples as agents of their own liberation.[2] Thus, one of my main arguments is that, through a method oppositional to the epistemology inherent in indigenismos (although certainly selective in specific aspects), Reinaga constructs a decolonizing Indigenous dialectic in indianista thought that transcends the inclusionist matrix hitherto employed by some indigenismos, without completely leaving behind some of the arguments advanced by indigenista intellectuals, which he consolidates in his *La revolución india* (1970).

Reinaga approaches the Peruvian indigenista author José Carlos Mariátegui with both ambiguity and selectivity because of the decolonial traces in Mariátegui's ideas. Reinaga comments extensively on his work in *El indio* and describes him as Indoamerica's greatest writer (the "más grande escritor de indoamérica") (*El indio*, 505), although he regrets that Mariátegui is affected by two opposing revolutionary modalities: the Europeanizing Marxist one and the Indigenous Inca one. In addition, he acknowledges Mariátegui's influence on other revolutionary movements such as the MNR in Bolivia and the guerrillas of Ernesto Che Guevara. Reinaga also appreciates that his ideas sought the liberation of Indigenous societies, albeit through a socialist revolution—that is, "in the Bolshevik style" ("a la bolchevique") (510).

Nevertheless, Reinaga quotes several passages from *Siete ensayos*, especially those in which Mariátegui emphasizes the cultural resistance of the Tahuantinsuyo (the name given by the Inca Empire to its united territories) and the racial resistance of Indigenous people. "There we have José Carlos Mariátegui, giving free rein to his Indian soul, daughter of the Andes, to his Inca spirit that emits cosmic fire. In Mariátegui's mental horizon, the Indian disappears at this moment, as a class (peasant class), to stand up and assert himself *as a race, as a people, as a spirit*. Instead of saying, 'The Indigenous proletariat awaits its Lenin,' he should have said: the Indian race, the Indian people, the Indian spirit awaits its Inka; or rather, the Indian awaits his Tupaj Amaru of our time."[3]

One of Reinaga's major objections to socialist indigenismo is that it categorizes Indigenous peoples as a social class in the interest of making them fit into a Marxist revolutionary dialectic.

In indianismo, by contrast, Indigenous peoples are both racialized colonial subjects and at the same time a national identity rooted in their ethnicity, which transcends the notion of social class as a differential variable in their struggles. This reading is best explained in *La revolución*, where Reinaga accuses liberalism and communism of being Europeanizing movements that seek to assimilate, integrate, and ultimately alienate Indians (141). He proclaims: "The revolutionary scream of the Indian is not assimilation; it is liberation. The hope of the Indian is not to follow: work donkey or political 'pongo,' the hope of the Indian is to liberate himself" ("El grito revolucionario del indio, no es asimilación; es liberación. La esperanza del indio, no es seguir: burro de trabajo o 'pongo' político, la esperanza del indio es liberarse") (142).

The indianista revolution does not set as an explicit goal the control of the means of production (cultivable lands, agricultural technologies, mining sites) and with it the seizure of power (governing the institutions of the nation-state). Such goals correspond to his Marxist phase of *Tierra y libertad*, before his crisis of consciousness. In his indianista period, the revolution transcends a conventional materialist sense of power and enters the realm of epistemology, since Indigenous peoples are defined as racial and colonial subjects living under the cultural, intellectual, and historical tyranny of the West. Therefore, they need to emancipate themselves from these symbolic units of oppression.

Reinaga rejects social class categories such as *mestizo*, *cholo*, and *campesino*, which he considers indigenista nomenclature, and centralizes the Indigenous subject as a colonized subject like the "naturales" of Africa, Asia, and America (*La revolución*, 137). In doing so, he asserts that Indigenous peoples must return to their sources of knowledge. In his de-Westernizing discourse, Reinaga not only opposes indigenismo but, in geopolitical terms and through a transnational empathy, positions Indigenous groups in the symbolic sphere of what is today called the Global South. This area extends to other territories that share experiences of oppression such as slavery, colonialism, and coloniality. He even openly expresses his empathy with the revolutionary philosophy of Frantz Fanon, whose ideas influence the construction of indianismo as a decolonizing dialectic.

The indianista revolution Reinaga proposes is not only a territorial and political liberation from the oppression suffered by Indians in Bolivia at the hands of other social classes (criollos and mestizos). My interest here is to illuminate an epistemological liberation that implies the reinstallation of Indigenous sources of knowledge and a system of values opposite to the colonial universalisms of the West, through a liberation that is at the same time racial, cultural, and epistemic. As Catherine E. Walsh ("'Other' Knowledges") points out in her political analysis of indianismo and zapatismo, both currents expose the geopolitical limitations of uncritical implementation of Marxism-Leninism as revolutionary praxis for Indigenous communities. For Fabiola Escárzaga (*La comunidad*) in *La revolución*, the socialist matrix of class struggle is inverted by a struggle of races. As a result of an initially political exercise, as described by Walsh and Escárzaga, Reinaga takes a step forward in the liberating struggle already anticipated by some indigenistas, since his proposal constitutes an act of detaching—as in Mignolo's understanding ("Delinking")—of the geopolitical referents that universalize knowledges of a certain ethnic group (Western Europe) toward territories dominated by the modern/colonial system. Indianismo also points to the need to decolonize the cultural, spiritual, and historical narratives that imprison Indigenous peoples. In so doing, its reorganizing approach dismantles the idea of History as an evolutionary narrative to which Indigenous societies must be subjected, an agenda that was already part of indigenista analyses.

THE ORDER OF THINGS

Reinaga first makes a direct allusion to a thesis formulated years before within the realm of indigenismo cuzqueño, whose main exponent was Valcárcel. The idea of the return of the Inca social system is not precisely a novelty introduced by indianismo, although Reinaga certainly makes significant modifications in both its substance and form:

> The "human nature" of the Indian is that of the Inka-man. Therefore, the Indian must return to the Inka, believe in the Inka, which is better than the man achieved by the West.... Return to the Inka to enlighten our future with faith and hope.... The Inka

for us is the recognition of the unity of our blood, of our spirit, and of our millenary culture; which Europe in four centuries has not been able to destroy. . . . We created a man who did not know how to lie, did not know how to steal, did not know how to exploit (ama llulla, ama súa, ama khella). The social ethics of Inkanato came out of the Cosmos.[4]

Whereas in political terms the aim of Valcárcel's idea of resurgence was to propose a regionalist alternative to Lima's indigenismo, Reinaga's resurgence is an explicit strategy of epistemological de-Westernization of Indigenous peoples—a return not only of the political and social system but of an Indigenous mode of being with a future horizon ("'naturaleza humana' del indio") (*La revolución*, 91).

In his formulation of an Inca resurgence, which focuses mainly on Qullasuyu (a region of the Tahuantinsuyo that involves what is now the Bolivian and Chilean altiplano), Reinaga constantly evokes the need to reactivate the insurgent heroic deeds of the anticolonial Indigenous rebellions that occurred between 1778 and 1781. That is, he invokes the rebellions led by Túpac Amaru II and Micaela Bastidas in Cuzco and by Túpac Katari and Bartolina Sisa in La Paz. From these historical events, Reinaga claims for indianismo those principles that are useful for the sociopolitical context of Bolivia in the twentieth century: the repudiation of Spanish subordination, which for Reinaga is manifest in the repudiation of the West and its heirs, as well as in the notion of an Indigenous autonomy that would be achieved with the recovery of certain Inca values that, in political and spiritual terms, precede colonial rule.[5]

On the other hand, whereas in Valcárcel the Andean philosophical notion of *nayrapacha* is a notion compatible with the emancipatory features of his andinismo, in Reinaga it becomes a structuring philosophical principle of the indianista revolution: "Return to the Inka to enlighten our future with faith and hope" ("Volver al Inka para iluminar de fe y esperanza nuestro porvenir") (*La revolución*, 91). This resurgence is prescribed by the proclamation of the Inca moral imperatives "don't be a liar, don't be a thief, don't be lazy" (*ama llulla, ama sua, ama khella*). In this way, the return to the values of Inca society proposed by the indianista revolution implies a process of construction of a future from the political, spiritual, ethical, and historical exteriority—or periphery—of the Western values imposed by the modern/colonial system.

The indianista revolution proposes a new order of things. It is the restitution of an authentically Indigenous epistemology that was not exterminated but subjugated from the onset of colonization by the various dichotomies that make up Western epistemology (Liberalism/Marxism, Christianity/secularism, etc.). Reinaga's indianista thought entails the relocation of the baseline of Indigenous values.

His philosophy seeks an integral rupture with the traits of Western influence because "Liberalism and communism, which came from Europe, want to assimilate us to Europe. . . . Assimilation, integration, is *enajenación*. And *enajenación* means: alienation" ("El liberalismo y el comunismo llegado de Europa, quieren asimilarnos a Europa. [. . .] Asimilación, integración, es enajenación. Y la enajenación significa: alienación") (*La revolución*, 140). With obvious remnants of Marxist terminology, Reinaga molds indianismo into a holistically liberating current of thought. He wants to divorce Indigenous peoples from the ideological polarization of his time (after all, he is also reacting to the imperatives of the Cold War) and construct an authentic discourse with an original historical basis. Thus, in one of the final chapters of *La revolución* he re-creates Indigenous values prior to the European invasion: "The man of Inka society is clearly aware of his dignity. . . . The land is a common good, everyone works it, and the Pachamama nourishes everyone, generously. The sun is the protective father of men. The principle that the man comes from the land and returns to it, here is the evidence."[6] Two striking aspects of this statement are the recurrence of tellurism as a device that provides empiricism to decolonizing arguments—akin to the role played by tellurism in Valcárcel's andinismo or by ayllu in Mariátegui—and the conjugation in the present tense of verbs that describe Indigenous peoples and Inca values. Reinaga constructs a sense of timelessness that is part of a larger decolonizing agenda that intervenes in conventionalized senses of time and space.

Within a decolonial framework, one of the major critiques against continental philosophy has been the tradition of imposing the problems or understandings of European philosophical currents on non-European territories and societies—for example, through the institutionalization of methods of knowledge forged in Western Europe. In his contrasting analysis of the theoretical frameworks of phenomenology and decoloniality, Mignolo ("Decoloniality") explains that the coloniality of knowledge is configured when a regional source of knowledge, which aspires to explain a totality, is universalized by hiding or undermining other local sources of knowledge. We can extract from this dynamic the conventional conceptualization of categories such as *time*, a linear succession of intervals containing events, and *space*, a unit of measurement through which the world is geographically categorized. Both concepts, separately, become empirically measurable notions that delineate the expansion of dominant epistemologies. Accordingly, Nelson Maldonado-Torres elaborates a critique of the geopolitical concepts of *temporality* and *spatiality* that emerged from continental philosophy and expanded toward non-European experiences. He suggests an alternative based on decolonial thought, or a post-continental alternative: the idea of "spatio-temporal epistemic fractures" ("Post-continental Philosophy," 2), which arise in those subjects whose life experiences are constrained by hegemonic discourses.

According to Maldonado-Torres, this is the case of Fanon—and for me, it is also the case of Reinaga. Ultimately, both are intellectuals who emerge from the colonial experience and who inhabit an epistemic fracture of spatial and temporal order when theorizing about the mobility of their respective societies, as they are subjected to hegemonic environments that question their temporal and spatial subjectivities. In response, Reinaga's indianismo proposes an Indigenous alternative. For instance, he asserts that pre-Hispanic peoples are subjects whose values—once de-temporalized or re-temporalized—have the capacity to intervene in an intolerable colonial present.

In *La revolución*, Reinaga proposes the integration of the philosophy embodied in indianismo within a programmatic framework that was both decolonizing and exogenous to the concerns of Western preoccupations. The promoted insurgency is not only satisfied with the de-Westernization of Indigenous peoples but advances to a resurgence of the Andean cosmological order that implies the revaluation of local knowledge without pretensions of universality, where Inca values operate as evidence that historically grounds his proposal. For example, Reinaga does not claim that the Inca moral imperatives (*ama llulla, ama súa, ama khella*) are universally applicable to or in tune with Western existence or lifestyles. Ultimately, they do not resonate with criollos and mestizos, social subjects resulting from the Andean colonial experience. Likewise, the dialectical structure from the principle of *nayrapacha* reflects an interest in dislocating the spatial-temporal episteme imposed by Eurocentric logic (the linear chronological view of time) to transplant Indigenous peoples into a *locus amenous* liberated in historical, cultural, ethical, political, and knowledge terms. In this context, categories such as *time* and *space*, in the ideology that articulates indianismo, are neither separate nor measurable units, since they embody ethical, ideological, and symbolic dimensions alternative to their universalized understandings. Thus, the indianista revolution aspires to create an epistemic autonomy related to the mobility, emergence, and utilization of Andean Indigenous knowledge. This would reorganize the ethical and spatio-temporal elements that regulate the vital experience of Indigenous peoples, creating an autonomous time and space through epistemological decolonization.

In other words, the indianista revolution posits the installation of an authentic model of time-space, borrowing Immanuel Wallerstein's binomial ("Inventions"), which is marked by the eventualities of Indian insurgency and which seeks to dismantle the universalisms of coloniality/modernity.[7] Nayrapacha in indianismo does not mean a leap to the past (nor does it in indigenismos). It means a rupture with linear global thinking and with time-space resonances in order to develop a future regulated by an Indigenous knowledge that remains subjugated under a time-space model that articulates present Andean life: that of coloniality and Eurocentrism.[8] In this sense, the nayrapacha philosophical principle subverts the idea of time as a chronological and linear category (it negates the forward and projects itself as upward/outward), and it breaks down the chronological principle of measurability). Moreover, Reinaga uses the sense of space as a symbolic place that emerges via the enunciative capacity of the subject liberated from colonial atavisms. The irruption of the concept of *time-space* in nayrapacha is linked to another Andean philosophical concept that is useful for understanding the revolutionary indianista dialectic: *pachakuti*.

Reinaga's intellectual production extends over more than twenty books and dozens of articles in which he elaborates on decolonizing political proposals linked to ancestral Quechua Aymara ideas, which he connects with the sociopolitical issues of the Bolivia of his time. Thus, indianismo gains ground in the Bolivian national debate and constitutes itself as an "insurrectional subjugated knowledge," as Juan Aparicio and Mario Blaser ("Lettered City," 85) call it—that is, as a pattern of mobilization that expresses an alternative to modernity. Or, as Arturo Escobar (*Territories*) would phrase it, a pattern of knowledge that interrogates the presuppositions of modernity and itself constitutes an alternative to modernity in terms of lifestyles and the organization of society. In both senses, this emerging Indigenous knowledge in Reinaga's literature is introduced in what he calls the *lettered city*, in the circuit of exchange of ideas that privileges written cultural productions, which, being produced by an Indigenous intellectual, connotes a reversal of the symmetry of knowledge production that has prevailed in Latin America since the early colonial period.[9]

In this sense, my reading of the scope and intentions of Reinaga's literature goes beyond the interpretation of María Elena Oliva's reading (*La negritud*). She understands Reinaga's writing as an attempt to overcome the protective and homogenizing mediation of mestizo indigenistas.[10] The intellectual purpose of Reinaga's writing and its corresponding ideological elaboration of indianismo is not only to counter the assimilationist agenda of indigenistas but also to activate the political, social, cultural, and philosophical agency of the Andean subject as a historically and epistemologically autonomous entity with respect to the Western imperatives that dominate Andean social life. Reinaga hopes to intervene in the present because he has a historical variable that supports him with respect to indigenistas of the early twentieth century—a literate Indigenous class. Indigenista policies after the 1952 revolution promoted access to education for Indigenous people, and this narrowed the literacy gap between indigenista cultural production and the Indigenous audience, a problem that was partially mitigated during Reinaga's indigenista period. Unlike Mariátegui and Valcárcel, Reinaga had a literate Indigenous audience who read and interpreted his texts and organized themselves according to his ideas. One of the young Indigenous activists who gained early access to and was influenced by Reinaga's literature was Quechua leader Felipe "El Mallku" Quispe. In the late 1960s, Quispe was a young union organizer and student at the Universidad Mayor de San Andrés. He was part of the revolutionary organization Ayllus Rojos (Red Ayllus) in the 1980s, where many of its members self-identified as indianistas.

FANON, REINAGA, AND DECOLONIAL AFFINITIES

In reaction to the conclusions of Fanon's *The Wretched of the Earth* (1963), which he quotes extensively in *La revolución*, Reinaga notes: "The Bolivian Indian cannot overlook the deadly crisis that the West is suffering. He must take advantage of it. But not to save his enemy. He must take advantage of this crisis to liberate himself. The Indian Revolution is an irrefutable logic in the field of ideas and in the phenomenology of facts. The Indian Revolution will burst like a natural law."[11] Reinaga makes several references to Fanon, specifically his *Wretched* and to a slightly lesser extent *Black Skin, White Masks* (1952). He speaks about the writer and philosopher in glowing terms and relies on his ideas to propose three fundamental principles for indianismo: (1) to argue for the need to oppose the influences of Western civilization and its modernizing project as a way to liberate colonized and enslaved subjects (Indigenous and Black people); (2) to racially theorize indigeneity in line with Fanon's racial categorization of Black people; (3) to equalize Indigenous and Black people in a transnational struggle against the slavery and the colonial system that emerges from Western civilization but penetrates different social layers in what ends up defining the ubiquity of Indigenous peoples in the symbolic and political space that today is called the Global South.[12]

Reinaga sees in Fanon's critique of the emerging postcolonial countries of Africa—particularly the new national bourgeoisie, which he considers to be the heir of European racism—an archetype for his critique of the Bolivian national bourgeoisie (criollos, mestizos, and cholos whom he considers to be alienated Indigenous subjects). On the epistemological expansion of the West in the former colonies of Europe, Fanon says: "This Europe, which never stopped talking of man, which never stopped proclaiming its sole concern was man, we now know the price of suffering humanity has paid for every one of its spiritual victories. / Come, comrades, the European game is finally over, we must look for something else. We can do anything today provided we do not ape Europe, provided we are not obsessed with catching up with Europe" (*The Wretched*, 236). It is understandable that, a few years later, such statements seduced Reinaga, who sought the epistemological liberation of Bolivian Indians.

Like Fanon for Black people, Reinaga seeks for Indigenous people a political liberation from the epistemological domain imposed by the West through the racialization of Indigenous and Black people to justify social oppression. By qualifying both ethnic groups, which for Reinaga are also ethical and political groups, as colonized, enslaved, and racialized subjects, he locates Andean Indians in the symbolic cartography of the Global South—that is, a reading of the world system where Indigenous peoples are recognized as peripheralized subjects. The Bolivian philosopher places Indigenous groups within a transnational setting in which oppressed subjects struggle for an integral liberation from the racial, political, and cultural imperatives bequeathed by Western European imperial expansion in territories such as the Andes, Africa, and the Caribbean.

Following this line of thought, I do not consider that Reinaga uses Fanon to position indianismo only in a "universal dimension," as Claudia Zapata and María Elena Oliva ("Frantz Fanon," 193–94) maintain. Rather, he uses Fanon's ideals to suggest anticolonial ideological alliances in a South–South dialogue where not only anticolonialism but also the struggle against the universal pretensions of the political, cultural, and racial values of Western civilization are discovered as a common factor. In that sense, universality does not relate to Reinaga's doctrine (indianismo) per se but, rather, to the condition of humanity of Indians, who, fully recognized as humans, would indeed embody a universal philosophical status—that is, to see Indians as beings, in existential terms, not only as entities lacking significance and humanistic values. In other words, if anything is to be universal, it is Indians and not indianismo, where tellurism and ethical commitment are directly geo-referenced to Andean reality.

In my view, what Reinaga finds compelling in Fanon's ideas is his racial theorization of Blackness because it allows him to racially theorize indianness. In *Black Skin*, Fanon questions the practice of "culturalization" that occurs in Black Antilleans or Africans who, having traveled to Europe to study, embrace European culture and civilization in order to legitimize their thoughts and sensibilities through a Western lens. In Reinaga's Andean context, these assimilated people resemble those "alienated" Indigenous subjects embodied in cholos and mestizos. This kind of "civilized" Black people, as Fanon (*Black Skin*, 50–51) asserts, no longer consider themselves authentically Black people because they attribute the cultural values of Blackness to barbarism. For Lewis R. Gordon (*What Fanon Said*, 24–25), in these passages of the book, Fanon elaborates a response to the expansion of a principle of anti-Black racism that establishes the cultural and racial values of the West as the correct form of humanity, so that his intentions are to revalue the condition of humanity that Blackness contains in itself, with its own cultural values.

Translated into the Andean setting, Reinaga formulates a criticism in the same sense toward mestizo social strata. For him, mestizos (racially mixed people) and cholos (urbanized Indigenous people) are social derivatives of Indigenous whitening—that is, processes of de-indianization that in Andean history resulted in subjects who allied with criollos to found what he calls the "colonial republic," the natural opponent of the desired "Indian republic" to whose re-creation Reinaga devotes the closing chapters of *La revolución*. Inspired by Fanon's ideas, the Bolivian writer emphasizes the need for an integral revaluation of the Andean Indians, with their racial identity and their condition of humanity. This reading of the historical significance of racialization for the inhabitants of the Andes enables us to find another ideological concomitance with Fanon with respect to the concept of national liberation.

In the context of the war for the independence of Algeria, Fanon wrote an article in *El Moudjahid* in 1958 in which he clarifies his perspective on what decolonization from the metropolis is, in the Algerian case of France, and real liberation of the colonized subject, which in this work is referred to as decolonization.[13] In this article, Fanon (*Toward*, 104–5) clarifies that national liberation does not imply the end of the "colonial pact," which would be the true liberation of colonized people, for which they must eliminate language, customs, and cultural designs imposed by oppressors. He understands that the liberation of colonized people does not end with political and economic autonomy but with epistemological autonomy, a cross-cutting claim in Reinaga's indianismo, which critiques in similar terms the "colonial republic" founded by criollos and mestizos and which seeks the alienation of the Indians through their *cholificación* (in an urban environment) and *campesinización* (in a rural environment), which Reinaga identifies as indigenista strategies of de-indianization. Despite the many indigenista traits running through the elaboration of indianista thought, Reinaga sees in the tempered emancipation from the metropolis a form of liberation that he associates with indigenista ideas, which can be inferred from the way he attempts to antagonize these two currents of thought: "Indigenismo was a vindictive current. Indianismo is a liberatory movement. Indigenismo was a pure vindictive idea. Indianismo is a political force for liberation. Even more. Indigenismo was a movement of the white mestizo *cholaje*; whereas indianismo is an Indian movement, a revolutionary Indian movement, which does not wish to assimilate to anyone; it proposes liberating itself."[14]

One could say that even the ignited rhetoric with which Fanon writes is reflected in Reinaga's scriptural style. But what is interesting in this analysis is that the way in which this Quechua Aymara intellectual opposes indigenismo is akin to how Fanon questions the tempered decolonization of Africa. While indigenismo, like indianismo, implies an anticolonial claim, both currents are not equally decolonizing, despite certain iterations between Reinaga's arguments and indigenista ideas illuminated throughout this chapter. What he takes from Fanon is that, by opposing less radical stances, it is possible to construct a radical decolonizing dialectic forged as the antithesis of all that is deemed not only colonial but also insufficiently liberatory.

At a congress of Black writers in Paris in 1956, a couple of years before writing his provocative article in *El Moudjahid*, Fanon points to racism as an instance of cultural domination from which Black people must free themselves. He highlights the benevolence of some social sectors that, protected by cultural relativism, justify the racial inferiorization of Black people through exoticism and paternalism (*Toward*, 34–35), a thesis that he elaborates in many ways throughout *Black Skin*. For Maldonado-Torres

(*Against War*, 130), Fanon is analyzing the state of Black people in a racial and colonial context, one of the main purposes of which he infers is the full acknowledgment of human status as a formula for overcoming the dehumanization to which colonialism subjected oppressed people. That being said, I argue that indianismo, which opposes the benevolence of the criollos and the paternalistic mediation of the mestizos indigenistas, constructs a uniquely Andean mode of thinking for the full acknowledgment of the human condition of Indigenous peoples as an unavoidable vehicle for the epistemic liberation of Quechuas and Aymaras in the Bolivian context. Reinaga opposes the indigenista humanitarianism of criollo mestizo intellectuals because he claims that this dynamic contributes to the dehumanization of Indigenous people, a perception that cannot be considered exaggerated if we understand that certain indigenista discourses, in addition to being dehumanizing, nullified the realization of a political agency in the Indigenous population.[15]

Ultimately, something that highlights the decolonial affinity between Reinaga and Fanon is that both writers situate Indigenous peoples and Black people within the global periphery as a politically insurgent symbolic space, one from which they both construct arguments that further the primary mission of decolonization: to liberate oppressed subjects by completely detaching them from the colonial matrix of power in epistemological terms. In a Cold War context, Soviet-oriented Marxism-Leninism might appear a feasible and popular alternative for de-Westernization.[16] Reinaga and Fanon step aside from this dichotomic tendency, however, and identify racism and the coloniality of being (rejection of the condition of humanity) as blind spots in the polarized struggle between the capitalist bloc of the West and the socialist bloc of the East.[17] That is why, for the indianista revolution, it is essential to declare the obsolescence of racial nomenclature promoted by the Bolivian "colonial republic" (mestizos, cholos, campesinos) in order to justify criollo domination through cultural relativism. It is my understanding that this dialectical distinction is one of the main contributions of indianismo to the ideological consolidation of subsequent Indigenous movements and to the decolonial discourse with which they articulated their political activism.

INDIANISMO IN MOTION

After the 1970s, indianismo expanded in the political and cultural life of Bolivia, influencing multiple thinkers, artists, and politicians. In its political party form, indianismo can be traced back to the Partido de Indios Aymaras y Keswas (Aymara and Keswa Indians Party), which was founded by Reinaga himself in 1962, and later renamed Partido Indio de Bolivia (Bolivian Indian Party, PIB). In its social movement form, as Waskar Ari (*Earth Politics*) points out, PIB draws on grassroots organizations and Indigenous activists who had already been operating for years in rural areas under the label of Alcaldes Mayores Populares (Popular Mayors), a form of Indigenous activism and leadership that in some areas of Bolivia could be detected as early as the 1920s.[18]

In the early 1970s, a number of unions and student and campesino movements were ascribed to indianismo. Among the groups that stand out is the Movimiento Universitario Julián Apaza (Julian Apaza University Movement), which enters the multitude of organizations claiming the figure of Túpac Katari (whose Spanish name was Julián Apaza) and forcing within these organizations the (re)appearance of a doctrine that would not take long to gain followers: *katarismo*.[19] The Tiwanaku Manifesto was signed in July of 1973, promoted mainly by several campesino organizations demanding the creation of a rural education system that would promote the cultural decolonization of Bolivia. For Escárzaga (*La comunidad*, 224–26), one of the consequences of this document was the promulgation of the autonomy of katarismo with respect to the PIB, not the autonomy of indianista ideology. The other consequence would be the division of the indianista movement into one half that privileged the racialization of the struggle, considering campesinos and workers as Indigenous subjects, and the other half of a more unionist nature that was fueled by the labor associations from the mining sector—that is, the proletarianization of Indigenous peoples. From these successive fragmentations emerged the Movimiento Revolucionario Tupaj Katari (Tupaj Katari Revolutionary Movement), Movimiento Indio Katari (Katari Indian Movement), and Movimiento Indio Túpac Katari (Tupac Katari Indian Movement); from the latter would surge the figure of Felipe "El Mallku" Quispe Huanca, an Indigenous Quechua activist who is crucial in the history of Indigenous movements in Bolivia and perhaps the person who most strongly embraced Reinaga's revolutionary ideas.[20]

Up to this point, in political party terms, Reinaga's proposal to materialize his ideology in a single party (the PIB) had faded. What was not lost were the revolutionary indianista principles, which, with different interpretations, would be present in the ideological design of all of these movements. However, from these divisions and regroupings, indianismo and katarismo merged as ideological trends that shared the stimulus to mobilize the Indigenous population. The figure of Tupac Katari was vindicated by multiple organizations born of indianismo-katarismo. In his historical study on the emergence of katarismo, Javier Hurtado (*El katarismo*) explains that this is due to the radical character with which Aymara movements historically claimed the uprising of Túpac Katari, together with his partner, Bartolina Sisa. According to Hurtado, unlike the Quechua rebellion of Túpac Amaru and Micaela Bastidas in Cuzco, that of Katari and Sisa promoted a radical rejection of any form of compromise with criollo mestizo minorities of the time, as well as an absolute refusal of Spanish authority and a cultural vindication of the Aymara Nation, starting with language. From this historical reinterpretation of the figure of Katari, we can understand the compatibility with Reinaga's indianista principles, which promoted a rejection of the civilizing influences of the West and demanded epistemic autonomy for Andean people.

Thus, the binomial indianismo-katarismo became a dualist doctrine that mobilized Quechua and Aymara Indigenous groups, regardless of their degree of organization, for more than a decade. The catalyst for the expansion of this doctrine was the emergence of an elite of Indigenous intellectuals who, in the 1950s and 1960s, benefited from the access to higher education promoted by MNR's indigenista administration. In the 1970s and 1980s, already consolidated as political activists in their different forms of organization (in parties, unions, workers' and campesino associations or as independent writers and artists), Bolivian Indigenous people burst into the political and cultural life of the country with a solid ideological basis that, tied to a strong ethnic claim, demanded the political, cultural, and spiritual decolonization of their country. Anders

Burman (*Indigeneity*) argues that the politicization of the Aymara and Quechua movements and their narrative of ethnic vindication and opposition to criollo mestizo elites would be reflected years later in the government plans and national policies implemented by former president Evo Morales. To this observation, I would add that the ideological consolidation of the Indigenous movements in Bolivia would end up paving the way for Morales's own political rise, creating not only a class and race consciousness among the various Indigenous organizations but also a sense of urgency for epistemological autonomy on which Morales later capitalized by linking it to his anti-imperialist struggle against the United States and US coca leaf eradication policies.

After the political persecution suffered by indianista-inspired activists during the military dictatorship of Hugo Bánzer Suárez between 1971 and 1978, many of them went into exile in neighboring Latin American countries or sought protection in secrecy. In the early 1980s, with the reestablishment of a fragile democracy, they returned and revived their activism. One of the returnees was the Indigenous leader Felipe Quispe who went back in 1983 and until 1986 organized a clandestine movement called Ayllus Rojos, which self-identified as pure indianistas and followers of Reinaga. However, in 1984, two other important figures would arrive in the historical account: the Bolivian Marxist intellectual Álvaro García Linera, coming to Bolivia after studying at the Universidad Nacional Autónoma de México (UNAM), along with his partner, the Mexican sociologist and activist Raquel Gutiérrez Aguilar. These two mestizos and Marxist intellectuals would initiate a work of grassroots insurgent mobilization with mining, campesino, and Indigenous leaders, and it would be under these circumstances that they would coincide with Quispe. In 1986, they cofounded the well-known Ejército Guerrillero Túpac Katari (Túpac Katari Guerrilla Army, EGTK).

From my point of view, the experience of the EGTK, which was active between 1986 and 1992, was the highest expression of organized insurgency achieved by indianismo, despite its being expressed as a strategic alliance with the Marxism-Leninism of García Linera and Gutiérrez Aguilar. In organizational terms, it was a clandestine movement that combined the revolutionary ideals of indianismo with the political-military structure of Marxist-Leninist guerrillas, who already existed in large numbers in Latin America in those years. In purely ideological terms, I must point out that EGTK represents a limitation or, in any case, a variation of the foundational indianista principles because, despite evoking Reinaga's revolutionary rhetoric, the mestizo side of this alliance never assimilated Aymara Quechua cosmovision as an aim in itself (a thought process embodied by Quispe). The mestizos of the EGTK revalued the ancestral cultural and political symbols as instruments to build affinities among the Indigenous populations. However, the other half of this alliance, the Indigenous half led by Quispe, was mobilized under the inspiration of indianista principles and from the revolutionary concept of cosmological irruption called *pachakuti*, which would reemerge in the Indigenous uprisings of the 2000s.

The EGTK experience ended in April 1992 when its main leaders, Quispe, García Linera, and Gutiérrez Aguilar, were arrested by the Bolivian Army's secret service. In the context of these detentions, Quispe would utter a statement that for many years resonated in the popular Indigenous and revolutionary Bolivian sectors. Being exposed on a public television channel, Quispe was asked by a journalist about the reasons for his struggle, to which he replied: "I would not like my daughter to be your maid" ("A mí no me gustaría que mi hija sea su empleada").[21] Quispe's statement addresses the cover-up of a quasi-slavery system to which many Indigenous Bolivian women are subjected when they work in conditions of underemployment for middle- and upper-class mestizo and criollo families. This quasi-slavery (which directly evokes the system of pongueaje) is employed with the same components of racism and dehumanization as were denounced by Reinaga in his texts and which over time articulate the social struggle of Bolivian Indigenous movements.

Quispe was released from prison in 1998, a year later than García Linera and Gutiérrez Aguilar, and since then they have taken different paths. Quispe founded the Movimiento Indígena Pachakuti (Pachakuti Indigenous Movement), a political party with which he sought to decolonize the Bolivian state from a legal perspective, but without much electoral success until his death in 2021. The other two would continue to engage in political activism together until 2001 when Gutiérrez Aguilar returned to

Mexico. By then, García Linera had already allied himself with Evo Morales, a coca farmer leader who was leading Indigenous protests against US coca leaf eradication policies in several South American countries. Coca leaf was widely consumed in Andean contexts in traditional rituals. It was a fundamental element in the culture, religiosity, and economy of Indigenous communities, and the eradication fostered by the United States was seen by Indigenous peoples in Bolivia as a neocolonial tactic aimed at culturally exterminating Andean societies.

AN ANDEAN REVOLUTIONARY THEORY ABOUT *PACHAKUTI* AND *NAYRAPACHA*

When Morales assumed the Bolivian presidency as the first Indigenous leader of a predominantly Aymara and Quechua country, he announced from the first days of his administration that it would be a new *pachakuti*. The term had been proclaimed by the various movements outlined above for decades, although its influence dates back to the colonial period (Millones, "Mesianismo"; Thomson, "Cuando sólo reinasen"). First, *pachakuti* is an Andean philosophical concept related to the Quechua and Aymara Nations that is etymologically born from the combination of the words *pachas* (world, space-time, cosmos) and *kuti* (change, return, overturn, reversal). Together they refer to an abrupt change of the present cosmos, a radical reordering of the political, cultural, and spiritual values of things. It is not a synonym of "social revolution," as it is usually translated for non-Indigenous audiences. For Rivera Cusicanqui (*Violencias*, 42–50), the term connotes a reversal of colonial order through a cycle of renewal and revolution. For Alejo Ticona (*Saberes*, 38–39), it reflects a drastic reinstatement that contains a promise of annihilation of colonialism. For Javier Sanjinés C., it is embodied in Indigenous mobilizations as a request that social institutions turn "the world upside down" (*Embers*, 33–34).

From all these interpretations it can be inferred that the concept *pachakuti* evokes an abrupt epistemological change in the hierarchies imposed by the colonial matrix of power and the oppressive logic of the modern/colonial/capitalist system—a change that is inspired by a sense of reversion of submerged values, in this case the knowledge and modes of existence of the Andean world.

Thus, it is understandable that in the elaboration of his indianista revolution, Reinaga argued that this would be "the substitution of the 'human nature' of the West by the 'human nature' of the inkanato" ("la sustitución de la 'naturaleza humana' del Occidente por la 'naturaleza humana' del inkanato") (*La revolución*, 76). The indianista revolution did not promote a return to the past but, rather, a construction of the future from the historical revaluation of the Andean subject, which had to pass through the revaluation of the social and moral imperatives of Inca culture. It is in this way that the two most influential philosophical principles of the Indigenous mobilizations promoted by indianista thought complement each other: *nayrapacha*, the time-space dislocation of a colonial present that allows the restitution of ethical, cultural, and political values; and *pachakuti*, the period of abrupt change, revolution, and reordering of the values that colonialism installed in Andean social existence. Accordingly, these two concepts become the fundamental philosophical principles of indianismo and its corresponding decolonizing endeavor.

In the field of Indigenous organizations influenced by indianismo, Gutiérrez Aguilar (*Rhythms*), who as we remember was part of them during their alliance with mestizos, explains that the notion of *pachakuti* moves through the mobilizations of the 1980s to the collectives that participated in the Bolivian Water War of 2000 (already with Morales leading) as a motive to invert the fundamental asymmetries of society as well as to make visible and to validate the internal logics of the Indigenous communities.[22] In her explanation of the practical unfolding of this concept, Gutiérrez Aguilar responds to Thomson's reading, which suggests that *pachakuti* corresponds specifically to the "time when only the Indians reigned" (50), warning that this interpretation would force this Indigenous philosophical principle to fit within the socialist dialectic of "the seizure of power" (50), since it would teleologically circumscribe *pachakuti* only to reverse the political asymmetries of the Andes. For her, the reversal of the fundamental asymmetries of Indigenous movements implies not only pulling up what is down but also bringing out what is inside (what remains hidden) in order to fully reverse the social pact that governs the world and to consolidate new conditions of existence. Popularized by indianista-inspired movements, the revolutionary concept of *pachakuti* and its interweaving with the philosophical principles of *nayrapacha* are derivative of what I consider a genuinely Andean theoretical revolution, achieving the construction of a decolonizing dialectic that transcends Western ideological imperatives.

Gutiérrez Aguilar's response to Thomson's interpretation makes it possible to examine two aspects of these concepts. The first is the logical and political disjunction that underlies the revolutionary nature of indianismo as partially opposed to that of Marxism-Leninism, a point that I am not interested in clarifying in this text, although I think it opens the door to a highly interesting analysis from the perspective of political science or philosophy.[23] The second thing, which I do consider pertinent for this study, is to ask, What is it that Indigenous people mobilize from within, what remains hidden, and what elements of the Indigenous decolonizing agenda describe a movement not only upward but also outward?

The question as to what is invisible and what needs a revolution to emerge contains not only the cultural and political values of Andean society but also the cosmological framework from which Indigenous people operate, their perceptions of the world, and their ways of relating to nonhuman entities. Thus, it is worth asking whether, in the Indigenous and campesino uprisings led by Morales, the coca leaf was an inert object politicized by the indianista discourse or whether it was, rather, a political subject with an agency that intervened in the political assembly of Indigenous organizations. My point is that these other forms of relating to the elements of the earth—these alternative world configurations to modernity—imply the emergence or recognition of ontologies that are alternative to the Western one structured by modernity/rationality. Indianista mobility offers us some signs of this ontological emergence that, in a more explicit way, is present in the analysis of the literature of Buen Vivir.

AN INDIGENOUS REVOLUTIONARY DIALECTIC

Taking Reinaga's ideas as a starting point, in this chapter I have illustrated the construction of an Indigenous revolutionary dialectic with a direct decolonizing teleology. By strategically selecting some notions elaborated by the most radical indigenista intellectuals such as Mariátegui and Valcárcel, Reinaga succeeded in setting the basis for the creation of a theoretical independence that would inspire Indigenous mobility in the second part of the twentieth century. However, we cannot forget that Reinaga was initially an ally of indigenistas who found himself trapped by the dialectical limitations of this intellectual movement and who, after a "crisis of consciousness," emerged from the decolonial cracks of indigenismo to articulate one of the most sophisticated Indigenous dialectics of the 1970s. Metaphorically, this Quechua Aymara intellectual is among the first to cross the dialectical bridge I have illuminated between the indigenista corpus and the decolonizing arguments of Indigenous intellectuals.

Now, one may ask, what does indianismo owe to indigenismo? In spite of the many things that can be criticized about the indigenista administrations of the MNR after the revolution of 1952, one contribution that should be recognized is that they created the objective conditions for the development of indianista ideas. The indigenista state policies, despite the marginalization reproduced by the MNR's elite, promoted the emergence of a generation of Indigenous activists who gained access to higher education and thus developed a class and race consciousness. Working as an official in the MNR, Reinaga perceived these conditions, and this is the reason his writing style oscillates between a deliberate monographic precision and a heated manifesto. Ultimately, Reinaga's indianista literature is a call to action that in a sense fits into the tradition of other texts with revolutionary pretensions such as Fanon's *The Wretched of the Earth* and, to some extent, Valcárcel's *Tempestad en los Andes* among other famous revolutionary manifestos.

However, another of my goals has been to demonstrate the impact that indianismo had on Indigenous mobility in Bolivia. Revolutionary indianista ideas sparkled in a constellation of political organizations, whether trade unions, political parties, or guerrillas. Indianismo and Reinaga's ideas, which circulated through publications accessible to grassroots sectors, were embodied in the mindset of many of these organizations. Forging the decolonial indianista discourse inspired the movements from which Evo Morales emerged in the early 2000s, the Indigenous leader who would later become president of Bolivia for thirteen years and implement—certainly with many shortcomings—one of the first deliberately decolonizing administrations in Latin America. On the other hand, indianismo also generates a theoretical revolution that is expressed not only in its strategic confluence with katarismo but also in the political updating of key concepts in Andean cosmology such as *nayrapacha* and *pachakuti*. In different ways, indianismo intertwines with these notions to forge an Indigenous revolutionary dialectic that had a correlate in political praxis.

Reinaga's literature is robust, and after publishing *La revolución india* he wrote at least a dozen more essays and manifestos. Although his ideas changed, it is difficult to say whether they evolved or convoluted. Toward the end of the 1970s, Reinaga wrote a book entitled *El pensamiento amáutico* (Amautic thought, 1978), which inaugurated what he defined as a superior phase in his decolonizing program. It certainly did not have major repercussions, and to a large extent it is a book in which he rewrites critical revisions of Andean history and engages in a self-celebratory style, which is perhaps the reason he did not participate in the Indigenous organizations of the 1980s. It could be said that from the 1980s onward his ideas were liberated from him and navigated independently through the Bolivian Indigenous decolonizing movements. Hence, I relatively coincide with Macusaya Cruz (*Del indianismo*, 69–71) who labels this period as a post-indianista phase in which Reinaga de-racializes his political agenda. After all, the convening power of indianismo resides in the fact that its dialectic centers Indigenous peoples as racialized subjects capable of developing an authentically Indigenous epistemology—in other words, a holistic vital praxis whose teleology is oriented toward the decolonization of all the spheres in which Indigenous daily life unfolds and that promises to bring down the logics that ground the modern/colonial Bolivian project.

CHAPTER 5

Marcos and the Zapatista Writing

Authority Upside-Down

On January 1, 1994, the Zapatista Army of National Liberation (EZLN) erupted onto the Mexican and international scene with an armed uprising that took place in the city of San Cristóbal de las Casas in the state of Chiapas, in southeastern Mexico. It was a guerrilla group made up mainly of Tojolabales, Tzeltales, Choles, and Lacandones; different ethnic groups from the Mayan territory of Mesoamerica. The Subcomandante Insurgente Marcos—now renamed Galeano (whose pre-insurgent identity would be revealed as the urban mestizo Rafael Guillén Vicente)—attracted special attention. From that moment on, the zapatista uprising in Chiapas has become one of the most emblematic of Indigenous insurgencies and decolonizing projects in Latin America. Although the EZLN's grassroots work dates back to the mid-1980s, it was between 1991 and 1992 that the movement became an essentially Indigenous project, despite the participation of some leaders of mestizo-urban origin who would gradually be replaced by Indigenous leaders in the formation of post-uprising committees.

The zapatista insurrection coincided with the implementation of the North American Free Trade Agreement (NAFTA), which they considered the consolidation of neoliberalism in the Mexican national project.[1] Since then, the EZLN, together with many Indigenous communities in Chiapas, has been building political, economic, cultural, and social autonomy in relation to the Mexican modern national project, whose colonial modality was one of the main motivations of the uprising. After a profound reorganization, since 2003 zapatista autonomous municipalities have been grouped in *caracoles* (the name used for a group of municipalities). These are ruled by the Juntas de Buen Gobierno (Good Government Councils), which are nonmilitary forums in charge of administering justice and regulating the social life of the communities. Their name is a clear reference to the emblematic denunciatory chronicle *Nueva Corónica y Buen Gobierno* that was written and illustrated by the Indigenous chronicler Guamán Poma de Ayala in the seventeenth century. In these collectives, men, women, children, and elders participate in a balanced fashion in what is described as the manifestation of a model of radical democracy. Likewise, these spaces follow Indigenous democratic principles such as *mandar obedeciendo* (ruling by obeying), a notion I will address later. After this organizational readjustment, the EZLN mainly assumed the role of a military ally of these Indigenous communities. The reasons for this change were amply explained in the *Sexta Declaración de la Selva Lacandona* (Sixth Declaration of the Lacandon Jungle).[2] It can also be interpreted as a step toward the indigenization of the struggle for zapatista autonomy, under which the EZLN breaks with the tradition of mestizo guerrillas and becomes an armed wing allied to an essentially Indigenous project.

Much has been written about the zapatista experience in Chiapas in recent years. In her analysis of Mexican media reception of the zapatista uprising, Analisa Taylor points out that the way the media tried to discredit them by claiming they were a group of Indigenous people manipulated by the urban mestizo Marcos is symptomatic of the indigenista cultural imaginary, which presumes intellectual incapacity on the part of Indigenous people, given that "Indigenous people simply do not have a role in interpreting or shaping their own positions within Mexican society" (*Indigeneity*, 77–78). Some studies have focused on the zapatista experience of autonomy as a radical response to the homogenization imposed by neoliberalism and its multiculturalist trap (Stahler-Sholk, "Resisting"), while other readings point directly to the colonial model with which it antagonizes the political action initiated by Indigenous Mayans in Chiapas and how a sense of autonomy emerges as a response to the legacy of dehumanization of the Mexican mestizo state toward Indigenous people (Mora, *Kuxlejal Politics*).

It is this latter, more historically encompassing understanding that I will pursue in my analysis of how the zapatista struggle—through the eclectic literary production, whether signed or not by Marcos-author (who is different from the actual writer)—transcends indigenista modalities framed by a decolonial struggle. Thus, I argue that such transcendence is made both in zapatista fictional and nonfiction literature and in the authorial construction process of Marcos, whose signature is on most of the zapatista texts that circulated between 1994 and 1999. Embodied in the individual corporeality of a person dissociated from his past mestizo identity, Marcos-author is not only a spokesperson commissioned by Indigenous insurgents (as his role as a writer has traditionally been explored) but is himself a literary and political device of Indigenous creation.

Marcos-author is illuminated in this chapter as a collective and anonymous Indigenous authorial construct that, through masking, neutralizes the possibility of transculturalizing interpretations. In this way, Marcos-author is inscribed in a non-Western tradition of authorial formation that exhibits the lack of a theorization about Indigenous authorship in the literary sphere, which prompts me to problematize some aspects of Eurocentric author theory. Along these lines, one of my main aims is to demonstrate that zapatista authorial construction does not fit within the objective conditions that forged the conventional Western sense of authorship. By reversing or subverting Western values attributed to the author such as individuality, originality, and authority over the text, the zapatista literary construct offers the opportunity to delineate a decolonial form of authoring texts by replacing the individual subject with an autonomous and anonymous collective. The authorial construction that results in Marcos-author is a method that stands in line with the zapatista political interest in reversing and transcending the mobility proposed by the Mexican state and its indigenista tradition as well as the modalities of internal colonialism within the country, by countering the intrinsic values of liberal thought. But how does the zapatista insurgency, in its struggle for the revalorization of Indigenous identity, transcend the values of official Mexican Indigenismo, rooted mainly in the ideas of writers and statesmen such as Gamio and Vasconcelos?

AN INDIGENOUS REASSEMBLAGE

The political agenda of the EZLN and the insurgent municipalities can be understood as a counterproposal to the official indigenista reformism carried out by the Mexican state after the revolution of the 1910s and 1920s and, more dramatically, to the neoliberal turn at the beginning of the 1990s. As precedents for the formation of the EZLN, Escárzaga (*La comunidad indígena*, 323–36) has identified the agrarian policies applied by the Mexican state, which in Chiapas privileged individual ownership by campesinos who self-identified as mestizos over the legacy of Indigenous communal property. By developing these agrarian policies, in parallel with the impulse of the Instituto Nacional Indigenista (National Indigenista Institute, INI), the main organ for the dissemination of Mexican official Indigenismo and whose creation was promoted by Gamio. The INI was part of a political attempt to impose mestizaje as the national identity in rural Mexico—that is, mestizaje was offered as an entry to the modern Mexican nation.[3] The distribution of land for agricultural work, applied by Mexico's indigenista policies throughout the twentieth century, was influenced by two principles of indigenismo at the turn of the century: (1) the idea of mestizo identity as a formula for building national unity, evoking in some way the radical mestizaje of Vasconcelos, and (2) the identification of land dispossession as the "Indian problem," recalling Mariátegui's thesis, although without forgetting that in Mexican history this has its own legacy of claims in the Mexican Revolution (e.g., Plan de Ayala).[4] Land distribution under the indigenista formula failed in Chiapas—and in many other parts of Mexico—because it ended up creating a class of mestizo ejido owners, which reproduced oppressive dynamics of labor exploitation, violence, and racism toward the Indigenous people in charge of agricultural labor.[5] Furthermore, as David Yetman ("Ejidos") illustrates, the ejido system was progressively manipulated by the PRI, which coerced ejidatarios to support its candidates in order to fortify its presence in the administration of the country.[6]

That is why one of the first actions of zapatista autonomous communities was the implementation of an agrarian reform that involved the reelaboration of a sense of social identity with their land. In other words, a counterreform to the official agrarian reform, and a counterreform against the failed indigenista policy of land distribution. As Mora (*Kuxlejal Politics*) explains, this zapatista reform was based not only on the reappropriation of land for communal collective agriculture but also on the redefinition of the communal identity of individuals based on their work with this land. Community identification was to be gained through the collective work of said land, not through a singular sense of ownership. This identification was articulated under the Mayan philosophical principle *lekil kuxlejal*, a holistic Indigenous principle that is articulated around the search for harmony with nature and between individuals, a human-nature link that resembles the heterogeneous Indigenous paradigm known as *Buen Vivir*. Mayan intellectual Juan López Intzín proposes to interpret this principle as a collective search for a harmonious life that forges a community network based on values rooted in wholeness, dignity, and justice ("*Ich'el ta muk'*," 87–95).

In the context of zapatista agrarian reform, the term *lekil kuxlejal* referred to the construction of a sense of Indigenous communal and territorial belonging that was defined by the participation of individuals in collective agricultural work. "The action of working the land is embedded in kuxlejal politics and plays a central role in the production of meanings associated with indigeneity," notes Mora (*Kuxlejal Politics*, 144). The zapatista project not only opposed the almost compulsive ethnic approach to mestizaje indexed in official Mexican indigenismo but also redrafted the meaning of Indigenous identity. In doing so, the zapatistas established that identity is constructed not only through ethnic self-identification but through community integration by way of participation in collective work, which acquired more relevance in the context of zapatista agrarian reform as it was equated to a process of identity construction.

Since the postrevolutionary period in Mexico, successive PRI administrations viewed the Indigenous multiethnic scenario through the lens of cultural relativism. Under this logic, the INI was created to be a space from which the Mexican state promoted the mestizo cultural identity as a way of assimilating Indigenous people into modern national life, a logic that was reproduced primarily in the Mexican state's educational and agrarian policies, and even in the cultural industry sponsored by the state apparatus, such as indigenista cinema.[7] It is from this moment on, in the mid-twentieth century, that an official Mexican indigenismo began to take shape, and according to Taylor "can be characterized as a hegemonic discourse and practice that has facilitated and justified an accelerated internal colonialism toward the second half of twentieth century" ("The Ends," 80). In her reading of official Mexican indigenismo, Taylor recognizes the reproduction of colonial dynamics, which from a decolonial viewpoint can be seen as the reproduction of the colonial matrix of power that, in this particular case, promotes the de-indianization of the Indigenous people of Chiapas for their subsequent incorporation into the modern/colonial system under the label of mestizos. Therefore, the irruption of the EZLN and of the autonomous communities and the reelaboration of their processes of identity construction suggest a reelaboration of the sense of indigeneity that until the end of the twentieth century had been captured by the agenda of the official indigenista discourse in Mexico.

Vasconcelos proposed racial homogenization through mestizaje and Gamio proposed cultural assimilation through education and the drafting of a new constitution, but the zapatistas reverse and, in some cases, go beyond these formulas through a process of decolonizing detachment. In this new approach they not only distance themselves from the modern Mexican national project but also propose an epistemological divorce with the forms of identity construction conventionalized by Western civilization, the implementation of the *lekil kuxlejal* principle being a case in point. How is this reversal of the modalities of official Mexican indigenismo embodied? In order to answer this question, the first task is to investigate the collective authorial construction condensed in Marcos-author by contrasting some values inherent to the Western sense of authorship. The second task is to explore some ideological and formal components that define the zapatista authorial construction as an Indigenous decolonizing praxis.

MARCOS-AUTHOR, AN INDIGENOUS CONSTRUCT

The figure of Marcos-author has traditionally been examined as that of a spokesman of and writer for the EZLN as well as a representative of zapatista communities, and it has been analyzed in different spheres: academia, media, and politics. Much has been said about the mestizo, mesocratic, and urban intellectual origins hidden beneath his balaclava before his incursion into the insurgency, which was a motive for criticism. Nevertheless, the communicative and literary capacities of this character—whether the real writer or Marcos-author—have been praised by allies and enemies of the zapatista movement alike.

I am interested in the authorial construction of Marcos and his conversion into an Indigenous vehicle for zapatista intellectual production. I posit a counterargument to the interpretations that illustrate him as an autonomous individual producer of knowledge from a mestizo subjectivity. I argue that, because of his trajectory and involvement with Indigenous cosmologies, Marcos-author—not the actual writer—constitutes, within the symbolic literary field, an Indigenous political device. He distances himself from the paradigm of an indigenista writer so as to subordinate his writing to the cultural production and modalities of the Indigenous zapatista communities, thereby realizing a trajectory that is the opposite of the one proposed by modern literary forms and, in general, one that opposes the Western sense of authority and authorship of Indigenous texts. Being an Indigenous symbolic device, Marcos-authored literary production reverses the sense of intellectual authority traditionally attributed to the single and visible author in the Western tradition—for a sense in which authority is a collective construct and not an individualizing one, as articulated by the radical sense of zapatista democracy.

In terms of genre, the zapatista literature signed by Marcos-author is vast and ambiguous. Although it could be said that his preferred genre is the communiqué, it is true that many of these are peppered with ample narrative and aphoristic passages. In addition, Marcos-author has also written children's stories such as *La historia de los colores* (1999); mythological tales gathered mainly in *Relatos de El Viejo Antonio* (Tales of Old Antonio, 1998), *Cuentos para una soledad desvelada* (Tales for an unveiled solitude, 1998), and *Don Durito de la Lacandona* (1999), where he gathers stories, communiqués, and lectures; the anthology *Desde las montañas del sureste mexicano* (From the mountains of the Mexican Southeast, 1999); and the detective novel *Muertos incómodos* (Uncomfortable deaths, 2005), written in collaboration with the Mexican writer

Paco Ignacio Taibo II. About the narrative and aphoristic style, aspects such as the ironic and sarcastic tonality with which he introduces references to Western culture stand out. Also noteworthy are the orality, musicality, and colloquialisms of his characters, which Ezequiel Maldonado ("Los relatos," 143) attributes to the influence of the oral tradition of Indigenous stories, which suggests interpreting these features not as the influence of the current Indigenous agency but as texts through which it is running.

In an interview Marcos-activist (without leaving Marcos-author completely behind) explains the role of one of his main literary characters—Viejo Antonio, an Indigenous elder who brought the EZLN guerrillas closer to the Indigenous communities of Chiapas. "The Zapatista Army of National Liberation, through him [Viejo Antonio], through those political and community leaders, begins to understand its history of political foundation, its consciousness, its historical consciousness. And the result is that we were not talking to an Indigenous movement that was waiting for a savior, but to an Indigenous movement with a long tradition of struggle, with a lot of experience, very resistant, very intelligent as well, to which we simply served as an armed wing."[8] Marcos-activist is at pains to emphasize that Indigenous decolonial mobility predated the alliance with the guerrillas: "we were not talking to an Indigenous movement that was waiting for a savior, but to an Indigenous movement with a long tradition of struggle, with a lot of experience" (Marcos, *El sueño*, 147).

The early twentieth-century notion expressed by indigenista thinkers Luis Valcárcel and José Carlos Mariátegui—that "the Indian is waiting for their Lenin," which back then offered a glimpse of an indigenista decolonial crack—is revisited in the elaboration of a decolonizing praxis within the ideological and strategic formation of the EZLN and the zapatista communities. The Indigenous sage Viejo Antonio, whether a real or fictitious character, helped the guerrillas plunge into an existing activist current. It is not Marcos-activist who stirs up the communities, but the opposite. In other words, the old indigenista claim that Indigenous communities were waiting for their Lenin is inverted.

In her examination of Rafael Guillén Vicente's scholarly thesis about Marcos's pre-insurgent identity, Catherine E. Walsh ("'Other' Knowledges") points out that Marcos was initially a Marxist-

Leninist intellectual with an indigenista slant who repeated the modality of "speaking on behalf of" Indigenous people. At some point, however, he developed a critical sense of his own intellectual position and discovered the geopolitical limitations of Marxist-Leninist thought, proposing the search for other critical perspectives on modernity. In this search, he found in the Indigenous insurgency and its anonymity an authentically decolonizing way to reevaluate subjugated or peripheral knowledge with respect to the modern/rational epistemological centrality. In this conversion, according to Daniela di Paramo, the balaclava helps him become an "'empty signifier,' which (in theory) can serve as a mirror of any of us" ("Beyond Modernity," 181). In this way, Marcos-activist neutralizes his former identity and manages not only to assimilate but to subjugate himself to the symbolic forces of Indigenous activism in Chiapas.

Once the symbolic identity of Marcos-author is constructed—reducing almost to obsolescence the mestizo identity that Guillén embodied during his years as a Marxist-Leninist indigenista and wearing a balaclava that concealed his previous identity and ethnicity—it makes no sense to read the zapatista writings transculturally insofar as they are not the result of an individual intellectual experience but, rather, the result of a collective literary creation. On the symbolic plane of his literature, since 1994, the writings signed by Marcos are a result of an Indigenous intellectual process, no longer that of a mestizo individual who deploys in his texts a humanitarian agency toward Indigenous people. In this sense, I agree with José Rabasa when he states that, "as an intellectual, Marcos no longer defines his task as one of representation. He does not speak for the Zapatistas (he is one more Zapatista and, as an intellectual, a subordinate) nor does he portray them" (*Without History*, 59).

From the first days of 1994, the beginning of the zapatista project, the zapatistas made it clear in a communiqué signed by the EZLN's Comité Clandestino Revolucionario Indígena (Clandestine Revolutionary Indigenous Committee, CCRI) that they rejected any attempt at paternalistic mediation or representation of the Indigenous word.[9] The texts signed by Marcos-author were previously commissioned, revised, and corrected by the CCRI, made up of men, women, children, and elders from the different Mayan ethnic groups involved in the project. This modality of radical democracy is articulated by the principle of *mandar obedeciendo* where authority is not singularized in any one individual but moves collectively from bottom to top. It is in this framework that the zapatista writings are created, constituting a collective authorial construction in which Marcos is only an instrumental derivation. Zapatista literary praxis challenges the notion of mere diversification that Manuel Gamio cautioned about in his evaluation of Indigenous cultures' role in forming a Mexican national literature. This praxis embodies in both form and content a rejection of the dominant vision of Mexican literature. This is evident in the very construction of the Marcos-author, which actively disrupts traditional notions of authorship within Mexican literature.

In one of the most comprehensive studies of zapatista literature, Kristine Vanden Berghe points to Marcos as a translator who "intervenes only to make the Indigenous message understandable to an external audience" ("interviene únicamente para hacer que el mensaje de los indígenas sea comprensible para un público externo") (*Narrativa*, 62–63). Vanden Berghe is right in the sense that Marcos-activist translates Indigenous content into letters and into Spanish on behalf of zapatistas, interested in communicating their thoughts to the outside world. But in talking about the translator role, she is referring to the actual person who sits down to write and not to Marcos-author as a symbolic entity and political device collectively created by the Indigenous activists who are part of the CCRI. The Indigenous origin of Marcos's authorial construct not only shows a decolonial activist submitted to Indigenous knowledge but also exhibits an authorial creation forged by Indigenous political agency, transcending transcultural indigenista modalities—especially if it's considered that, in this authorial formation process, authority does not rest in the individual writer but in the collective agency of the CCRI.

The way in which the zapatista authorial construct forges Marcos highlights the need to discuss what kind of authorship this is. Authorship has always been a matter of discussion within Indigenous literary production. In his analysis of the autobiographical testimony of Maya Quiche activist Rigoberta Menchú, John Beverly brings into discussion the risk of written forms as devices that assert lettered privilege against the agency of the subaltern.

For him, this crossroads is primarily triggered by liberal guilt that overemphasizes the authority deposited in the written text (*Subalternity*, 69–71). Gloria E. Chacón, in her studies of contemporary Mesoamerican writers, argues that alternative authorial construction processes have the symbolic value of challenging the "widely held assumption that the oral tradition is intrinsically a more authentic indigenous practice" (*Indigenous Cosmolectics*, 67). Drawing on these delineations of Indigenous authorship, I am interested in illuminating the authorial construction process of Marcos, shaped by the political orders of the CCRI and Maya philosophical principles (*lekil kuxlejal* and *mandar obedeciendo*). This process, I argue, is unique in that, far from reemphasizing mestizo mediation, it instead overturns some of the tenets of liberal authorship without stripping Marcos's literary praxis of political content.

The conventional author theory of recent years is born of the seemingly oppositional proposals of Roland Barthes and Michel Foucault. In a canonical essay entitled "The Death of the Author" (1967), Barthes promotes discarding the author's intentionality from the analysis of any literary text and suggests paying attention only to the text as the principal signifying element in literature. In a not-so-indirect response to Barthes, Foucault reframes this discussion in a lecture entitled "What Is an Author?" (1969) where he refocuses attention on the author and suggests that, instead of questioning intentionality, functionality should be critically explored. For him, the author, not the actual writer (a distinction I endorse) functions as a device that singularizes discourses into an identifiable subject that "permits one to group together a certain number of texts, define them, differentiate them from and contrast them to others" (210). As can be deduced, both theories end up being problematic for exploring the zapatista authorial construct that—instead of individualizing discourse—collectivizes and anonymizes the circulation of its ideas in lettered platforms.

Barthes's and Foucault's theories of authorship, which focused on dismantling the liberal values conferred by European tradition on literary authorship, constitute a response to capitalism and its intervention in the cultural sphere. Is this the same process that forges the zapatista authorship? Colonialism and coloniality—in an oppressive continuum that encompasses capitalist expansion—are the reality against which the zapatista project struggles.

Hence, I argue that the modality of creation and circulation of zapatista literature exposes the limitations of Western author theory for non-Western forms of authorship. I argue that it is necessary to explore the analytical particularities of zapatista authorial formation.

This formation can be understood as a decolonial praxis inscribed in the search for a locus of enunciation for Indigenous literatures. This search was initiated by the intercultural claims of the indigenista tradition (e.g., Gamio and Arguedas). However, in zapatista literary practices, this search is consecrated as the expansion of an Indigenous decolonial agency that instrumentalizes the symbolic figure of Marcos-author to achieve its communicative purposes. After all, the individualistic authorial construct is not a structural element of Indigenous authorship in Mesoamerica. As David Távarez ("Zapotec Time") demonstrates, in Mesoamerica there was a preexisting collective and anonymous form of authorial construction that survived colonial devastation through the circulation of anonymous Indigenous knowledge in booklets and calendars. This means that collectivism and anonymity as strategies have been part of cultural life in this region for centuries and have articulated Indigenous literary production since before the emergence of the singularized romantic author.

The individualizing vision of intellectual creation made the Mexican state seek to discredit the zapatista movement by blaming Marcos individually for manipulating Indigenous communities, unable to identify that it was a collective construct where authority resided in the Indigenous collective. This is how, in the field of intellectual production, Marcos-activist finds himself subjected to the zapatista principle of *mandar obedeciendo*, according to which the practice of power is inverted, with the authority being the one who receives the orders and not the one who imparts them. For Mora (*Kuxlejal Politics*, 187–92), this modality is inscribed in the zapatista interest of representing a sovereign idea of power by reversing the classical liberal model of decision-making. Thus, Marcos-author is actually a political, literary, and intellectual instrument with which zapatista communities communicate with the outside world in order to avoid what Jérôme Baschet calls an "ethnicism" that would isolate the zapatista movement, given that "the zapatista struggle is Indigenous but not only Indigenous" ("la lucha zapatista es indígena, pero no solo indígena") (*¡Rebeldía!*, 201). The alliances that the zapatista project built with other groups and the sense of epistemological multiplicity inherent in the literature are illustrative of this interest in avoiding isolation—something that, certainly, is in line with the concerns expressed by Gamio, who in *Forjando patria* warned, through an indigenista perspective, about the risks of the isolation of the Indigenous peoples in small homelands ("pequeñas patrias").

With this explanation of the zapatista authorial construct, I intend to clarify that my understanding of Marcos-author is not that of a cultural sympathizer who decides to become indianized but, rather, that of a symbolic identity created by and functional for the zapatista Indigenous project, an identity that goes beyond the methodological and ideological tenets of indigenista discourse and inaugurates a decolonial praxis within the cultural dimension. This construct is what allows me to read Marcos-author's texts as Indigenous cultural products and practices and not as the textualization of a solidary approach as formulated by some of the various indigenista discourses analyzed in the first part of this book. Always in a symbolic realm, in this authorial construction, the balaclava becomes a useful mechanism for the purpose of dispelling a sense of individual authority over the intellectual content of zapatista literature.

However, returning to the controversial role as translator, it is worth mentioning that Mignolo posits that an ideological translation occurs in Marcos-activist since, given his Marxist-Leninist indigenista background, he unmasks Western universal abstractions (Marxism and liberalism) and cultural relativism as a reproducer of colonial differences. I would add that the authorial construct derived from zapatista literature unmasks the constrained analytical lens through which the material conditions of Indigenous textual production are traditionally explored. However, Mignolo points out that Guillén (it is problematic that he continues to speak of Guillén) "infects himself with Amerindian cosmology" ("Zapatistas's Theoretical Revolution," 247) and therefore abandons converting the Indigenous people of the Lacandon jungle into Marxists and transforms himself conceptually under the identity of Marcos. I partially agree with Mignolo's contention to the extent that an ideological translation takes place in the literature signed by Marcos-author. After all, the unmasking of universal Western abstractions also explains indigenista ideological controversies (e.g., Mariátegui's polemic in Buenos Aires). Yet I disagree with describing this process as an infection of "Amerindian cosmology" to refer to what in essence is the construction of a new symbolic entity and identity based on the political agenda and Mayan Indigenous knowledge. And, on the other hand, in view of what has been argued above, I disagree with locating this process in Guillén, who ultimately was left behind with the balaclava and the 1994 uprising. I would propose to index Guillén entirely in the zapatista literature authored by Marcos, understanding Marcos as the result of an Indigenous construct and zapatista writings as the final outcome of a cultural creation that ideologically describes a trajectory from the inside out (to use the same terms used to describe Bolivia's indianista mobility in the previous chapter).

VIEJO ANTONIO, INDIGENOUS SUBJECTIVITY, AND INSURGENT NARRATIVE

In the prologue of *Relatos de El Viejo Antonio* (1998), Armando Bartra conveniently recalls an old Tzotzil myth according to which the "ladino"—that is, mestizos or hispanized Indians—stole the book from the Indigenous Chiapanecos, in a rhetorical sense that refers to the written word and the symbolic support of the knowledge it contains. Bartra also comments on how ironic it is that the book has been returned to these people with the appearance of Marcos, not elaborating on Marcos-author and literary production as an Indigenous construct. As I have been arguing, insisting on Marcos as a mestizo writer obscures the Indigenous intellectual agency that runs through this authorial creation and the collective authority over the intellectual content of zapatista texts. One can understand that what Bartra's mythological reference elliptically contains is precisely the centuries of displacement of Indigenous knowledge and forms of wisdom because of the ongoing colonial system. That is why he states:

> And so the first gods saw that "the one" is necessary, that it is necessary to learn and to work and to live and to love. But they also saw that the one is not enough. They saw that "the all" is needed

and only the all is enough to make the world go around. And that was how the first gods, the greatest gods, the ones who gave birth to the world, became good at knowing. These gods knew how to speak and to listen. And they were wise. Not because they knew many things or because they knew much about one thing, but because they understood that the one and the all are necessary and sufficient.[10]

The impossibility of communicating in a world that was first viceroyal and then republican—which sanctioned or made invisible the languages and knowledge systems that were alien to the Eurocentric matrix—becomes evident. In *Relatos*, Viejo Antonio is presented as a deceased and therefore timeless Indigenous character, a Chiapaneco who laid the foundations of the zapatista struggle in its purely guerrilla period and the subsequent assimilation of the EZLN to Mayan indigeneities. In the zapatista narrative, Viejo Antonio channels Indigenous knowledge and historical readings that have remained hidden under the overwhelming colonial knowledge regime that privileged only thought with Eurocentric sources and, ultimately, made visible only the intellectual production of mestizos who were recognized as valid cultural subjects. The literary strategy with which Viejo Antonio is presented, as in almost all zapatista literature, is ideologically explicit, which also makes this character explicit as an alter ego of Marcos himself.

Featured in various zapatista texts, Viejo Antonio is a literary character with whom the zapatista narrative constructs an Indigenous subjectivity and a symbolic genealogy with direct political intentions. Viejo Antonio recounts to the first-person narrator in the tale "La historia del uno y los todos" (The story of one and all) how the conglomeration of gods forged the world through a collective and self-critical process. The portrait conveyed by Viejo Antonio shows collective agency as an original mode of Indigenous mobility ("the one and the all are necessary and sufficient") (Marcos, *Desde las montañas*, 389) in an effort to oppose the individual re-creation of the origin of Indigenous societies.

For Vanden Berghe ("Nativismo," 200–206), this character embodies a hybrid stereotyping of the material conditions of Indigenous communities as being poor, ailing, and yet morally superior because of his harmonious connection with nature. On a discursive level, Martin Baxmeyer highlights the political value of Viejo Antonio—mainly in his mythological stories since, with ambiguous language (because of unconventional phonetic and syntactic interventions in Spanish) and through the mythologization of political principles, he creates a "direct contradiction to the dominant technocratic discourse of our times" ("contradeclaración directa al discurso tecnocrático dominante de nuestros tiempos") ("El mito universal," 183). Baxmeyer's reading makes sense given the political conjuncture with which the zapatista movement contends. After all, technocratic discourse articulates the valorization of knowledge in the policymaking processes of liberal administrations, such as the Mexican state in the context of NAFTA implementation.

Thus, in the literary sphere, Viejo Antonio operates as a wise Indigenous spokesman who aspires to re-create a Mayan subjectivity (regardless of the degree of authenticity) that runs through a profoundly decolonizing discourse: "Our greatest grandparents had to face the foreigner who came to conquer these lands. The foreigner came to give us other manners, other words, other beliefs, other gods, and other justice. His justice was only for him to gain and to dispossess us. His god was the gold. His belief was his superiority. His word was lies. His mode was cruelty. Ours, our greatest warriors confronted them, there were great fights among the natives of these lands to defend the land from the hand of the foreigner. But great was the strength that the foreign hand brought."[11] In this monologue, Viejo Antonio gives visibility not only to the vision of the defeated (*visión de los vencidos*) but also to the fields in which the oppression imposed by the colonial invasion was reproduced (religion, economy, culture, and the justice system).[12] In addition, he also denounces the sense of otherness that becomes a burden for the "natives of these lands" ("naturales de estas tierras") (Marcos, *Relatos*, 70).

This process of becoming an *other* in your place of origin is exhibited as the result of the colonial dynamics that Viejo Antonio ascribes to the foreigner, a subject whose ambiguity can refer directly to the European occupier or to the Mexican national subject represented in the criollos and mestizos. Renaming Latin America as Abya Yala, a term adopted by zapatista communiqués as well, is a political strategy to cease being the *other* in their own land, since it re-creates the symbolic and factual space as and from an Indigenous locus of enunciation. In a reading of zapatista insurgent poetics, Hannah Burdette (*Revealing*) argues that their strategy seeks, on the one hand, to recall the condition of invisibility of subaltern subjects and, on the other hand, to explicitly criticize the policies of racial exclusion and cultural segregationism. We can see that the same policies are reproduced in Marcos's writing, which seeks not only to illuminate Indigenous knowledge and invisibilized subjects but also to denounce these policies of exclusion and degradation, as shown by Viejo Antonio: "to dispossess us" ("despojarnos a nosotros") (Marcos, *Relatos*, 70).

But one characteristic of zapatista literature is that it does not serve merely as a denouncing device; rather, it advances toward communicating its political program and formulating its unique sense of autonomy. In another passage of *Relatos*, Viejo Antonio recounts the origin of the words granted by the founder gods: "The first three of all words and all languages are democracy, liberty, justice" ("Las tres primeras de todas las palabras y de todas las lenguas son democracia, libertad, justicia") (*Relatos*, 65).[13] Unambiguously, zapatista literature introduces the fundamental ideas of its political program aimed at autonomy, as well as the regulatory principles of its sociability: "That the word of command obeys the word of the majority, that the staff of command has a collective word and not a singular will" ("Que la palabra de mando obedezca la palabra de la mayoría, que el bastón de mando tenga palabra colectiva y no una sola voluntad") (66), which refers directly to *mandar obedeciendo*, the system of democratic regulation of zapatista Indigenous communities that not only articulates Marcos's authorial construction but also runs through zapatista literature.

On *Relatos* and mythological rewriting from an Indigenous perspective, Vanden Berghe notes this is how "Marcos escapes to a kind of ahistorical zone where poetic and mythological vision replaces factual historical knowledge and rejects historiography as an imposition of non-Indigenous Mexico on Indigenous traditions" ("Marcos escapa a una especie de zona ahistórica donde la visión poética y mitológica suplanta el conocimiento histórico factual y que rechaza la historiografía como una imposición del México no indígena sobre las tradiciones autóctonas") (*Narrativa*, 113–14). In my view, Vanden Berghe refers to Marcos-activist, who not only makes Indigenous historiography visible but also revalorizes it by introducing the Indigenous mythological narrative as a crucial element, contrary to what is imposed by the factual precision of Western historiography. This literary strategy also legitimizes the sources of Indigenous knowledge by embodying Mesoamerican cosmology in this alternative mythology. On the other hand, according to Armando Bartra, Viejo Antonio represents the possibility of Indigenous singularity as opposed to the dominant tradition of collectively and anonymously representing Indigenous communities. "Undoubtedly, rural communities have in the preeminence of collectivity their condition of survival within a hostile world, but this does not imply the absence of individuation" ("Sin duda las comunidades rurales tienen en la preeminencia de lo colectivo su condición de sobrevivencia dentro de un mundo hostil, pero esto no implica ausencia de individuación") ("Mitos," 16). Through Viejo Antonio, zapatista literature breaks with the stigma of anonymity that hangs over the classic collective representations of Indigenous communities for non-Indigenous audiences and advocates the centrality of Indigenous communities as a source of dissemination of knowledge and as crucial agents in the rewriting of history—that is, in cultural decolonization.

Returning to the quote about ancestors in *Relatos*, the zapatista mythological narrative seeks to reposition indigeneity in the historical narrative in opposition to the official version where Indigenous societies are othered. Thus, as Viejo Antonio claims, the Indigenous peoples did not allow themselves to be inertly invaded by foreigners, but rather their "greatest warriors confronted them" (Marcos, *Relatos*, 70). In this tale, Indigenous mobility is mythologized and exalted and a legacy of insurgency among the natives of Chiapas is vindicated. Accordingly, the myth explains the domineering origin of a radically different system of existential conception and construction of reality ("give us other manners, other words, other beliefs, other gods, and other justice") (70). From a decolonial analysis of this enunciation, I identify advocacy in favor of a radical change in the terms of Indigenous sociability, alluding to a change of the ontological order that is also part of the zapatista struggle, specifically their interest in decolonizing their beingness by bringing in the organizing principles of Mayan cosmology.

It should be recalled that, read as an Indigenous-based instrument, Marcos-author translates Mayan cosmology into Spanish to explain the constitutive elements of the zapatista insurgency. Thus, I suggest reading it in terms of the insurrection of knowledge defined by Aparicio and Blaser as a pattern of mobilization that, by engaging with Indigenous cosmologies, brings forward other worlds and knowledges. From the epistemological divorce from the Eurocentric civilizing process and concepts, the zapatista insurgency is inscribed as an insurrection of subjugated knowledge that not only questions the power and knowledge regime of modernity/coloniality but also challenges "the ontological grounding of modern institutions" ("Lettered City," 64).

The state apparatus as a regulatory or objective entity is no longer a protagonist in this struggle since it is only an object of desire within a multipolarity limited by modern politics. Instead, in their search for epistemological and ontological autonomy—that is, for sources of knowledge and modes of existence—zapatistas are advocates for the fragmentation and diversification of ways of being and world-making processes. It is in this decolonizing principle that their famous slogan in favor of "a world where many worlds fit" ("un mundo donde quepan muchos mundos") (Marcos and EZLN, "Cuarta") is rooted. This is how *pluriversality* articulates many of the sovereignty claims of the Indigenous peoples of Mesoamerica. Marcos-author's conceptual development is constituted as a crucial element for the construction of decolonial solidarities with and from the zapatista movement and, simultaneously (to displace the state apparatus from this discussion), a key factor for the emergence of an Indigenous decolonial critique. After all, the decolonizing principles of the Mexican Revolution were dissipated throughout the twentieth century due to the Mexican state's coaptation and institutionalization of its revolutionary values.

PLURIVERSALITY AND ZAPATISTA DISCURSIVITY

The *Cuarta Declaración de la Selva Lacandona* (Fourth Declaration of the Lacandon Jungle) was a communiqué signed by the zapatista CCRI that reveals to a significant degree the pluriversal matrix that articulates its decolonial dialectic. "Many words are walked in the world. Many worlds are made. Many worlds make us. There are words and worlds that are lies and injustices. There are words and worlds that are truths and true. We make true worlds. We are made of true words"[14] ("Muchas palabras se caminan en el mundo. Muchos mundos se hacen. Muchos mundos nos hacen. Hay palabras y mundos que son mentiras e injusticias. Hay palabras y mundos que son verdades y verdaderos. Nosotros hacemos mundos verdaderos. Nosotros somos hechos por palabras verdaderas") (CCRI-EZLN, *Cuarta*, 1996).

Before exploring this decolonial dialectic, however, let us pay attention to another recurring character in zapatista literature (albeit a fictional one)—that is, Don Durito de la Lacandona, a beetle who intellectually militates for the insurgency and who constantly appears either in dialogues with the narrative "I" as Marcos's literary alter ego or in offering lectures on specific topics. The beetle's sarcastic reference to Don Quixote de la Mancha made clear in the naming of the character, the playful method with which he theoretically antagonizes issues such as neoliberalism, capitalism, and globalization, as well as his promotion of armed struggle are the main features of this nonhuman figure with high intellectual values. He also allows the narrative "I" to mock the conventionalized institutions for the legitimization, production, and administration of knowledge. What could be less intellectual and sophisticated than an insect?

In *Don Durito de la Lacandona* (1999), a compilation of tales, communiqués, speeches, and lectures featuring Don Durito as a central character, some issues that are addressed complement the sense of autonomy previously delineated by Viejo Antonio's mythological narratives. Don Durito does not speak of the colonial origin of the struggle nor of the first gods and the emergence of zapatista moral principles. Rather, he discusses the present and the modern/rational political system and prescribes solutions to articulate solidarities with other movements.

For example, analyzing the history of neoliberalism, Don Durito claims that in this ideology the villains are "Blacks, yellows, chicanos, latinos, Indigenous people, women, young people, prisoners, migrants, fuck-ups, homosexuals, lesbians, marginalized people, old people, and most especially, rebels" ("los negros, los amarillos, los chicanos, los latinos, los indígenas, las mujeres, los jóvenes, los presos, los migrantes, los jodidos, los homosexuales, las lesbianas, los marginados, los ancianos, y, muy especialmente, los rebeldes") (*Don Durito*, 125). With this intersectional enumeration, Don Durito positions their struggle in the global context of domination—that is, in the periphery, from a framework of world-system analysis. This is how this character establishes a sense of solidarity between the Indigenous people and other wretched of the earth because, as Baschet warned, the zapatista struggle is Indigenous—but not only Indigenous. Recalling Marx and Engels's statement, Don Durito calls for unity among the subalterns of the world. In that sense, zapatista literature performs an exercise in ubiquity such as that of Reinaga when he establishes an empathetic connection between the struggle of the Andean Indians and the enslaved people of Africa and the Caribbean. However, this enumeration also reveals the sense of multiplicity inherent in the ideological battlefield of the zapatista project as it refutes various Western universalisms.

In most of his interventions, Don Durito reiterates the threefold statement *democracia, libertad y justicia* as the main programmatic demands of the zapatista movement—the same three foundational words as were proclaimed by Viejo Antonio as the principles of the zapatista idea of revolution. In a 1995 story/communiqué, Don Durito explains the significance of the zapatista revolution and its implications: "Any attempt to 'reform' or 'balance' this deformation is impossible from inside the state party system. There is no 'change without rupture.' A profound, radical change is needed in all social relations in Mexico today. A revolution is necessary, a new revolution. This revolution will only be possible from outside the state party system."[15] Zapatista literature thus discloses that revolution is not the creation of a revolutionary party, as the Latin American socialisms of previous decades attempted, but the creation of a world—that is, it reframes revolution as a world-making praxis, somewhat setting a difference with the type of revolutionary praxis promoted in the 1920s by Mariátegui. Revolution is not about the seizure of power ("no se trata de la conquista del poder") but about building the prelude to a new world ("construir la antesala de un mundo nuevo") (*Don Durito*, 57).

To this end, the zapatista struggle is framed in what Mignolo ("On Pluriversality") defines as a pluriversal way of conducting decolonization, which implies changing the terms of the conversation—in this case the conversation about what a revolution means—and detaching oneself from the nation-state model by recognizing it as the paradigm that universalized Western ideals. In other words, from a pluriversal revolutionary framework, the state apparatus and the means of production are no longer objects of desire. Therefore, zapatista pluriversality also dissociates itself from the tradition of inclusivism promoted by indigenista state policies.

In her analysis of the zapatista revolutionary imaginary, María Josefina Saldaña-Portillo (*Revolutionary Imagination*) explains that it proposes creating a new history, one that takes into account the silenced Indigenous legacy and that offers itself as an alternative to the legacy of the modernization discourse of the Mexican liberal nation, which we can interpret as an alternative to modern politics. Some of this is exhibited in Viejo Antonio's mythological narrative, but at this point, we already know that the zapatista literary endeavor is to communicate more than just a historical rewriting of what is unique in the zapatistas' quest for an Indigenous decolonial critique.

In his analysis of contemporary Indigenous movements, Arturo Escobar points out that since the 1990s a form of mobility has emerged that is oriented toward the promotion of a different mode of relationality of worlds—that is, a mobilization of ontologies.[16] By understanding ontology in the context of Indigenous movements as the study of world-making processes that (re)define what exists and what does not, these ontologies in motion, without being homogenized, interrelate constantly in order to challenge the founding epistemes of modern politics. In that context, Escobar highlights that the slogan "a world of many worlds" was popularized by zapatistas so as to disseminate the notion of pluriversal-oriented autonomy as a mode of liberation of "worlds and knowledges constructed on the basis of different ontological commitments, epistemic configurations, and practices of being, knowing, doing" (*Designs*, 74).

Don Durito's enumeration and the phrase from the *Cuarta Declaración* quoted above uncover in zapatista literature, whether signed by Marcos-author or by the CCRI, the recognition of an ontological multiplicity inherent in decolonizing struggles. Ultimately, zapatista insurgent municipalities are composed of different Indigenous nations (Tojolabales, Tzeltales, Choles, and

Lacandones) that, while sharing a common legacy of colonial oppression and in some cases being part of the same ethnolinguistic family, differ in their ontological commitments—that is, in their interrelationships with nature, their dynamics of internal democracy, and their world-making processes. Pluriversality constitutes an organic step forward in the critical and diversifying vision anticipated in the indigenista decolonial cracks of the early twentieth century, as Gamio envisioned in his critique of the nature of laws in the formation of Mexican nationality.

For the zapatista movement, revolution does not constitute the abrupt replacement of one model of social organization by another. From their literature (in any of its genres, but above all through their insurgent praxis), we understand that, under their teleological principle of revolution, Indigenous autonomy (and not only Indigenous) is seen as a process of opening up different ontological relationalities, a process structured under the heterogeneous principle of *pluriversality*. This coexistence of multiple ontologies "chicanos, Indigenous, Blacks, yellows" ("chicanos, indígenas, negros, amarillos") (*Desde las montañas*, 19) embodied in the slogan *a world of many worlds* implies the liberation not only of political and cultural epistemes but also of the very modes of reality creation. By breaking with the social control of the nation-state, the zapatista insurgency discards the relativism inherent in the dominant multiculturalist discourse of the time. With that purpose of communicating visions of insurgent Mayan ontological autonomy, zapatista literature skillfully chooses Viejo Antonio and Don Durito, a poor Indigenous man and an insect, as rhetorical devices that decolonize both past and present with the intention of channeling a future-oriented idea of autonomy imbued, for the zapatista case, with the varied Mayan cosmology.

Unlike the ageless Viejo Antonio, a local character whose main references are rooted in Mesoamerican culture, Don Durito is an animal character who constantly elaborates on the future while being indexed in the present. He is an insect that personifies the various oppressed subjects of the world. After all, every subaltern is an insect under the modern/colonial/capitalist structure. Thus, Don Durito triggers a global empathy among the "wretched of the earth" (in the most Fanonian sense) but, at the same time, appeals to Western intertextualities using Shakespeare and Bertolt

Brecht and being himself a parody of Don Quixote, the literary symbol of Hispanic culture, the dominant episteme. For Di Paramo, the use of parody and irony in the zapatista narrative is an attempt to "break away from conventional political rhetoric and put forward an alternate rhetoric that, in some respects, is indeed original, particularly in its use of ironical and poetic language" ("Beyond Modernity," 183). Although she localizes this rhetorical strategy in Marcos's individuality (which I disagree with because Marcos-author is a collectively constructed Indigenous device), I agree with Di Paramo's interpretation of irony as a decolonizing dialectical strategy that runs through the zapatista narratives as an antithesis to conventional political discursivity.

Bringing us back to the pluriversal axis, Don Durito argues for solidarity among the different oppressed groups around the globe, with their unique forms of world-making and reality creation, and with that world-making praxis reveals that the zapatista project does not enact a uniform model of autonomy. The zapatista narratives exhibit the horizontal acceptance of a radical diversity that transcends cultural relativism and makes incursions into pluriversality—that is, into the mobilization, interrelation, and independence of distinct world-making processes, Indigenous or not. Zapatista literature does not engage in multiculturalism or pluriculturalism. It avoids academic jargons, including those institutionalized by official leftist parties, and assembles the diversity of decolonizing struggles under the not-so-ironic label of "intergalactic" movements, a term I interpret as a pragmatic euphemism for the multiplicity of worlds (ontologies). Thus, in a May 1996 communiqué, the zapatistas invited their allies to an "intergalactic summit" (*Don Durito*, 103–15) in which the different insurgent sectors of the world could share experiences at a panel entitled "En este mundo caben muchos mundos" (In this world many worlds fit) (112), one of the first times this slogan was used as a call to the multiplication of insurgency and autonomy that has inspired several movements in different parts of the world. This slogan is repeated as a leitmotif of zapatista literature that is one of the main influences of the decolonizing narrative popularized by this movement, whether signed by Marcos-author or by CCRI. Ultimately, the texts produced by the zapatista project between 1994 and 1999 (the period analyzed here and corresponding to its formative stage) consolidate the pluriversal discourse within an Indigenous-rooted intellectual framework.

AUTHORITY UPSIDE-DOWN

In both form and content, zapatista literature is strongly impregnated by the insurgent political program of the Mayan communities and the EZLN, in which they attempt to materialize an alternative to the modern/colonial/capitalist system through a liberating model articulated in Indigenous political principles, expanding in many ways the decolonial claims anticipated by the indigenista tradition of the early twentieth century. This unique mode of liberation transcends political and economic independence. It not only encompasses the revalorization of Indigenous wisdom and sources of knowledge (without claiming to be a universal model) but also encourages interrelations with other forms of world-making praxes that are subjugated by the multiple realms of coloniality. These interrelations mark the fundamental difference between the zapatista type of liberation and other revolutionary formulas tested in Latin America, including some that had active Indigenous participation. Thus, my aim has been to exhibit that, framed in this political program, zapatista literature and the collective creation of Marcos-author operate as communicative devices of an original decolonizing agency that transcends the indigenista representational ethos.

However, one of the most interesting lessons left by the zapatista literary processes is the inversion of power between individuals and collectives. The inverted authority that formulates Marcos's authorial construction also runs through the ideas, plots, messages, and cosmological content that make up the decolonizing dialectic of zapatista literature. In her historicization of the emergence of Indigenous intellectual agency in the Americas, Florencia E. Mallon highlights a decolonial approach such that, "as part of this new political and cultural dynamism, Native peoples have generated their own intellectuals, who have taken center stage in debates over cultural interpretation and translation and over the narration of Native histories" ("Introduction," 2). It is as part of this straightforwardly decolonizing political dynamic that the authorial construction that created Marcos-author and the political content of the zapatistas' writings must be understood as pieces that go beyond the representational limits of indigenista literature and authorship. By reversing the sense of authority, which is limited not only to author construction but also to the dialectic that inspires characters such as Viejo Antonio or Don Durito, the zapatista project consolidates an Indigenous decolonial discourse in a unique way both in its form (political praxis) and content (ideology) that engages in a dialectical dialogue with the indigenista decolonial cracks.

If literature is a process (recalling Mariátegui's terms), zapatista literature, and mainly that produced between 1994 and 1999, was part of an eminently political process in which the zapatistas were setting the ground rules of their decolonizing project. In his study of contemporary Maya narrative, Arturo Arias asserts that Maya literature frames its claims in Mayan epistemological contexts, from which it is possible to identify its "socio-political and cosmopolitical implications" (*Recovering*, 223). To some extent, this is the type of analysis I employ when I explore zapatista literariness through the lens of normative Mayan principles such as *lekil kuxlejal* and *mandar obedeciendo*. Like Arias, I do not believe it is possible to formulate a common analytical framework for all literatures produced in Abya Yala, as sometimes this is not even possible within the same Indigenous linguistic family where different communal formulas and processes of cultural creation coexist—as in the heterogeneous Maya Nation, as well as the Quechua, Mapuche, and Nahuatl (among other Indigenous) Nations. Each nation carries its own political praxis and its own cosmological content. The zapatista literary experience, framed in the context of Mayan insurgency, is an illustrative example of how intellectually sophisticated Indigenous decolonial thinking is—and how skillful communicative strategies can be when employing local modalities of democracy.

CHAPTER 6

Poetics of *Buen Vivir*

Political Ontology of Indigenous Poetry

It has been perhaps three decades since the concept of *Buen Vivir* entered the Latin American political and environmental debate through the door of the Indigenous movements—that is, through a door traditionally ignored, if not deliberately closed, by the factual and symbolic forces of coloniality of power.[1] In this specific field, Buen Vivir has lived long enough to go from being an innovative concept that held the promise of a radical eco-social paradigm shift in the face of the environmental devastation brought about by neoliberalism in Latin America during the 1970s–1990s to its subsequent institutionalization by leftist and neo-indigenista political movements, particularly in Ecuador and Bolivia where it was introduced in their constitutions during the 2010s. On the the subsumption of Buen Vivir in constitutions, Catherine E. Walsh ("Development") and Eduardo Gudynas ("Buen Vivir") have described convincing instances of the conversion of Buen Vivir into a functional rhetorical device for the continuity of developmental models dependent on extractivism.[2] What is certainly true here is that the usages and meanings of Buen Vivir have multiplied, being at the same time a modernist political instrument invoked by positivist socialist politicians and a vital paradigm that mobilizes Indigenous communities to respond from their own socio-ecological assemblies through an alternative coexistence between humans and nature.

However, from the sphere of Indigenous cultural studies, we have so far missed the opportunity to identify, in multiple Indigenous social texts, the detailed political agenda that is communicated through the plurality of archives containing direct or tangential evocations of Buen Vivir. Poorly essentialized as Indigenous environmentalism, Buen Vivir is more than a possible ecological empathy or another environmentalism of the poor. I argue for a deeper understanding of Buen Vivir, moving beyond environmentalist interpretations. I contend that *Buen Vivir* is a concept rooted in the specific context of the Quechua Nation, one strongly linked to its cosmological components. Through literary works, Buen Vivir communicates the complexities of an onto-political agenda (which refers to the intersection of cultural identity and political systems) that constructs an Indigenous decolonial discourse. I illuminate Buen Vivir as both an expression of Indigenous cultural production and a continuation of decolonial ideas previously developed by Andean-based indigenismos—and in some cases, by early manifestations of Indigenous decolonial discourse such as indianismo.

This is not an attempt to bring Indigenous texts into the discussion of "multiple" or "alternative modernities" (Grossberg, *Cultural Studies*, 80) but, rather, to particularize the political ontology inherent in such texts in order to identify Indigenous critical instruments through an exercise of cultural analysis.[3] In this case, I focus on a specific corpus of contemporary Indigenous poetry from the Andes, paying particular attention to the topics represented by the Quechua Peruvian poets Ch'aska Anka Ninawaman and Washington Córdova Huamán. My selection of poetry to be the genre to study stems from the role that poetry as a form plays within the Indigenous literary tradition. It functions as a political tool that builds upon the Andean oral tradition. In this sense, I follow the line previously developed by scholar Miguel Rocha Vivas (*Mingas*, 89) who, in his study of Quechua Colombian poet Fredy Chikangana, emphasizes that Chikangana's literary practice based on orality (or *oralitura* as it's termed) operates as a form of political positioning that reaffirms the formal independence of Indigenous literatures.[4]

I interpret Buen Vivir as a heterogeneous discursive trope that is forged through the thematization of specific cultural devices when they are subjected to the cosmological conjunctures of the Indigenous nations that produces them. For this purpose, I will review some of the most influential definitions of this concept and compare them with the notion of political ontology applied to cultural analysis. I examine examples from the book *Poesía en quechua. Chaskaschay* (Quechua poetry: Chaskaschay, 2004) by Ninawaman, where the notion of Buen Vivir is manifested through the dynamic re-creation of *Allin Kawsay*, an eco-social Quechua principle, paying particular attention to the poetic and political agency of coca and commenting briefly on the revitalization of the trope of Inca resurgence, an old component of the Cuzco indigenista agenda. I also explore poems from Córdova's *Parawayraq Chawpinpi / Entre la lluvia y el viento* (Between rain and wind, 2019), discussing how the vibrant portrayal of nature and the connection to Andean and leftist political symbols weave the trope of Buen Vivir into a radical political tradition, thereby contributing to broadening the Indigenous decolonial discourse historicized in this work.

BUEN VIVIR AS A LITERARY TROPE

Although there seems to be consensus on the futility of positing an absolute and fixed definition of Buen Vivir, it is possible to identify thematic and political patterns in the conceptual descriptions formulated in recent years by different disciplines. The Ecuadorian economist Alberto Acosta ("El Buen Vivir," 2010) defines *Sumak Kawsay* (the Kichwa version of Buen Vivir) as a regime that safeguards the protection of nature based on Indigenous traditions, which is materialized in the achievement of rights for nature as a post-development alternative.[5] In his comparative analysis between the Kichwa and Aymara versions of Buen Vivir (*Sumak Kawsay* and *Suma Qamaña*, respectively), Uruguayan ecological theorist Eduardo Gudynas highlights that, as a praxis, it is manifest in "decolonial efforts" that "should not be understood as a return to a distant Andean past, precolonial times. It is not a static concept, but an idea that is continually being created" ("Buen Vivir," 443). For Bolivian environmental activist Pablo Solón (2016), Buen Vivir is a *pachacentric* response to the anthropocentric human-nature relationship inherent in capitalism, and this response is embodied in multipolar communities composed of human and nonhuman members through a bond based on a set of meanings such as "plentiful life," "sweet life," "harmonious life," "sublime life," or "inclusive life" ("vida plena," "vida dulce," "vida armoniosa," "vida sublime," "vida inclusiva") (*¿Es posible?*, 13). For Solón, these components are constantly overlapping and modifying each other, as the core of the concept, *pacha*, refers to an Andean cosmic integrality in constant movement and reconstruction, a dynamic that also modifies progressive notions of time and space. The prefix *pacha* plays a crucial role in the revolutionary philosophical framework that defines the programmatic agenda of various forms of indianismo. This connection with the philosophical principle of *pachakuti* is key to understanding its significance. Inspired by political debates and forged in proximity to Indigenous movements, these three readings of Buen Vivir formulated in and about different Andean Indigenous contexts, coincide in the sense of dynamism and constant edification epistemically influenced by sources of Indigenous knowledge and social practices, each conditioned by the variables of its own political purpose—and I would add, conditioned by its own socio-natural assemblies.

Buen Vivir has also fostered interpretive efforts in the humanities, although the focus of most of these efforts is on the analysis of the political content of Indigenous representations in environmentalist documentaries. Roberto Forns-Broggi notes the lack of theorization on the topic of environmental justice as a recurring theme in Latin American eco-cinema, where he points out that Buen Vivir appears as a "guide to alternative well-being" ("una guía de bienestar alternativo") that, interestingly, can foster "possible dialogues between Andean and Mesoamerican communities" ("posibles diálogos entre las comunidades andinas y mesoamericanas") ("Los retos," 321). In the same vein, Jorge Marcone (2015) emphasizes the lack of rigorous analysis of Indigenous ontologies represented in a corpus of environmentalist documentaries that tend to focus on the description of Indigenous resistance and environmental degradation. Within this framework, Marcone notes that, among the diverse Latin American popular environmentalisms, Buen Vivir is a component that represents "an innovative Indigenous thinking on ecology and decolonization," which embraces a sense of "well-being and cohabitation with others and other-than-humans" ("Filming the Emergence," 215, 216). He adds that, seen as a network of information and knowledge generation, it approaches what Ursula Heise (2008) defines as "eco-cosmopolitanism," insofar as it "values human difference derived from tradition, history, and location, yet presupposes a shared humanity that wishes to engage in the conversation about Buen Vivir, alternatives to development, and 'imagined communities' of both humans and non-humans" (217). Finally, in her analysis of Juan Carlos Galeano's documentary *El río* (2018) and Guillermo del Toro's fictional film *The Shape of Water* (2017), Joni Adamson identifies a didactic evocation of Buen Vivir in the form of "knowing how to live" with other beings, presumably nonhumans, without arrogance or prejudice ("People of the Water," 12). All these readings of Buen Vivir converse with the interpretive and theoretical efforts of Solón, Gudynas, and Acosta as well as with those of Thomas Fatheuer ("Buen Vivir") in terms of Buen Vivir and legislation and those of Marisol de la Cadena ("Indigenous Cosmopolitics"; *Earth Beings*) in relation to the practices between human and nonhuman entities, specifically the political role of the latter. From all of this, it can be inferred that, for both social sciences and humanities, *Buen Vivir* is a heterogeneous concept that, when identified in contexts of Indigenous activism, refers to a philosophical notion containing a promise to change vital paradigms and that deploys a decolonial political potential involving Indigenous cosmopolitics.

Thus, on the one hand, Buen Vivir is not only an Indigenous social movement. That is to say, it is only one of the many faces of popular environmentalisms, which discards the anthropocentric dominant society/nature paradigm in exchange for a biocentric one that includes Indigenous philosophies and social practices in its decolonial struggle against the environmental and ecological devastation provoked by neoliberal capitalism. But, on the other hand (and strongly tied to the foregoing), Buen Vivir is also the radical enunciation of a set of ground rules that constantly construct and reformulate the identity of the communities and the sense of being and existence derived from those communities' respective cosmologies.

In other words, and in light of the claims made by the humanities, Buen Vivir can be a vocalizable device that thematizes a number of cultural products, which regardless of its authorship, incorporates Indigenous ontological constructs in their content.

Brought to the table of cultural analysis, Buen Vivir serves as a trope forged in the specific cosmological context of each community, where the sense of collectivity is redefined according to the nature of its members. This positions Buen Vivir as a cultural concept that embodies how the Indigenous decolonizing agenda evolves and modifies themes from the lineage of political movements that came before it, such as indigenismo and indianismo.

The *Sumak Kawsay* of the Kichwas, the *Allin Kawsay* of Quechuas, and the *Suma Qamaña* of Aymaras—three of the most popular versions of Buen Vivir—generally overlap as Indigenous-based agendas that decolonially resist the alienating interpretation and usage of nature by anthropocentric Western stakeholders. However, these forms of Buen Vivir differ in essence, rhythms, and interveners because they are conditioned by different cosmological contexts: the Kichwa, Quechua, and Aymara Nations. Similarly, the *Lekil Kuxlejal*, a Mayan concept relatively close to Buen Vivir, differs from the *Allin Kawsay* of Quechuas and the *Suma Qamaña* of Aymaras because it does not complicate the role of nonhuman actors but, instead, is defined as a labor, collective, and meritocratic interaction inspired by a principle of radical democracy, as Mariana Mora (*Kuxlejal Politics*) has rigorously described in her study of the zapatista communities of Chiapas. All these Indigenous organizing principles are unique forms of Buen Vivir. Homogenizing them would be an oxymoronic strategy, despite the political commonalities that may be identified. What I perceive as the main differential variable among all these forms of Buen Vivir that socially activate the Indigenous population of Latin America is the political ontology with which each community establishes its own existential and political commitments.

The identification of all these variables in diverse Indigenous (and not only Indigenous) literary texts allows me to interpret Buen Vivir as a heterogeneous trope that even predates the emergence of Buen Vivir in its visible form of social activism and that is manifest in communication of the mythical, performative, practical, cosmological, and cultural details that describe the ontological commitment of any given Indigenous community. Here, political ontology, as defined by Mario Blaser in "Political Ontology," plays a crucial role because it helps to identify the political scope inherent in the cultural representation of each Buen Vivir. Blaser argues that political ontology is a framework of study in which the ontological transcends a discussion of explicit or implicit assumptions about things that may or may not exist. Instead, political ontology moves toward a series of practices and interactions between human and nonhuman actors. For example, I suggest understanding Evo Morales's decolonizing activism before he became president as a manifestation of a more-than-human coalition in which he (human) struggled alongside coca leaves (nonhuman peers) against an imperialist doctrine such as the coca leaf eradication promoted by the United States.

Blaser adds that ontologies are also manifest "as 'stories' in which the assumptions of what kinds of things and relations make up a given world readily graspable.... Although stories are a good entry point to an ontology, attending only to their verbalized aspect and not to the way in which those stories are embodied and enacted only give[s] us half the story. In other words, ontologies must be understood as total enactments involving discursive and non-discursive aspects" ("Political Ontology," 877). As a literary trope, at first glance, Buen Vivir addresses only the verbalized side of Indigenous ontologies, but what Blaser overlooks—perhaps being more interested in intervening in ethnography than in cultural studies—is the capacity of social texts to reflect explicit or implicit enactments and, perhaps more importantly, the capacity of literary and cultural texts to be themselves a signifying device that transcends its representational value.

Thus, I propose that the trope of Buen Vivir in Quechua poetry helps overcome the disconnect between Indigenous cultures and their representation in literature. The manner in which indigenista writers portrayed Indigenous cultures has always complicated this relationship, something foreshadowed by José María Arguedas, who advocated reviving Quechua literature as a way to encourage Indigenous cultural and political agency in the Andes. Ninawaman and Córdova embody this process through their politicized poetry, reaffirming the formal and thematic independence of Indigenous literatures in the Andes. I argue that, as a discursive trope in cultural texts, Buen Vivir is a complex and intellectually sovereign decolonial discursive construct through which Indigenous writers retake, refute, or expand some decolonial ideals, a few of which were previously suggested by indigenista discourses.

QUECHUA COSMOLOGICAL ITERATIONS IN NINAWAMAN'S POETRY

Ch'aska Anka Ninawaman (1973–) is a Quechua writer who was born in the province of Yauri-Espinar (Cuzco, Peru) with the name Eugenia Carlos Ríos, which she replaced by the pen name she uses as a public persona and with which she reasserts her Indigenous Quechua identity. Ch'aska responds to the specific Indigenous and peasant community where she was born (Ch'isikata), while Anka (eagle) and Ninawaman (fire hawk) are the Indigenous surnames of her father and mother, respectively. Her renaming says a lot about her interest in creating a space of Indigenous enunciation endorsed by her professional trajectory, as she has worked for many years as a Quechua-Spanish translator. She was trained as an educator in language and literature at the Universidad San Antonio Abad in Cuzco, a city to which she migrated in early adulthood. Then she moved away from Peru and completed graduate studies at the renowned Latin American Faculty of Social Sciences in Ecuador and then gained a doctorate at the Universidad Autónoma de Barcelona. She eventually settled in Paris, where she works as a language instructor at the National Institute of Oriental Languages and Cultures.

There is a well-known anecdote about her life that illustrates her activism in favor of Quechua intellectual production and the adversities she had to face. The incident occurred when she was defending her undergraduate thesis "Literatura oral en la Escuela Choqecancha" (Oral literature in Choqecancha School), which was written entirely in Cuzqueño Quechua: none of the members of her committee was fluent enough in this language to perform the oral debate. The problem was solved with the providential appearance of the American anthropologist Bruce Mannheim, a fluent Quechua speaker, who at the time was conducting field research in Cuzco and teaching at the Instituto Bartolomé de las Casas. He was invited to join Ninawaman's dissertation committee and to help her successfully defend her research project. I believe that the anecdote can be read as a major success as it describes the sense of urgency she seeks to communicate through Quechua writing in her scholarly production and her literary production. Quechua for Ninawaman is not only a linguistic site of enunciation but, more importantly, a symbolic space of cultural intervention that she enacts with decolonial intentions.

Among the scholars who have studied her most rigorously are Ulises Zevallos Aguilar, who has noted that "in her construction of popular imaginary, she evokes Andean elements such as coca, condenado, *wakcha*, sirens, and Kukuli" ("Peruvian Quechua Poetry," 66).[6] Claudia A. Arteaga focuses on the political potential inherent in the assessments and lexical choices with which nonhuman elements are identified in Ninawaman's poetry ("Función poética," 572). Alison Krögel states that her poems "use a popular register of Cuzco Quechua and celebrate the symbolic and ritual richness of the flora, fauna and multiple sacred and malevolent beings of Quechua culture" ("utilizan un registro popular del quechua cuzqueño y celebran la riqueza simbólica y ritual de la flora, fauna y múltiples seres sagrados y malévolos de la cultura quechua") ("Sara mamacha," 335). These observations on Ninawaman's poetry coincide in an aspect that is key for my particular analysis—the preeminence and valorization of natural elements in her attempt to portray the cultural identity of the Quechua Nation, a form of Indigenous subjectivity that thematically connects with the elements that ontologically compose the heterogeneous Buen Vivir as a particular political stance.

Concerning Indigenous poetry of the Americas at large, Jean Franco has pointed out that this is the platform that "best stages the versatility and beauty of languages and suggests the emergence of new kinds of Indigenous subjectivity" ("Some Reflections," 461–62). I infer that the innovative character of these subjectivities is portrayed in instances such as the emergence of Buen Vivir as a vocalizable discursive device. About Quechua poetry, Franco states that "written poetry in Peruvian Quechua has often been written by bilingual intellectuals who are not Indigenous but [who] have defended Quechua in a gesture of defiance against the hegemony of Lima" (464). Franco is clearly alluding to poetry in Quechua written by white mestizo authors such as José María Arguedas or César Guardia Mayorga but seems to suggest that there was no properly Indigenous written Quechua poetic tradition in the second half of the twentieth century. However, Martin Lienhard had by 1988 already highlighted a particular poetic tradition in Andean Quechua with strictly Indigenous roots, which developed throughout the twentieth century in two ways: orally, performed mainly in community rituals and festivities, and written, as a derivation of the former, based on the urban life experiences of Quechua intellectuals during mid-twentieth-century migration. Lienhard makes an effort to clearly differentiate between what he calls *Misti* poets (including the mestizo poets mentioned by Franco) and Quechua poets.

Complementing these two readings, different and divergent in their respective ways, Zevallos Aguilar historicizes Quechua poetry by pointing out that the Quechua poets of the contemporary generation, among them Ninawaman, "have chosen poetry as a literary medium of expression, continuing a long tradition established in the sixties by, among others, Andrés Alencastre, César Guardia Mayorga and José María Arguedas" ("Peruvian Quechua Poetry," 56). Zevallos Aguilar identifies a formal and thematic connection between the generation of indigenista poets he mentions and the current generation of Indigenous poets, which in no way suggests a dissociation of Ninawaman from the community-based oral poetic tradition anthropologically traced by Lienhard. Ultimately, I infer from this discussion that there are good reasons to assume a double bond between the two poetic generations, particularly if we can assume that Ninawaman has read and revisited the literary modalities of the indigenista poets who wrote in Quechua and, at the same time, has experienced and been instructed in the community-based oral poetic tradition.[7] Therefore, she partially embraces the indigenista agenda, but in her poems she appropriates its denunciatory intentions and, in so doing, reformulates a decolonial agenda that represents the continuity of an Indigenous intellectual tradition forged under the influence of the Quechua cosmovision.

VITALISM OF COCA AND CUZQUEÑO TROPES IN A DISRUPTIVE TOTALITY

Kuka mamacha
santa remidio,
tanteo qukuqcha
kallpa yuyay churakuq,
wiksa nanaypaq santa remidio

kiru nanaypaq santa remidio
chhaynallataq
sunqu nanaypaq santa remidio

Hojitas de coca,
santa remedio
tanteadora de suertes.
Siempre noche y día
estás dándome
mucha fuerza y mucha vida
(*Chaskaschay*, 80–81)

Little leaf of coca,
holy remedy
scorer of luck.
Always night and day
you are giving me
much strength and much life.[8]

Chaskaschay is divided into six sections that are thematically organized into different areas of the Quechua universe that she portrays. The poems are presented in a self-translated bilingual Quechua-Spanish version. Most of her poems are dedicated to animals from Andean regions such as pumas, vicuñas, and condors; to mythological characters such as mermaids; and to natural elements that she represents with intense vitality such as mountains, stars, and coca leaves. For example, the above stanza belongs to the short poem "Hojitas santa remedio"—"Cocacha santa remidio" (Little leaves, holy remedy) where the coca leaf is represented as a vehicle transmitting energy and vitality to the human body, which, it could be assumed, is enunciated in the poem as follows: "estás dándome / mucha fuerza y mucha vida."

Ninawaman describes a unique trajectory in the way she illustrates that the coca leaf is the subject of her verses, the active entity that triggers most of the actions. In this poem, coca embodies the concept of *k'intu* (small bunch of coca leaves). *K'intu* refers to the ritualistic role traditionally played by a handful of coca leaves in rituals such as offerings to the Earth and Mountains or in reciprocity ceremonies involving coca chewing, as described by Catherine J. Allen ("To Be Quechua," 159–61). For Arteaga ("Función poética," 569), who translates coca leaves directly as *k'intu*, the poetic function of *k'intu* establishes a connection with the references to coca leaf use found in the *Manuscrito de Huarochirí*, a collection of sixteenth-century Quechua oral histories compiled by Fray Francisco de Ávila and translated into Spanish by J. M. Arguedas. Ninawaman's poem expresses a vitality that itself embodies the core of Quechua cosmopolitics, where political action is forged through a reciprocal interaction between humans and nonhumans.

Unlike essentialist readings that identify Buen Vivir as a new form of environmentalism, for Ninawaman the vitalism of coca leaf does not communicate an ecological thought but, if anything, an enunciation of the political agreement that articulates her collectivity and grounds her Buen Vivir. As a trope in Indigenous literature, Buen Vivir is expressed as a discursive device that channels knowledge patterns inherent to Andean cosmology. That epistemic immanence emerges not just from a vital Indigenous trajectory but mainly from the intrinsic ontological commitment that balances the life of a more-than-human collective. Through her political commitment to coca leaves, Ninawaman embodies a form of vital materialism that transcends conventional understandings of personhood through a Quechua-based knowledge production process.[9] After all, as Arturo Arias notes, "all Indigenous texts embody knowledge that is already available discursively to the community, by orally and performatively tapping their traditions and cosmologies. They embody what just about every member of the community already knows" (*Recovering*, 28). I must add that, as I have repeatedly pointed out in this analysis, the members who integrate these communities are not only human in a conventional sense. In fact, the category of *humans* seems insufficient to define the role of stakeholders in this assembly.

To avoid the naturalization or socialization of members of a more-than-human collectivity, Bruno Latour proposes the term "actant" to refer in a non-anthropomorphic way to the active agents or interveners of an association in which categories such as *subjects* and *objects* may be insufficient. In this association, "its members act, that is, quite simply, that they modify other actors. . . . Humans and nonhumans for their part can join forces without requiring their counterparts on the other side to disappear. To put it yet another way: *objects and subjects can never associate with one another; humans and nonhumans can*" (*Politics*, 75–76, emphasis in original). I propose that we interpret the partnership between the human lyrical voice and coca in this way—that is, as a coalition in which coca plays an acting role insofar as it intervenes in the political agenda communicated through the poems. As Jorge Marcone states, "an actant is something that acts or to which activity is granted by others. . . . By virtue of location and timing, an actant makes a difference, makes things happen" ("Latin American Literature," 80). In this case, coca is an allied actant, as it is stated in the poem "Coca Mama"—"Kukacha mamacha": "chhiripipas wayrapipas / vida pasaq masichay"—"compañera en los fríos, / amiga en las lluvias" (companion in the cold, / friend in the rains) (*Chaskaschay* 95), or it is an actant whose presence not only consolidates the Quechua ontological association but also conveys vitality.

This interpretation can be extrapolated to other cases, given the specific relevance that coca has in the cosmovision of different Andean contexts. For instance, it is possible to infer the acting or intervening role of coca in the Indigenous mobilizations led by former Bolivian president Evo Morales in the early 2000s against the coca leaf eradication policies promoted by the United States with local criollo politicians as allies. These colonial policies of eradication affected Indigenous communities neighboring the village in which Ninawaman was born. In recent decades, promoters of the pro-eradication discourse have used the coca leaf as an excuse to criminalize Indigenous communities in the Andes. Thus, it can be inferred that both in Ninawaman's cultural and intellectual activism and in Morales's political activism, coca is a trigger for Indigenous decolonial mobilizations that, in demanding safeguards for coca, are at the same time demanding safeguards for their own ontological commitments. I use the discursive platform through which these claims run to define Buen Vivir as a cultural trope, since they emerge as a socio-natural political instrument from decolonial activism that seeks to safeguard the physical, symbolic, and spiritual well-being of Indigenous communities.[10]

Other relevant aspects of Ninawaman's poetry for this study are the points raised in the section entitled "Inkantuyuq

Llaqtakunamanta"—"De diosas montañas y ciudades" (Of the goddess mountains and cities) in which she reinstates Cuzco, the former spatial and urban epicenter of the cuzqueño indigenista agenda of the early twentieth century, as a symbolic place of Indigenous enunciation that articulates her lyrical subject. In Valcárcel's work, Cuzco becomes the backbone of the trope of Inca resurgence as a dialectical formula that allows him counteract the criollo national project and *costeño* (or coastal) indigenismos. However, decades later, Ninawaman resumes the Cuzco trope in her poem "Qusqumama sumaq llaqta"—"Cuzco mama buena tierra" (Cuzco mama, good land) to re-thematize Cuzco, no longer as a regional indigenista platform (that is, as a rhetorical object) but as an Indigenous telluric subject

Qusqu sumaq llaqta
Wik'uña wich'unawan awasq
pachakamaq sunqun ukhupi
t'ikariq qhantu t'ika

Cuzco mama, tierra fértil
tejido con fibra de vicuña,
flor de cantuta floreciente
en el corazón de la tierra
(*Chaskaschay*, 64–67)

Cuzco mama, fertile land
woven with vicuña fiber,
flowering cantuta flower
in the heart of the land

This stanza congregates several notions of the natural balance embedded in the Quechua Buen Vivir, since it highlights the agricultural vitality of the land, the harmonious participation of people through vicuña fiber, and the telluric force that centripetally joins these elements in Cuzco. In the poem, Cuzco is referred to neither as a modern city nor as a metropolitan space. Rather, Ninawaman expands the semantic tradition of *Qosqo* as a geo-cultural topic, a literary tradition founded by the Inca Garcilaso—albeit toponymically inaccurate, but symbolically charged with significance, as stated by Rodolfo Cerrón Palomino.[11] Thus, in the poem, Cuzco is a symbolic individual that accompanies the lyrical subject who collectively articulates the actions re-created in the verses; actions presented also in a prophetic tone (that strongly resembles the tone used by Valcárcel) when she says:

> Ashkhamantaqa,
> qaqatapas rumitapas
> tanqallasunmi,
> rumipas
> qaqapas puririllanqan
> Suma kawsaywanqa;
> chaypiña munakusqay wawachay
>
> De miles y miles
> cerros y barrancos
> empujaremos nomás
> cerros y barrancos
> volverán a andar
> con paciencia y amor,
> nuestro tiempo volverá
> mi huahua, me dijiste
> (64–69)
>
> From thousands and thousands
> mountains and cliffs
> we'll just push
> mountains and cliffs
> will walk again
> with patience and love,
> our time will come back
> my huahua, you told me

The poem expresses a sense of community that, when translated into Spanish or English, can only be expressed through the word *nosotros/we*.

This concept reflects a form of collective action, as Quechua poet and scholar Odi Gonzales points out. According to Gonzales, "the gravitation of the collective over the individual does not flow in statements, it prevails in the attitude, in the interaction of individuals" ("[la] gravitación de lo colectivo sobre lo individual no discurre en enunciados, rige en la actitud, en la interacción de los individuos") (*Nación*, 178). In this case, there is a collective voice that includes Cuzco and pleads for a sense of restoration that will be achieved through the mobility of mountains and cliffs, a strategic and affective mobility that invokes the restitution of a singular sense of time. The notion of return, resurgence, and past-as-future that is invoked in the Andean principle of *nayrapacha* has been extensively analyzed throughout this book in the indigenista literature of Valcárcel and in the Indigenous proposals of Reinaga's indianismo. With the vital inclusion of nonhuman actants, Ninawaman represents a step forward in the development of the *nayrapacha* principle and its inclusion in the decolonial discursive network articulated in her poems. This dialectical evolution is most visible in the poem she dedicates to her hometown "Chuqik'irawchaw"—"Chuqik'iraw":

Q'umir kuka k'intuwan
saminchasqa k'intusqa
inka llaqta; yachay wasi
Sara aqhawan ch'allasqa,
llama pichuwan saymasqa;
inkakunaq samaykusqan llaqta.

Pueblo de incas
templo de coyas,
casa de sabios
pueblo al revés,
a ti siempre te sueño
escondido en el espacio
perdido en el tiempo;
envuelto en hojas de coca.
(*Chaskaschay*, 70–72)

Inca Town
temple of coyas,
house of wisemen
town upside down,

I always dream of you
hidden in space
lost in time;
wrapped in coca leaves.

The incaism expressed by Ninawaman in the first four verses of this stanza is rounded in a time-space disorder ("pueblo al revés") that, dialectically speaking, re-creates the conflation of *nayrapacha* and *pachakuti* constructs, going beyond the indianista discursive usage where these constructs were operated for Reinaga as destabilizing principles of colonially imposed hegemonic notions of time-space and revolutionary action. Here it is worth recalling the suggestion of the Bolivian environmental activist Solón, who defines Buen Vivir as a *pachacentric* response to Western anthropocentrism. Catherine J. Allen (1998) explains that *pacha* in Quechua is a suffix that "may refer to the whole cosmos or to a specific moment in time" and "is simultaneously a material order of concrete nature and a moral order" ("When Utensils Revolt," 22). *Pacha* then refers to a cosmic totality in the Quechua worldview, a disruptive time-space unity that Ninawaman's poem straightforwardly re-creates in its Spanish self-translation ("escondido en el espacio; / perdido en el tiempo"). However, unlike Valcárcel and Reinaga who together construct a historical trajectory of the decolonial indigenista–Indigenous dialectical bridge, Ninawaman introduces nature as a vital political actor ("Q'umir kuka k'intuwan"—"envuelto en hojas de coca"), which, as we have seen above, is a mode of conveying her political ontology. In different instances of Ninawaman's poetry, coca in its *k'intu* mode is a political actant that, in this case, surrounds a sense of disruptive totality embedded both in the poem and in the trope of resurgence that was installed in the early twentieth century by indigenista writers of Cuzco.

Coca is an actant that in the Quechua socio-natural assembly operates as a political partner with an influential agenda. In the poem "Chuqik'raw," coca is introduced by Ninawaman as a pivotal actant that envelops, covers, seals, and solidifies the promise of return that runs through Ninawaman's discursive incaism, and which had been enunciated previously by Valcárcel and Reinaga. Embedded in the dialectic of Buen Vivir, the trope of Inca resurgence is less messianic than it is in indigenista discourse, but it is also narrowly bound to the Quechua cosmological singularity that gives meaning to Ninawaman's socio-natural assembly. Hence, the former indigenista prediction finds a solid landing strip in the coca. In this way, coca is not only an ally in the more-than-human political coalition portrayed by Ninawaman, it is also an eco-social element that corrects and complements the indigenista agenda by accurately illustrating the ontological politics of the decolonial discourse in the poems. Aside from the evident relational ontology between Ninawaman and coca, which the poem exhibits through the lyrical *we*, coca reemerges in this part of the poem to assert its central position in the discursive trope of Buen Vivir.

POLITICAL SYMBOLISM AND BUEN VIVIR IN WASHINGTON CÓRDOVA HUAMÁN

Washington Córdova Huamán (1952–) is a Quechua poet and writer born in the town of Circa in the province of Abancay (Apurímac, Peru). Córdova's role as a translator of works into Quechua reflects his broader mission as a disseminator of Quechua material culture. He is also a scholar of Andean oral literature, as evidenced by his master's thesis, "Tinkaywankay, discurso poético quechua en las comunidades campesinas del distrito de Circa (Abancay–Apurímac)" (Tinkaywankay, Quechua poetic discourse in the peasant communities of the district of Circa [Abancay-Apurímac]) (2013), from the Universidad Nacional Mayor de San Marcos. In 2020 he won the National Literature Prize in the category of native languages with his bilingual Quechua-Spanish poetry book *Parawayraq chawpinpi—Entre la lluvia y el viento* (Between rain and wind, 2019). Córdova embodies the concept of *locus of enunciation* as defined by Indigenous literary critics such as Emil Keme' ("For Abiayala to Live") and Yásnaya Aguilar ("Is There"). This concept refers to a symbolic space forged by Indigenous writers through their ability to create and circulate works in their native languages. However, as with Ninawaman, the Quechua-Spanish bilingual praxis seems to be a precondition for wider circulation.

In Giovanna Iubini Vidal's view, Córdova belongs to a generation of writers, intellectuals, and artists she calls the "Andean neovanguard" (*"Tinkuy,"* 182). This group contributes to the aesthetic diversity of the region through a transcultural and transdiscursive attitude. Iubini Vidal highlights the visual imagery re-created by Córdova's poems, which, she argues, dialogues with the visual aesthetics promoted by a first wave of Andean vanguardists such as the Orkopata Group, whose most notable work was the *Boletín Titikaka* (1919–1930).[12] This connection between an Indigenista movement such as Orkopata and Córdova's contemporary Quechua production suggests the possibility of a political and ideological link supporting the existence of a decolonial Indigenous discourse. Following Mauro Mamani Macedo in "Literatura quechua" (143–46), the natural elements in Córdova's poetry are linked to a broader panorama of social transformation. Mamani Macedo argues that Córdova's work recovers Andean myths and recontextualizes them within a historical framework, aiming to achieve an "updating of the past or refreshing of time through living memory" ("actualización del pasado o refrescamiento del tiempo a través de la memoria viva") and "the enactment of the *pachakutiy*, the transformation of the world, as an action of drastic change in time-space" ("la ejecución del pachakutiy, la vuelta del mundo, como acción de cambio drástico del tiempo-espacio") ("Literatura quechua," 144). These analyses of Córdova's poetry allow me to situate him within a literary tradition that reuses political elements previously developed by what I term "indigenista decolonial cracks," whose dialectical evolution transforms into a decolonial discourse with distinctively Indigenous roots.

In the *Parawayraq chawpinpi*'s poems Córdova constructs decolonial political imaginaries deeply rooted in the Andean cosmovision, employing nature not always metaphorically. My main argument concerning Córdova's poetry is that he redefines Buen Vivir as a literary trope emerging from the development of Andean political discourse, not solely as an environmental defense. If Buen Vivir is primarily a decolonial construct anchored in Andean cosmopolitical symbols, then Córdova's poetry allows us to examine the imbrication between nature and Andean political myths from a socially and historically grounded perspective within the decolonizing Indigenous tradition. Nature serves as a literary device for Quechua expression, but it also represents a political coalition that resonates with Indigenous mobilizations demanding political, cultural, and territorial sovereignty. Córdova's background as a scholar in environmental studies specializing in socio-environmental conflicts involving mining projects and local irrigation and agricultural systems imbues his bilingual poems with an ecological consciousness.[13] Thus, navigating these variables that define Córdova's political and social engagement, I read his poems as the cultural development of a broader decolonial political agenda that he advances through other forms of intervention.

A NATURAL READING OF INKARRI

In the history of Indigenous political thought in the Andes, be it Quechua or Aymara, myth plays a crucial role in discursive constructions that define cultural historiography and Andean intellectual autonomy. The *Inkarri* myth stands out as a prime example, embodying the restitutive political spirit that emerged in response to colonization. Despite variations in its telling, or as Mercedes López-Baralt ("El retorno") terms them, "cycles," the *Inkarri* refers to the mythological return of an Inca who, having been decapitated by the Spanish, restores the Andean social order. Flores Galindo (*Buscando*, 40) argues that the *Inkarri* myth arose from the confluence of Christian discourse on the body's mystical value and the death of Tupac Amaru I, the last Vilcabamba Inca, who was beheaded after capture by the Spanish. López-Baralt ("El retorno," 22–24) posits that the *Inkarri* cycles extend through literary production, with foundational moments in Guamán Poma de Ayala's *Nueva Corónica* and the anonymous poem "Apu Inka Atawallpaman," circulated in the Andes since the sixteenth and seventeenth centuries and translated into Spanish by J. M. Arguedas in the mid-twentieth century.

Córdova's poem "Llaqtaq Rimariynin"—"Eco de multitudes" (Crowd echo) exemplifies a new cycle of the *Inkarri* in Córdova's work, where it is ideologically intertwined with components that define the Quechua Nation's Buen Vivir (*Allin Kawsay*) philosophy:

Allinta qawariy, ama pantaychu
mach'aqaqaypa churinmi,
Anta panpakunapi
tiqsi muyuq k'anchariynin,

manchakuy qapariyninqanmi
tinpuq urquhina t'uqyarispa
millay runaq uyanta phatachinanpaq
ukhu pachamanta rikurimun.

Observa bien, no te confundas
es el hijo de la serpiente,
crisol del universo
en las pampas de Anta,
emergió desde el ukhupacha
estallando como el volcán
para quebrar con su estruendo
la mirada del bribón.
(Córdova, *Parawayraq*, 256–57)

Look carefully, do not get confused
he is the son of the serpent,
crucible of the universe
in the pampas of Anta,
emerged from the *ukhupacha*
bursting like the volcano
to break with its roar
the gaze of the rascal.

Aymara scholar Idón Chivi ("Una democracia") argues that Buen Vivir emerged in the Andes as a collective search to establish "linguistic, ideological, and collective imaginary positionings" ("posicionamientos lingüísticos, idearios, imaginarios colectivos"). Through the figure of the Inkarri destined for vindication ("mach'aqaqaypa churinmi"—"es el hijo de la serpiente"), Córdova expresses the decolonial desire inherent in both Buen Vivir and *Inkarri*. This figure's return signals the social and political reversal of an unsustainable status quo ("ukhu pachamanta rikurimun"—"emergió desde el ukhupacha").

The telluric reference to the *ukhu-pacha*, a specific space in Andean mythology representing the "lower world" or "underworld" often visualized as a serpent (*amaru*), situates this poem within the Inkarri narrative tradition. Peruvian sociologist Nelson Manrique ("Historia y utopía," 204–5) also associates *ukhu-pacha* with the spatial origin of the Inkarri's reemergence. However, Manrique cautions that this event does not necessarily guarantee better times, potentially signifying an apocalypse as well. The *Inkarri* myth, previously explored as part of the revolutionary indigenista discourse developed by Mariátegui through the *ayllu* concept, is utilized in Córdova's poetics with the same decolonizing aspirations. The symbolic description that directly conveys the myth's revolutionary potential employs telluric metaphors like roar or explosion ("manchakuy qapariyninqanmi / tinpuq urquhina t'uqyarispa / millay runaq uyanta phatachinanpaq"—"estallando como el volcán / para quebrar con su estruendo / la mirada del bribón").

In the poem "Wiñay pachaq qawariynin"—"Imagen del tiempo" (Image of time), Córdova also re-creates the sense of resurgence implicit in the *Inkarri*, but this time he expands more on the political vitality of natural elements that are not merely metaphorical artifices. For example:

> mayukunan kallpacharikuspa
> qapariyta qallaeimurqaku,
> rawrariq sunqukunapitaqmi
> musquykunata rawrarichispa
> urpikunaq wiqinta ch'akichirqaku
>
> iniciaron su grito los ríos
> transformándose en heroísmo
> y en cada corazón ferviente
> secaron sus lágrimas las torcazas
> atizando un torbellino de ilusiones
> (Córdova, *Parawayraq*, 108–9)
>
> the rivers began their clamor
> transforming themselves into heroism
> and in every fervent heart
> the wood pigeons dried their tears
> stirring up a whirlwind of illusions

The political resurgence (which we explored previously in some indigenista decolonial cracks such as the one that inspires Valcárcel's

Tempestad en los Andes) is grounded in the agency of natural agents such as the river or the torcazas. These elements are not merely annunciating the resurgence to human agents but are operating it through their physical actions. The physicality embodied in the descriptions of the natural elements is central to the thematization of Buen Vivir as a political more-than-human agency. After all, in this poem, it is the actions of nonhuman actors that trigger the revolutionary political awakening of humans:

> Phiñakuyninta raphapapachispan
> pinchinku phawayta qallarirqa,
> sunsuq llanllarinankaman
> chiwaku hayllinta takirqa
> qunqasqa k'uchukunapitaq
> musuq kawsayta wankarispa
> llaqtakuna hatarirqaku.
>
> Rompió los aires el gorrión
> enarbolando su cólera,
> entonó su himno el zorzal
> hasta estallar de emoción
> y en los rincones del olvido
> se alzaron los pueblos
> coreando cánticos del mañana
> (Córdova, *Parawayraq*, 112–13)
>
> The sparrow broke through the air
> and raised his wrath,
> intoned his hymn
> until bursting with emotion
> and in the corners of oblivion
> the peoples rose up
> chanting songs of tomorrow

The reparative claim lies in the affective agency of nonhuman elements. Their political action reactivates the more-than-human alliance that typically characterizes the manifestations of Buen Vivir in its form of social activism. This stands in contrast to the misappropriation exercised by neo-indigenista politicians such as the technocrats in the administrations of Rafael Correa in Ecuador and Evo Morales in Bolivia.[14] In this poem, the elements of nature function as what Marisol de la Cadena (*Earth Beings*, 24–25) defines as *earth-beings* within Quechua cosmopolitics. These are sentient entities that are not human but which inhabit the landscape, such as mountains, rivers, lagoons, and other visible marks of the environment. Earth-beings are not mere physical objects; they have the capacity to act and to maintain reciprocal relationships with humans. In Quechua, these entities are referred to as *tirakuna* (nonhuman beings) who coexist with *runakuna* (humans).

The re-creation of the Inkarri political awakening contained in the poem "Wiñay pachaq qawariynin" represents this coexistence as a dialectical relationship in which the political awakening of the nonhumans (*tirakuna*) preexists the human political awakening (*runakuna*). Thus, I consider the political action re-created and longed for in Córdova's poetry as a step forward in the evolution of Indigenous decolonial discourse because it revisits the call for an epistemological reevaluation proposed by the revolutionary indianista thesis through several of the recurrent topics in the postulates of Andean indigenismo (tellurism, myth). Córdova's poetry dialectically fuses the Indigenous philosophical trends of his time (Buen Vivir) within a literary tradition that amplifies the constellation of decolonial interventions that exist in Latin America in general and in the Andes in particular. "Wiñay pachaq qawariynin" ends with a political message that clearly defines the decolonial telos running throughout *Parawayraq chawpinpi* and the role that played by the *tirakuna*:

> haqaypin ñawpa runakuna
> paykunapura yanapanakuspa
> wayllukuyninkuta mat'iparispa
> musuq kawsayta almitirqaku
> chaypin salq'a Yanawarakuna
> taytachakunaq yanapakuyninwan
> ñawpa llaqtakunata amachaspa
> musuq p'unchawta illarichisparaq
> wañuyta llallirqaku . . .

allí donde las voces subyugadas
gestaron su destino
afirmando la fe inquebrantable
de sus ayllus solidarios,
allí donde los indómitos Yanawaras
protegidos por los dioses montaña
vencieron la muerte
perfilando el porvenir
de los pueblos legendarios . . .
(Córdova, *Parawayraq*, 118–19)

where the subjugated voices
gestated their fate
affirming the unbreakable faith
of their solidary ayllus,
where the indomitable Yanawaras,
protected by the mountain gods
defeated death
outlining the future
of the legendary peoples . . .

The poem concludes with a deliberate rearticulation of the resurgence trope. This trope in the context of the 1920s–1930s cuzqueño indigenista school served to articulate a political agenda. Córdova's version presents a new interpretation, functioning as a kind of natural re-creation (though not necessarily overtly environmentalist) of the *Inkarri* myth. Here, the active and political role of nature is reconfigured as the telluric foundation that mobilizes the revolutionary human collective, personified through religious and political deities (*Yanawaras*).

Córdova's poem aligns with Andean philosophical developments. The political telos it transmits transcends a simple resurgence; it envisions a future horizon not a return to a past form. This aligns with the *nayrapacha* (past-as-future) principle that is central to the resurgence thesis in Valcárcel's indigenista and Reinaga's indianista revolutionary discourses. Here, Córdova utilizes a prophetic tone to describe the coming of a transformative social moment:

ñawpa llaqtakunata amachaspa
musuq p'unchawta illarichisparaq
wañuyta llallirqaku

defeated death
outlining the future
of the legendary peoples

Córdova's poetry, then, is not simply a glorification of the past. Rather, it is a highly politicized work inscribed within the expansion of what Flores Galindo termed the "Andean utopia" (*Buscando un inca*, 17). This utopia represents a cultural imaginary envisioned as a future horizon for Andean societies, attainable through social and political struggle.

Córdova's work is crucial for delineating a contemporary Indigenous decolonial discourse, which emerges not through spontaneous generation but, rather, as a continuation and expansion of a decolonizing tradition with diverse subjectivities. While Córdova draws from both indigenista intellectuals and the Indigenous literary tradition, the historical context of his work is heavily influenced by the emergence of Buen Vivir in its various forms. Thus, it becomes essential for us to understand Buen Vivir in his poetry, as it represents a further development of the decolonizing tradition across the Andes and other Indigenous regions of Latin America.

BUEN VIVIR LITERATURE

I do not intend to restrict or conceptually alter Buen Vivir, an onto-political framework/instrument/paradigm forged in the sphere of Indigenous political philosophy and activism. If anything, I seek to expand the conceptual possibilities of Buen Vivir through the identification of certain themes that are intrinsic to Indigenous literatures (in this case, to those of the Quechua Nation) as well as to highlight the decolonial dimension conveyed through these texts as pertaining to a wide tradition dating back to indigenista decolonial cracks. In the Indigenous literature of Latin America, there are multiple instances in which Buen Vivir can operate as both a specific theme and a productive framework of analysis, although, as I have repeatedly emphasized, always being subjected to the cosmopolitical variables of each Indigenous nation. The opposite could lead us to fall into the analytical error of homogenizing different cosmologies, which in this case would be to render invisible the intellectual singularities of the various Indigenous nations of Latin America. The literary tradition during the colonial period (and that of its criollo mestizo heirs) has already perpetrated this invisibilization through misrepresentations and hasty generalizations embodied in its portraits of Indigenous societies, with a few notable exceptions.

On the other hand, it is true that not all Indigenous communities in Latin America embrace the few concomitant principles of Buen Vivir. There is no room for conceptual absolutisms, and this is made clear by Kichwa scholar Armando Muyolema in his passionate criticism against the role of the indigenista discourse in the forging of a "Latin American reason" or Latin Americanism. For him, indigenismo is a movement that addresses the "Indigenous problem" and, through the formation of Latin Americanism, "expands throughout the continent as a homogenizing promise that reduces the autonomy and relativizes the specificity and militant character of those [indigenista writers]" ("se expande por el continente como una promesa homogeneizante que resta autonomía y relativiza la especificidad y el carácter militantes de aquellos (escritores indigenistas)") ("América Latina," 244). Although I must admit there is much evidence to support Muyolema's criticisms against the representational telos of various Latin American indigenismos, paradoxically his references to indigenismos seem to suggest a divorce between the indigenista tradition and contemporary Indigenous writers. As I have demonstrated in this book, not all indigenistas are benevolent or paternalistic, and in some cases, certain indigenista writers anticipated the failures of their political and cultural projects. Along these lines, homogenizing the various indigenismos can be as problematic as homogenizing Indigenous literary production in Latin America.

Fortunately, Buen Vivir as a literary trope enables us to approach different cosmopolitical contexts with a genuine recognition of their unique intellectual genealogies and ontological commitments embodied in a diverse literary corpus. Thus, I argue that Ninawaman's and Córdova's literary works position them as Buen Vivir writers. Their works are defined by the political aims of Buen

Vivir and shaped by the experiences of the Quechua Nation and its decolonial tradition, alongside the influence of nature in articulating Andean cosmopolitics. Furthermore, these writers embody the evolution of a counter-hegemonic discourse that has been circulating in the Andes since the beginning of the twentieth century. Reading them through a dehistoricized lens would be inaccurate, as their poems clearly demonstrate a dialogue with the Andean indigenista tradition that preceded them.

Although it is true that Indigenous and indigenista writers can be located in distinct social bodies, primarily through a structuralist analysis, the decolonial discourse embedded in their literary tradition reflects a dialectical bridge that is evident in the resemanticization of Cuzco as a literary trope in Ninawaman's poetry or in the Inkarri's iterations conveyed by Córdova's poems, in tandem with the insertion of natural elements into a literary discourse that forges Buen Vivir as a discursive construct. Gloria E. Chacón states that "a discussion of Indigenous literature in Latin America cannot discount the indigenista tradition that inevitably Indigenous writers interrupt" ("Cultivating Nichimal K'op," 168). Conversely, recalling some ideas put forward by Edward Said, Chacón suggests that "a contrapuntal reading of indigenista and Indigenous texts illuminates the epistemic and ontological stakes of contemporary Indigenous writings in the decolonization process: a process that obviously is marred with contradictions" (169). Analytical strategies such as these have allowed me to construct a different narrative about a relevant body of Latin American literature.

Buen Vivir touches on many aspects of Latin American Indigenous politics, cultures, and ecologies, though with a major emphasis on South America. Among Indigenous movements, it is a relatively recent political discursive construct that inspires many of the activisms that the social sciences have labeled as environmentalist. And although it is true that Buen Vivir is strengthened by presenting a paradigm shift in response to the environmental destruction caused by neoliberalism in Indigenous ecosystems, it is also a discursive device that conveys the cosmopolitical, cultural, and aesthetic features that make up such an alternative paradigm. A close examination of the literature of Buen Vivir sheds light on it not only as a biocentric concept but as a complex theoretical fabric that intervenes in many layers of Indigenous cultural and political life in Latin America today. Its core is attached to Indigenous ecological notions and has been altered in institutional proposals for alternative development, but constraining it to the exclusive sphere of what would be community-based environmentalism might result in missing the political implications that the ongoing expansion of Buen Vivir offers in other spheres such as Indigenous literature. Similarly, overlooking the decolonial aspect of this literature entails a depoliticization of a literary corpus that is quite straightforward in its political intentions with the proposal of a paradigm shift.

Ultimately, the identification of intellectuals and writers of Buen Vivir and the theoretical illumination of the expansive waves that mobilize and agitate their rhetoric and political praxis allow for the identification of complex thematic axes in Quechua poetry. It is worth mentioning that there are other areas where this thematic emergence can be explored. For example, one of the favorite genres of Indigenous movements is the documentary, whether directed by Indigenous filmmakers or with Indigenous performative intervention. Here, I think of films such as *Hija de la laguna* (Daughter of the lake, 2015) by Ernesto Cabellos, *El maíz en tiempos de guerra* (Maize in times of war, 2016) by Alberto Cortés, or the series of short documentaries *Conversaciones con la Madre Tierra* (Conversation with Mother Earth) directed by Indigenous communities of the Peruvian Andes. All of these, together or dispersed, compose an Indigenous cultural corpus that is transmitted in a variety of cosmovisions that, with a heterogeneity of onto-political commitments, shows different forms of Buen Vivir. After all, contemporary Indigenous literatures and their multiple dialectical conversations with other critical traditions in Latin America continue to be unexplored pathways. Those interested, as I am, in the appreciation of critical independence of Latin American literature have the duty to navigate these pathways, paying attention and dialoguing horizontally with the theoretical instruments provided by Indigenous sources of knowledge.

AFTERWORD
An Indigenous Decolonial Critique

My main purpose in this book has been to trace a genealogy for the dialectical bridge that spans the course of a century, connecting two seemingly dissociated traditions: indigenista and Indigenous literatures. From a broad theoretical perspective that encompasses mostly decolonial critical tradition, I have touched on specific aspects such as race, culture, economics, and epistemologies. I have investigated those ideological connections that are traceable between the vast corpus of indigenista essays explored in Part I and the heterogeneous Indigenous literary corpus explored in Part II. In recent decades, a certain assumption has been accepted reminiscent of (post)structuralism, which presumes that the indigenista tradition and the Indigenous activist writers belong to divorced ideological spheres.[1]

It is as if indigenista writers—especially those dedicated to fiction—were embodying another form of orientalism applied to Latin America. I suspect that this separatist tendency, which often invokes its interest in privileging exclusively Indigenous agencies, has more presence on university campuses than in the social venues of Indigenous interaction. While working with pro-Indigenous civil organizations in Peru, my country of origin, I witnessed how various Indigenous political leaders, activists, and artists from the Peruvian Andes and the Amazon invoked indigenista tradition embodied by criollo mestizo writers and artists. Does this make their arguments less Indigenous? Not at all. It merely exhibits the ideological and programmatic connections between the two traditions, which I try to demonstrate in all the chapters of this book. Ultimately, my point has been precisely to pose a counterargument to perspectives that strive to separate or gloss over these points of connection.

The particularity of the dialectical bridge I illuminate in this book is that it is constituted as a trope that navigates different lettered cultural products (essays, communiqués, short stories, poems) and that, in turn, has a correlate with indigenista and Indigenous social mobility (with the Andes and Mesoamerica being the areas given the most attention throughout these chapters). In Part I, I explored a fairly canonical corpus of indigenista texts such as the essays of Alcides Arguedas, Manuel Gamio, José Vasconcelos, Luis E. Valcárcel, José María Arguedas, and José Carlos Mariátegui, considering these authors as the promoters—not always purposefully—of a particularly Latin American discourse aimed at problematizing modernity/coloniality from the centrality of Indigenous peoples as forgers of their respective national projects. My interest was not only to demonstrate the act of ideological opening that is embodied in their writings (and in some cases also in their political activism) but mainly to describe the indigenista decolonial cracks they opened—a symbolic baseline sustaining the dialectical connection created years later by Indigenous writer activists. Even as I highlight the limitations that indigenista intellectuals themselves had to contend with (e.g., in Mariátegui's Comintern polemic or J. M. Arguedas's epistemological quest), these limitations enlighten the path that would later be explored by other Indigenous dialectical formulation (e.g., Reinaga's ideological edification and the symbolic construction of the zapatistas).

What all these traditions have in common is a broad sense of insurgency, expressed in ways ranging from nonconformity and structural reformism of the criollo national project (Gamio and Arguedas) to eloquent revolutionary claims (Indo-Marxism, andinismo, indianismo, zapatismo, Buen Vivir). In different ways, the radical changes promoted in these examples entail the intrinsic recognition of an intolerable present linked to the marginalization and subjugation of Indigenous societies in the Andes and Mesoamerica. The starting point of this present, as it is located by this corpus of indigenista-Indigenous intellectuals and writers, is the foundation of colonialism and the correlated capitalist expansion in Latin America.

AFTERWORD

The texts showcased various critical perspectives challenging the multiple forms of coloniality. To this end, I have engaged with the extensive theoretical contributions of scholars such as Dussel, Quijano, Mignolo, Rivera Cusicanqui, Sanjinés, Lugones, Grosfoguel, and Walsh, among others, who examine the critical intersections of the modernity/coloniality/capitalism trinomial. Their ideas about the diverse spheres of action and the domination of the colonial hegemonic system were extremely helpful in identifying a particularly decolonial and Indigenous type of Latin American discourse that I call an *indigenous decolonial critique.*

AN INDIGENOUS DECOLONIAL CRITIQUE

Altogether, and in their diversity, the literary texts of Reinaga, Subcomandante Marcos-EZLN, Córdova, and Ninawaman provide an ideological backbone that transcends the rhetorical scope of a literary trope and embodies an Indigenous decolonial critique. By capitalizing on, reversing, or expanding motives advanced by indigenista decolonial cracks, these Indigenous writer activists forge a particularly Latin American type of decolonial discourse that, in many cases, correlates with the anti/decolonial praxis they deploy in their activism. Thus, I argue that, in the second half of the twentieth century in Latin America, there was a progressive and solid emergence of a decolonial Indigenous critique. It resides in the Indigenous dialectic that counteracts the ideological, epistemological, and structural imperatives of the West reproduced by the arbitrariness and marginality of modern national projects.

This type of critique does not reside in a homogeneous paradigm or a new way of theorizing a sort of Pan-Amerindianism, since such a reading would invisibilize the epistemological and ontological singularities of each ethnic group. Mayas, Quechuas, and Aymaras construct a process of intellectual agency that adheres to their socio-natural contexts and their respective Indigenous nationalities. Even if there were some concomitances between their dialectics (after all, they all contend with colonialism and capitalism), it is not possible to speak of a homogeneous stream of thought. Of course, the fact that they construct/unfold their agencies from their respective epistemic singularities does not mean they are less solidary but, rather, that they embrace from an original positionality a sense of historical-structural heterogeneity, which allows them to intervene, fissure, or subvert the colonial matrix of power. In this way, they manage to empower the content of their literary productions and build a circuit of circulation that transcends the local community scope. Quite illustrative of this critical development is the consolidation of the term "Abya Yala" to refer to the Indigenous enunciative space of Latin America, which in recent decades has been embraced by both Indigenous and non-Indigenous people as a sense of liberated symbolic spatiality with a clear decolonizing intentionality.

Based on the symbolic spatiality that flows in between literary texts and social mobilities (that is, in essays, poems, and communiqués but also in protests, revolutions, guerrillas, and insurgent collectives), this Indigenous decolonial critique operates from an epistemologically liberated vision against modern/colonial praxis: racism, patriarchy, segregationism, labor exploitation, and environmental destruction. Each in their unique way, the Indigenous writers examined in Part II grapple with all these variables from a still-in-construction and plural Indigenous dialectic whose teleologies always aspire to land in a decolonial praxis. Whether promoting an Indigenous revolution, declaring an eco-social paradigm shift, or reclaiming the political autonomy of certain communities, Indigenous decolonial critics grapple with many modern/colonial/capitalist fronts and do so from diverse and changing modalities. For example, *autonomy*, a key concept in the study of Indigenous decolonial mobilities in recent years, does not reflect a homogeneous sense of independence, given the sense developed by the zapatistas in Chiapas—and a quite different one being built by the Wampís Nation in the Peruvian Amazon through the Autonomous Territorial Government of the Wampís Nation (GTANW) where, unlike zapatistas and according to the circumstances, the Wampís governance model individualizes authority and delineates their territorial autonomy in dialogue with the Peruvian state. Are the Wampís less decolonial than the Maya zapatistas? Not at all. The Wampís' methodology follows another path toward the construction of an equally decolonizing and insurgent sense of autonomy, taking advantage of a certain flexibility—or indifference—of the Peruvian state apparatus regarding the Amazonian forest that Wampís people claim to control.[2] The same plurality with which autonomy is shown is applicable to the different epistemologies and dialectics forged from each of the Indigenous experiences in Latin America.

In my endeavor to illuminate the Indigenous decolonial critique, I put my arguments in conversation with many insights forged by the decolonial critics mentioned above, most of them urban academics who theorize from structural and institutional privilege from which I myself write this book. It is not my intention to divert the thread of analysis toward a deconstruction of the mesocratic privileges of the average scholar.[3] I do mention this, however, because it is necessary to point out that I am not trying to supersede or compare the ideas of these scholars with the decolonizing notions forged by Indigenous writer activists. Rather, I wish to highlight the originality and diversity of the latter. At the end of the day, if I have proved anything in this book, it is that Reinaga, the zapatistas, and the other Indigenous writer activists who intervened in Latin America in recent decades, as well as those who are still active, did not need to be schooled in theories of decoloniality, postcoloniality, or dependency in order to construct together an original decolonial critique strongly rooted in their indigeneities. What I highlight is not a resonance of the scholars' theoretical work but the emergence and consolidation of an authentically Indigenous type of decolonial critique that dialogues—not without problematization—with some of the dilemmas posed by indigenista discourses against the modernity/coloniality/capitalism trinomial. Ultimately, the decolonial theoretical corpus is a support for my arguments, not for the Indigenous critical formation that has constructed its own genealogy over the course of the last hundred years.

AN OPEN FIELD

It might seem obvious that there are connecting vessels between the indigenista literary tradition and the corpus of Indigenous intellectuals consolidated in recent decades. However, as I have sought to demonstrate, less obvious are the particular dialectical connections that run through those vessels. These are notions critical of modernity that, to a large extent, intervene in the antitheses that forge the dialectics of the Indigenous decolonial critique.

AFTERWORD

Authors of further works interested in exploring other types of connections could, for example, revisit the ideological threads in long-form narrative works such as the novel (a literary genre that until recently was not the preferred one in the Indigenous literary tradition, which was more inclined toward orality, testimony, and poetry) as well as visual production. In the last decades, in the Andes and Mesoamerica (mainly in Mayan nations), a robust cohort of Indigenous novelists have appeared, producing from urban spaces and channeling a decolonial discourse inspired by their Indigenous positionality.[4]

Another pending account in this still understudied open field is to examine contemporary relations between the Indigenous nations of Latin America and those of North America (United States and Canada). A disconnect and mutual unawareness between the two traditions has long been presumed to the point that, for example, in many North American universities, with programs typically labeled as Native American Studies, there is little or no exploration of the Indigenous groups that mobilize below the Rio Grande. And yet, these connections exist—and not only through the solidarity shown by some North American Indigenous organizations that have expressed camaraderie with the zapatista project but also in the organizational and agenda-building spheres. In October 2019, the International Meeting of Indigenous Communication took place in Cuzco, which traditionally brings together Indigenous organizations from the Andes, Amazon, Araucanía, and Central America. For the first time this year, the meeting included representatives of the Cherokee and Navajo Nations. Meetings such as this one, which in a way resembles the transnational and cooperative spirit of Pátzcuaro, could become more frequent in the coming years because of the growing political and cultural mobility of Indigenous organizations in the Western Hemisphere. Thus, it is not difficult to imagine that, sooner rather than later, there will begin to circulate interesting literary or cinematic productions inspired by the cultural exchanges of these interethnic encounters and by other forms of international solidarity among Indigenous collectives and intellectuals.

NOTES

INTRODUCTION: INDIGENISTA INQUIRIES AND THE FORMATION OF CRACKS

Epigraph: The quotation is from Marjory Urquidi's translation, *Seven Interpretive Essays on Peruvian Reality* (1971, 274). In the main body of the text, I will refer to Mariátegui's book by the abbreviation of its Spanish title, *Siete ensayos*.

Epigraph: "Esta polémica del cholaje blanco e indio es una literatura de mestizos. Escritores cholos y neo-indios engendran una raposa ideología: el indigenismo y el cholismo. [. . .] Mas llegará la hora, como que ha llegado ya, en que los auténticos y verdaderos indios, indios de sangre y espíritu, irrumpan en la 'república de las letras,' y aparezcan cerebros indios, produciendo pensamiento indio. Y entonces, hay que estar seguro de ello, que se cantará el responso para el 'indigenismo' como para el 'cholismo.' Quedando el 'espacio vital' libre para la literatura *indianista*" (my translation). In this book, I work with the edition of *El indio y los escritores de América* (1968) compiled in *Fausto Reinaga. Obras completas* (2014). Unless otherwise indicated, all translations hereafter are mine.

1. Decoloniality refers to the intellectual, political, and theoretical movement that challenges a world system structured by colonial and capitalist principles. For further details, see the extensive theoretical work of Quijano (1992, 2010).

2. The historical events outlined in this paragraph provide the political and social context in which the indigenista discourse emerged as a reevaluative agenda at the turn of the century. This context also serves as a framework for delimiting the corpus addressed in this book. This rationale explains the noninclusion of a pioneer author of the indigenista narrative, Clorinda Matto de Turner, whose novel *Aves sin nido* (1889) marks a pivotal point in the revision of what

my work describes as the failure of the criollo national project to incorporate Indigenous peoples. For further exploration of Matto's work, I recommend consulting Efraín Kristal's *The Andes Viewed from the City* (1987), Antonio Cornejo Polar's *Escribir en el aire* (1994), and Vanesa Miseres's chapter devoted to Matto's itinerant work in *Mujeres en tránsito: Viaje, identidad y escritura en Sudamérica (1830–1910)* (2017).

3. The "trinomial modernity/coloniality/capitalism" is a term typically used by decolonial critics to refer to the interconnected framework that shapes the modern system. For more information, see Walter D. Mignolo, *Darker Side of the Renaissance* (1995), and Aníbal Quijano, "Prologue: Coloniality of Power" (2000).

4. The use of the term *Abya Yala* has a relatively modern origin and derives from the native language of the Guna tribe in Panama. Commonly translated as "lands of maturity" or "land of vital blood," the term was popularized by Aymara activist Takir Mamani in the 1970s when the Guna ethnic group was fighting for territorial sovereignty against transnational corporations. For more information on this event, I recommend consulting Emil Keme"'s "For Abiayala to Live, the Americas Must Die: Toward a Transhemispheric Indigeneity" (2018).

5. I must clarify that it is not my intention to engage in a terminological discussion of the sort that, for example, Latin American decolonial and subalternist theorists influenced by postcolonial theory had in the 1990s and early 2000s. For a rigorous exploration of their differences and concomitances, I recommend exploring books such as Walter Mignolo's *Local Histories/Global Designs* (2000) and John Beverly's *Subalternity and Representation* (1999).

6. It cannot be ignored that Quijano is strongly influenced by his Marxist formation. To open this line of discussion would force us to reevaluate to what extent all his theorizations on the coloniality of power are, in reality, a project to transcend the loop in which the Marxist critique of dependency seemed trapped after the collapse of the Soviet bloc. Of course, although interesting, this discussion is much more akin to a study of a different nature (political science, sociology, et al.).

7. Here I am referring to the work of Eduardo Viveiros de Castro ("Exchanging"), Bruno Latour (*Politics, We Have Never*), and Philippe Descola (*Beyond Nature*), which constitute a corpus that responds to the limitations of continental philosophy for explaining the relationship between society and nature.

8. These other definitions allude to the (post)structuralist use of the word "genealogy" and the genealogical method, as it was inaugurated by Friedrich Nietzsche. For example, the conceptualization implicit in the essay "Neitzsche, Genealogy, History" (1971) by Michel Foucault would resonate deeply in the conceptual journey of genealogy through the humanities and social sciences.

9. For the purposes of this work, I cite "El indigenismo en el Perú" from the version compiled in Arguedas's *Indios, mestizos y señores* (1989). I cite "No soy un aculturado" from the version included in Arguedas's *El zorro de arriba y el zorro de abajo* (1988).

10. To use a definition that will be repeated in chapter 6, Marcone states, "an actant is something that acts or to which activity is granted by others. . . . By virtue of location and timing, an actant makes a difference, makes things happen" (*Latin*, 80).

CHAPTER 1. ARGUEDAS AND GAMIO

1. Manuel Gamio constantly alludes to the German American anthropologist Franz Boas and his work *The Mind of Primitive Man* (1911). In this essay, Boas questions scientific racism and social Darwinism as methods of social classification. He also formulates one of the first approaches to ethnic diversity by forging the analytical approach known as cultural relativism.

2. Criticism about colonial literature has agreed that Bartolomé de las Casas was shocked by the devastation and extermination suffered by the aboriginal populations of the Caribbean, which he witnessed during his years as an itinerant preacher. Later, after being appointed bishop of Chiapas, he would assume a seemingly paternalistic and protective stance toward the Indigenous population.

3. For more information, see "The Uses of Diversity" (1985) by Clifford Geertz and "Multiculturalismo y racismo" (2011) by Peter Wade.

4. By "empleomanía," Arguedas refers to people's tendency to look for work in the public sector, creating a kind of useless bureaucracy and producing a vicious circle that prevents Bolivian institutions from spearheading any modernizing projects.

5. As Paz Soldán rightly points out, the hierarchical vision of races will not be a permanent stance from Alcides Arguedas (*Alcides*, 81), although he always showed skepticism of racial mixtures. Around 1937, in the third edition of *Pueblo enfermo*, Arguedas makes a significant modification of this point, bringing his perspective closer to Nazism's racial ideas. Nevertheless, Arguedas did not go to the extreme of promoting a project of racial cleansing, but rather, emphasizing his pessimism, he affirmed that modernity would be an unrealizable project in Bolivia, given the atavism caused by the large proportion of Indigenous blood in the population.

6. "Cuando un patrón tiene dos ó más pongos, se queda con uno y arrienda los restantes, sencillamente, cual si se tratase de un caballo ó de un perro, con la pequeña diferencia de que al perro y al caballo se les aloja en una caseta de

madera ó en una cuadra y á ambos se les da de comer; al pongo se le da el zaguán para que duerma y se le alimenta de desperdicios" (*Pueblo*, 61–62).

7. "Pero el indio no sólo puede ser alquilado, sino que tiene la obligación de transportar las cosechas por cuenta y á riesgo suyo, desde la finca á la morada urbana del patrón. El traslado se efectúa á lomo de asno ó llama, y se recorre 100 ó 150 kilómetros de esta manera. Muchas veces la parte de la cosecha que le corresponde trasladar, traspasa sus medios de locomoción" (Arguedas, *Pueblo*, 62).

8. "Calle abajo, en desorden, venían grupos de chiquillos astrosos precediendo á las comparsas de bailarines indígenas que avanzaban lentamente soplando en sus zampoñas tristes. Iban los indios vestidos con sus mejores ropas de gala y los jefes de las agrupaciones hacían tremolar en las manos las banderas sacadas á lucir en los solemnes días de la fiesta parroquial de cualquier otro inolvidable acontecimiento. Detrás de las comparsas, varios cholos conducían á distancia de algunos metros, dos bandas de tela blanca desplegadas en todo lo ancho de la calle y sobre las que, en letras negras, los partidarios habían pintado dos inscripciones : ¡ ¡ ¡ VIVA EL EGREGIO CIUDADANO DON COSME ENDARA ! ! !" (Arguedas, *Vida*, 71)

9. With this, I refer to the European philosophical tradition that embodies *cultural pessimism* as an anti-progressive discursive construct with a tendency to identify instances of decadence in the Western civilizing process. I am alluding to the ideas of philosophers such as Emil Cioran or Oswald Sprengler, among other adherents of Arthur Schopenhauer's philosophical pessimism. For further exploration of this philosophical current, I suggest consulting Oliver Bennett's *Cultural Pessimism* (2001).

10. In fact, Gamio and Vasconcelos would occupy public positions, the former as head of the Department of Anthropology and the latter as secretary of education, from which they would promote their respective indigenista visions in a confrontational manner. About these conflicting perspectives, Dalton posits a possible explanation for the failure of the assimilation of the Mexican Indians (*Mestizo Modernity*, 37).

11. For Osamu Nishitani, the social sciences are the realm in which the superiority/inferiority schemes that lead to *cultural racism* are defined. In this structure, the civilized subjects (heirs of European culture and social scientists) assume the role of *humanitas*, or producers of knowledge, while the Indigenous ones (the others, the uncivilized ones) embody an inferior status called *anthropos*, or subject of study. For more information, see Nishitani, "Anthropos and Humanitas: Two Western Concepts of 'Human Being'" (2006).

12. "La civilización europea contemporánea no ha podido infiltrarse en nuestra población indígena por dos grandes causas: primero, por la resistencia

natural que opone esa población al cambio de cultura; segundo, porque desconocemos los motivos de dicha resistencia, no sabemos cómo piensa el indio, ignoramos sus verdaderas aspiraciones, lo prejuzgamos con nuestro criterio, cuando deberíamos compenetrarnos del suyo para comprenderlo y hacer que nos comprenda" (*Forjando*, 40).

13. "La mayoría que en nuestra población actual representa la raza indígena, sugiere la tentación de conferir a su literatura filiación nacionalista. En efecto, de escaso número de curiosos es conocido el asombroso número de relaciones, cantos, poemas [. . .] que atesoran nuestros indígenas, pero, precisamente, por ser casi ignorada esa literatura de quienes no pertenecen a la raza indígena o no son investigadores de nuestra población indígena, no puede llamarse nacional" (*Forjando*, 204–5).

14. I recommend consulting Gloria Elizabeth Chacón's *Indigenous Cosmolectics* (2018) for an in-depth exploration of the thematic and ideological scope of this group of Indigenous Mesoamerican writers.

15. The INI was created in 1940 within the framework of the Indigenista Congress of Pátzcuaro in Michoacán, Mexico. The resolution was supported by countries such as Ecuador, Nicaragua, Bolivia, Peru, Cuba, Honduras, Costa Rica, and the United States. Its headquarters was established in Mexico City, and it began operations in 1942 under the direction of Manuel Gamio, who remained in office until 1948. The institute responded to interest in the stimulation of indigenista policies in Latin America under a pan-indigenista vision promoted by a group of intellectuals and technocrats.

16. I would like to note, however, that there is already a large body of critical literature that reinterprets conventional social scientific approaches to the different projects of autonomy within the various Indigenous movements in Latin America and other areas of the Global South using the perspective of multiple ontologies. For more information, see *Designs for the Pluriverse: Radical Interdependence, Autonomy, and the Making of Worlds* (2018) by Arturo Escobar; *Constructing the Pluriverse: The Geopolitics of Knowledge* (2018), ed. Bernd Reiter; and *A World of Many Worlds* (2018), ed. Marisol de la Cadena and Mario Blaser.

17. "El indio no tiene remota idea de lo que es la ley. Según su criterio simplista, es bueno lo que llena sus necesidades y malo lo que se opone á la satisfacción de ellas; y para imponer sanción, preciso es que el que de ella sea objeto, tenga idea, por lo menos, de lo que es malo ó bueno, justo ó injusto en su aceptación corriente. Hablar lenguaje de código al indio analfabeto y embrutecido, es incurrir en grave falta de lógica, porque ante ese curioso lenguaje, no muy bien comprendido ni aun por los alfabetos, por las muchas interpretaciones á que se presta, permanece mudo, y si alguna consciencia llega a poseer, es al último,

cuando cargado de grillos, agarrotado en el fondo de un inmundo calabozo, tiene hambre y piensa que debió haber cometido acción mala cuando así le tratan y tan airados se muestran los hombres" (Arguedas, *Pueblo*, 67–68).

18. "Que las Constituciones y leyes de casi todos los países latinoamericanos, son copia más o menos fiel de la Constituciones y leyes europeos o norteamericana, y, por lo tanto, exclusivamente apropiadas al elemento social que por origen, cultura o idioma, o por las tres características, es semejante a elementos sociales europeos o norteamericanos. [. . .] Sugiérase a las Repúblicas latino americanas, en las que predomina la población indígena, la conveniencia de revisar las Constituciones vigentes, a fin de que respondan a la naturaleza y necesidades de todos los elementos constitutivos de la población y pueda alcanzarse el desarrollo armónico e integral de la misma, fortaleciéndose así, positivamente, la que es base del verdadero pan-americanismo" (Gamio, *Forjando*, 129–30).

19. It is interesting to note that Gamio's proposal was partially assumed by successive Mexican administrations. It became more noticeable during the governance of Lázaro Cárdenas del Rio, who created the ejidatarios system, aimed at ending the revolution-era agrarian reform process by distributing land to peasants. This reformist stance in national laws would find its most radical expression in the new constitutions in Ecuador (2008) and Bolivia (2009), when both countries were ruled by intercultural administrations.

CHAPTER 2. VASCONCELOS AND VALCÁRCEL

1. Most of the cuzqueño intellectuals who were part of this current of thought were grouped within the Grupo Resurgimiento: in addition to Valcárcel, José Uriel García, Luis Felipe Aguilar, as well as the brothers Félix Cosío and José Gabriel Cosío. A text that illustrates very well the political profile that unites these intellectuals is the article "La violenta situación de los indios en el departamento del Cusco" (The violent situation of Indians in the department of Cuzco) signed by the Grupo Resurgimiento and published in no. 6 of the magazine *Amauta*, directed by José Carlos Mariátegui.

2. I use the term "anthropological place" in the sense given by Marc Augé who refers to these places as spaces with historical and cultural significance, opposed to non-places or places of transit created by postmodernity. See Augé, *Non-Places* (1995).

3. For further information, consult Charles F. Walker, *Tupac Amaru Rebellion* (2014), where he reveals details about the political and economic interests that mobilized the uprising of Túpac Amaru II in Cuzco.

4. "La restauración del orden cósmico—que la idea de un tiempo histórico

lineal y progresivo rehúsa comprender, a no ser como un 'volver atrás la rueda de la historia'—puede ser aprehendida también con el concepto *nayrapacha*, que nos sirve de epígrafe: pasado, pero no cualquier visión de pasado; más bien, 'pasado-como-futuro,' es decir, como una renovación del tiempo-espacio. Un pasado capaz de renovar el futuro, de revertir la situación vivida: ¿No es ésta la aspiración compartida actualmente por muchos movimientos indígenas de todas las latitudes que postulan la plena vigencia de la cultura de sus ancestros en el mundo contemporáneo?" (*Violencias*, 51). This quote, drawn from Silvia Rivera Cusicanqui's book *Violencias (re)encubiertas en Bolivia* ([Re]covert violences in Bolivia) (2010), initially appeared in the anthology of essays entitled *Violencias encubiertas en Bolivia* (1993), where the article was titled "La raíz. Colonizadores y colonizados" (The root: colonizers and colonized). Silvia Rivera Cusicanqui has clarified that the editor, Xavier Albó, in 1993 took poetic license with the title of this article. She has specified that the dualistic formulation anticipated in the title does not represent her analysis of the origins of mestizaje in Bolivia. For this reason and trying to respect the nominal will of Rivera Cusicanqui herself, I choose to quote the 2010 edition.

5. I should point out that what Aníbal Quijano calls "cultural coloniality"— that is, the oppressive reproduction of European cultural paradigms to explain non-European cultures—has also been noted, albeit with different nomenclature, by other authors who belong to both decolonial and subaltern studies. In this sense, and just to mention a few names, the same approach can be explored in Néstor García Canclini's *Culturas híbridas* (1990), Edgardo Lander's "Modernidad, colonialidad y posmodernidad" (1997), and Dipesh Chakrabarty's *Provincializing Europe* (2000), among others.

6. Although in the main body of the text I refer to Vasconcelos's essay using its Spanish title (*La raza*), the pages cited correspond to the English translation published by Johns Hopkins University Press in 1997.

7. The expression "deus ex machina" is, apparently, used by José Vasconcelos in its best-known meaning as introduced by the ancient Greek theater—that is, as the irruption in a certain situation of an event or person (in Greek theater it was usually a god) in order to suddenly resolve the problems of the narration, without corresponding to the linearity of the plot.

8. "El Cusco y Lima son, por la naturaleza de las cosas, dos focos opuestos de la nacionalidad. El Cusco representa la cultura madre, la herencia de los inkas milenarios. Lima es el anhelo de adaptación a la cultura europea. Y es que el Cusco pre-existía cuando llegó el conquistador y Lima fue creada por él, ex-nihilo. [. . .] Solo el Cusco está reservado para redimir al indio" (Valcárcel, *Tempestad*, 213). For the purposes of this study, I work with one of the most

recent editions of this book (2020), that of the Cuzco publisher Rey de Abastos, which includes two recent studies by the historian Ramón Pajuelo Teves and the cuzqueño writer Enrique Rosas Paravicino.

9. In a specific essay on this topic, I analyze how the rediscovery of Machu Picchu and the intellectual battle to impose a regionalist historical and aesthetic interpretation—as opposed to the universalizing readings disseminated in *National Geographic* magazine by the North American archaeologist Hiram Bingham—contributed to the formation of the intellectual agenda of cuzqueño indigenismo, through the intellectual production of Valcárcel and Uriel García. For more information, see Díaz Zanelli, "Writing Machu Picchu" (2021).

10. "El día que todas las conciencias sientan nacer el orgullo de ser de esta madre sublime—la raza—que aguarda largos siglos la hora de su rehabilitación, habrá desaparecido el problema indígena. [. . .] Solo un gran amor fraternal, comprensivo, uno de esos amores que arrancan de la génesis de la especie y son el grito de la sangre, tendrá el poder de salvar al Perú, dignificando al indio" (Valcárcel, *Tempestad*, 214).

11. It is worth mentioning the thesis of Javier Sanjinés who suggests that Franz Tamayo's pro-mestizaje ideas preexisted those of other more influential indigenists in Latin America such as Vasconcelos who would have had access to Tamayo's essays before publishing *La raza cósmica* (*Mestizaje Upside-Down*, 64–65).

12. Derived from the Greek word *tellus* (earth), in the context of Latin American literature, *telurismo* refers to a discursive approach that emphasizes the deep cultural connections of a specific human collective with the earth and nature. This style is characterized by portraying cultural identities through landscapes, local traditions, or rural experiences. Two classic examples of telluric literature in twentieth-century Latin America are the indigenist novel *El mundo es ancho y ajeno* (*The World Is Wide and Alien*, 1941) by Ciro Alegría and the critical essay *Radiografía de la pampa* (*X-Ray of the Pampa*, 1933) by Ezequiel Martínez Estrada.

CHAPTER 3. MARIÁTEGUI'S INDO-MARXISM AND ARGUEDAS'S CULTURAL PROGRAM

1. Although I keep the Spanish abbreviation of the title (*Siete ensayos*) in the main text, page citations will be to the translation made by Marjory Urquidi and published in 1971 by the University of Texas Press under the title *Seven Interpretive Essays on Peruvian Reality*.

2. "Tahuantinsuyo" is a term used by the Inca state to refer to its unified territories during the imperial period.

3. Here I am following the notion of Western Marxism put forward by the Italian historian Domenico Losurdo, who refers in this way to the Marxist current that arose in European countries that were not officially socialist. Among the founding voices of this current were Georg Lukács and Antonio Gramsci. Losurdo emphasizes that, unlike the Marxism implemented in the Soviet Union (which he calls Eastern Marxism) defined by Leninism, Western Marxism deploys a deep concern for theorizing revolutionary praxis and its cultural dimensions. For more information, I recommend consulting, Losurdo's *Il marxismo occidentale* (2017).

4. Bolivian Marxist critic Álvaro García Linera provides an interesting interpretation of how Marx identified the pre-Hispanic agrarian community in the Americas as a precapitalist social formation that differed from other precapitalist communities such as those of China, India, and Algeria, among others. Through this singular view, García Linera proposes a new understanding of the historical role of the Inca community in the critical anti-capitalist panorama of Latin America. For more information, see "Introducción al cuaderno de Kovalevsky" in García Linera, *La potencia plebeya*.

5. The main scholarly reference on which Mariátegui relies to make such strong statements about the ayllu and its survival in the Andes is the work of Peruvian sociologist Hildebrando Castro Pozo, which he references repeatedly throughout *Siete ensayos*. The specific work that Mariátegui cites is *Nuestra comunidad indígena* (Our Indigenous community) (1924), where Castro Pozo presents a detailed sociological study of Indigenous communal organization in the Andes. This study also influenced other indigenistas such as Luis Eduardo Valcárcel, José Uriel García, and Víctor A. Belaunde.

6. Actually, indigenista intellectuals themselves are part of this discussion. Valcárcel contributed to this open conversation with a historical study entitled *Del ayllu al imperio* (From ayllu to empire) (1925), which Mariátegui also read before the publication of *Siete ensayos*. In addition, the ayllu was constantly invoked in the indigenista literature of the time, as in Enrique López-Albújar's *Cuentos andinos* (Andean stories) (1920).

7. Leibner himself has rigorously explored the accommodative and zigzagging uses given to the concept of *ayllu*, which, introduced by the social sciences, was a relatively new debate in the early twentieth century.

8. The Soviet kolkhoz (collective farm) was a collective agricultural formation created by order of Lenin during the first years after the Russian Revolution of 1917. Under the cooperative model, the project collectivized agrarian production in the rural areas of the Soviet Union. One could assume that Mariátegui's reference is selective and constrained, among other reasons, because the kolkhoz

experience did not offer the same historical, ethnic, and racial dimensions as the ayllu did. Rather, it seemed the result of a form of socialist modernization. For further information on the kolkhoz, I recommend consulting Alexander Vucinich's "The Kolkhoz" (1949) and R. W. Davies's *Soviet Collective Farm* (1980).

9. Indigenous social unrest in the southern Andean regions of Peru such as Ayacucho and Puno was indicative to Mariátegui of an Indigenous social mobility and revolutionary spirit. For more information on the simultaneity of these Indigenous uprisings in the Peruvian Andes and the articulation of an indigenista discourse, I recommend Carlos Arroyo Reyes's *Nuestros años diez. La Asociación Pro-Indígena, el levantamiento de Rumi Maqui y el incaísmo modernista* (Our ten years. The Pro-Indigenous Association, the Rumi Maqui uprising, and modernist Incaism) (2005).

10. For the historical reconstruction of this event I rely on the historiographical works of Eugenio Chang-Rodríguez, *Poética e ideología en José Carlos Mariátegui* (1983) and Alberto Flores Galindo, *La agonía de Mariátegui* (1989), as well as some essays that are part of the compilation edited by José Aricó, *Mariátegui y los orígenes del marxismo latinoamericano* (1978).

11. Flores Galindo explains (*La agonía*, 30–40) that the reason it was decided to name it a socialist party and not a communist one was in response to an analysis of the Peruvian social base made by Mariátegui, who had pondered the possibility of creating a less ideologized organization in a first phase, with the intention of incorporating the most significant number of members from the social sectors (workers, peasants, trade unions).

12. In this book, I work with the version edited by Mariátegui's successors in the anthology *Ideología y política* (Ideology and politics) (1987).

13. "Una conciencia revolucionaria indígena tardará quizás en formarse; pero una vez que el indio haya hecho suya la idea socialista, le servirá con una disciplina, una tenacidad y una fuerza, en la que pocos proletarios de otros medios podrán aventajarlo" (Mariátegui, *Ideología*, 43). This quotation, attributed exclusively to Mariátegui, appears curiously repeated in the second part of the paper, which was cowritten with Pesce. However, it is relevant to point out that this statement belongs to Mariátegui.

14. As a counterpoint to my interpretation, I recommend reviewing the arguments put forth by Mijail Mitrovic and Sebastián León, who historicize the way Latin American Marxism introduces the category of *race* in historical materialism in their "Raza y clase en el materialismo histórico: notas sobre América Latina" (2022).

15. It is worth mentioning that this nondeterministic view of history has

inspired some recent readings that interpret Mariátegui together with another current of socialist intellectuals who promote an Open Marxism. For more information on this point, I recommend consulting Curtis Kline's "The Open Marxism of José Carlos Mariátegui" (2022).

16. The speech known as "No soy un aculturado" was read by J. M. Arguedas during the ceremony to receive the Inca Garcilaso de la Vega Award in recognition of his intellectual trajectory in 1968. However, in this text I work with the reprint of the speech published with his posthumous novel *El zorro de arriba y el zorro de abajo* in 1971.

17. "*Amauta* se convierte en una tribuna de difusión de la ideología socialista marxista, y como alcanza a tener una vastísima circulación en el país y en América Latina, se convierte, al mismo tiempo, en un medio de expresión de los escritores provincianos rebeldes que denuncian, mediante la narrativa o el ensayo, el estado de servidumbre en que se encuentra la población indígena" (Arguedas, *Indios*, 13).

18. This text was initially published in "Notas sobre la cultura latinoamericana y su destino" (Notes on Latin American culture and its destiny, 1966), a volume edited by Peruvian philosopher Francisco Miró-Quesada with contributions from artist Fernando de Szyszlo and Arguedas. I work with the reedition of the text made by literary critic Ángel Rama. He compiled this essay in a collection of anthropological and cultural interventions entitled *Formación de una cultura nacional indoamericana* (Formation of an Indo-American national culture, 1975).

19. The *Manuscrito de Huarochirí*, a Quechua text containing Andean myths and legends, was compiled in approximately 1598 by priest Francisco de Ávila with the title of *Dioses y hombres de Huarochirí* (1966) in the early seventeenth century during the Spanish eradication of Indigenous religions. This cornerstone of Quechua literary history circulated in Latin America only after its first Spanish translation by Peruvian indigenista writer José María Arguedas in the mid-1960s.

20. In many ways, the figure of J. M. Arguedas continues to resonate in the cultural production of the Indigenous movements in the Andes. For example, in the documentary film *Sigo siendo (Kachkaniraqmi)* (2012) by Peruvian filmmaker Javier Corcuera, the evocative and ideological presence of Arguedas in contemporary Andean musical production is explored during several passages. Likewise, his role as a Spanish-Quechua translator inspired many of the bilingual writers and intellectuals who today diversify Andean cultural production, such as Ugo Carrillo, Pablo Landeo, Sócrates Zuzunaga, Ch'aska Anka Ninawaman, and Washington Córdova Huamán.

INTERLUDE: THE INDIGENOUS TURN OF THE MID-TWENTIETH CENTURY

1. Some exceptions can be mentioned, such as Mexico, where this process began in the 1920s because of the influence of José Vasconcelos in the administration of Álvaro Obregón (1920–1924). In this period, rural education programs were created and, in the urban sphere, so were spaces for indigenista artistic development that would foment the emergence of the Mexican muralist school. Along the same lines, some Indigenous community recognition policies carried out in Peru during the administration of Augusto B. Leguía, known as the Oncenio (1919–1930), can be taken into account.

2. I know that, in the Peruvian case, that radical indigenista event was the Revolutionary Government of the Armed Forces, led by Juan Velasco Alvarado between 1968 and 1975. The agrarian reform and the cultural promotion of Andean society through the National System of Support for Social Mobilization played a crucial role in the emergence of decolonizing Indigenous discourses in Peru. However, I have decided not to include in this brief chapter an analysis of this period because, when Velasco erupted on the Peruvian scene with his indigenist policies, there were already Indigenous decolonizing discourses in the Andes, such as the indianismo of Fausto Reinaga in Bolivia. After all, it is important to remember that the history of Indigenous mobilizations in Latin America and of the insurgent genealogy that I illuminate, is not free of overlaps and mismatches inherent to the particular material conditions in which these events took place. For more information, I recommend consulting Franklin Pease's *Breve historia contemporánea del Perú* (1995) and Enrique Mayer's *Ugly Stories of the Peruvian Agrarian Reform* (2009).

3. Actually, there is considerable scholarship devoted to historicizing the performance of Indigenous intellectuals during the colonial period. For more information, I recommend consulting Gonzalo Lamana's *How "Indians" Think* (2019) and the compilation *Indigenous Intellectuals* (2014) edited by Gabriela Ramos and Yana Yannakakis.

4. For more information for policies of distribution and the economic impact of the Cárdenas agrarian reform, consult María Eugenia Romero-Ibarra's "La reforma agraria de Cárdenas" (2010).

5. For a rigorous history of the ejidatario system, I recommend consulting Jorge Martín Trujillo's "El ejido, símbolo de la Revolución Mexicana" (2015).

6. As Yoer Javier Castaño Pareja argues, the ejidatario credit system was envisioned by Cárdenas as the realization of a revolutionary goal. For more information, see Castaño Pareja, "Estrategias de fomento" (2014).

7. Fallaw describes other interesting examples such as the promotion of cul-

tural and sports festivals whose propagandistic rhetoric was aimed at redeeming the Mayan population.

8. In fact, the designation of La Paz as the initial location of the congress occurred in 1937 on Mexican soil, in the context of the Third Pan American Conference on Education held in Mexico City (Alvin Martin, "El Primer Congreso," 224).

9. The way in which I use the term "spirit" echoes the use made by the Spirit of Bandung, an international conference that brought together countries from Asia and Africa in 1955 in the Indonesian city of Bandung. At this meeting, policies were outlined whereby most of these countries (which were still experiencing or living under conditions of colonialism) dissociated themselves from the polarization resulting from the Cold War. Constituted as nonaligned countries, this conference established the political intentions with which at least twenty-nine countries would seek original alternatives for their development and decolonization. For more information, see "The 'Bandung Spirit' and Solidarist Internationalism," by Heloise Weber and Poppy Winanti (2016).

10. Through remarkable historical research, Jennifer Jolly reconstructs in detail how the Cárdenas administration turned Pátzcuaro into a cultural laboratory where the image of Mexican indigeneity was reconstructed and manipulated in the process of national identification. A politics that, in a way, aspired to counteract Mexico City's indigenista centrality. For further information, consult her *Creating Pátzcuaro, Creating Mexico* (2018).

11. The Bolivian economy depended on its mining industry and imports of raw materials. The fall in international prices during the Great Depression generated a deficit in Bolivian revenue years later. The Chaco War was a conflict between 1932 and 1935 in which Bolivia fought Paraguay for the control of a portion of the Chaco Boreal, an area geographically connected to the southern side of the Amazon Basin. The conflict negatively impacted the economies of both countries, but the final agreement benefited Paraguay, which obtained most of the claimed territory. For further information, see Alejandro de Quesada's *The Chaco War* (2011).

12. In a comprehensive study of the formation of the movement prior to 1952, Lora points out that the MNR's success in praxis was due to the ideological flexibility or porosity in which party members fit their nationalist discourse fit. However, this also ended up being problematic when they had to manage the country because it was not possible for them to fulfill all of the previously assumed commitments. For more information, see Guillermo Lora, *History of the Bolivia Labour Movement, 1848–1971* (1977).

CHAPTER 4. INDIANISMO

1. For this book, I work with a version of this essay, originally a book, that was compiled in the series *Fausto Reinaga. Obras completas* (2014), volumes edited and put into circulation by the Vice-Presidency of the Plurinational State of Bolivia during the government of Evo Morales, which illustrates the intellectual dialogue between Reinaga's ideas and the decolonizing administration of Morales.

2. Perhaps the statement that most eloquently describes Reinaga's split with the MNR is in *La revolución india*, where he says: "No one in the MNR thought or dreamed of a Bolivian Indian Party, and even less that the Indian could aspire, as a race, Nation and people, to Power" ("Nadie en el MNR pensó ni soñó en un Partido Indio de Bolivia, y menos todavía que el indio podía aspirar, como raza, Nación y pueblo al Poder") (303). The question of Indigenous political agency is crucial in what I elaborate here as an epistemological rupture.

3. "Ahí tenemos a José Carlos Mariátegui, dando rienda suelta a su alma india, hija del Ande, a su espíritu inka que echa fuego cósmico. En el horizonte mental de Mariátegui desaparece en este instante el indio, *como clase* [clase campesina], para erguirse y afirmarse *como raza, como pueblo, como espíritu*. En vez de decir, 'El proletariado indígena espera su Lenin,' debió haber dicho: la raza india, el pueblo indio, el espíritu indio espera su Inka; o bien, el indio espera su Tupaj Amaru de nuestro tiempo" (*El indio*, 509).

4. "La 'naturaleza humana' del indio es la del hombre-inka. Por ello, el indio debe volver al Inka, creer en el Inka, que es mejor que el hombre logrado por el Occidente. [. . .] Volver al Inka para iluminar de fe y esperanza nuestro porvenir. [. . .] El Inka para nosotros es el reconocimiento de la unidad de nuestra sangre, de nuestro espíritu y de nuestra cultura milenaria; que Europa en cuatro siglos no ha podido destruir. [. . .] Nosotros formamos un hombre que no sabía mentir, no sabía robar, no sabía explotar (ama llulla, ama súa, ama khella). La ética social del Inkanato salía del Cosmos" (*La revolución*, 91, my ellipses).

5. Through his analysis of eighteenth-century Indigenous documents, Sinclair Thomson has shown that even notions of a resurgence of Indigenous autonomy predate the insurrections that occurred between 1778 and 1781, as these notions are already present in short-scale communal uprisings that occurred in the Andes in the 1740s. For more information, see his article "'Cuando sólo reinasen los indios'. Recuperando la variedad de proyectos anticoloniales entre los comuneros andinos (La Paz, 1740–1781)" (2006).

6. "El hombre de la sociedad inkaica tiene nítida conciencia de su dignidad. [. . .] La tierra es un bien común, todos la trabajan, y la Pachamama a todos nu-

tre, generosamente. El sol es el padre protector del hombre. El principio de que el hombre viene de la tierra y torna a ellos, aquí es una evidencia" (*La revolución*, 396).

7. Immanuel Wallerstein defines the concept of *time-space realities* as a single structural unit governed by its determined geohistorical systems. Coloniality would be the geohistorical system that determines the time-space reality in which Reinaga finds himself. Wallerstein further adds that the division of the concepts of *time* and *space* is the product of the intellectual foundations of the Enlightenment and the consequent maturation of history and geography as fields of the social sciences in Europe. For more information, see "The Inventions of TimeSpace Realities: Towards an Understanding of Our Historical Systems" (1988).

8. I use the expression "linear global thinking" in the interpretation of Walter Mignolo ("Global South")—that is, as one of the intellectual principles that grounded Western civilization by temporally dividing the planet according to the internal criteria of European history (Middle and Modern Ages), thus justifying the imperial expansions and social hierarchies of colonialism.

9. I clarify that, with this, I am not suggesting Reinaga is the first Indigenous intellectual to create literary texts from a subjugated knowledge in the interest of questioning the social paradigms and hegemonic knowledge imposed by the modern/colonial system. The history of Indigenous intellectual production that intervenes in the literate spaces of Latin America goes back to the very origins of the colonial period. For more on this point, I suggest Gonzalo Lamana's *How "Indians" Think* (2019) and the compilation *Indigenous Intellectuals* (2014) edited by Gabriela Ramos and Yana Yannakakis.

10. While identifying his decolonizing contributions, María Elena Oliva's interpretation (*La negritud*, 104–7) of the emergence of indianismo as an ideology opposed to indigenismo emphasizes that Reinaga's main interest was to overcome the paternalistic indigenista mediation, from which other points of the indianista agenda were articulated. On the contrary, the overcoming of mestizo mediation is only one consequence of a larger decolonizing agenda that addresses epistemology as the battleground.

11. "El indio de Bolivia no puede dejar pasar la crisis mortal que padece Occidente. Tiene que aprovechar. Pero no para salvar a su enemigo. Esta crisis tiene que aprovechar para liberarse. La Revolución india es una lógica irrebatible en el terreno de las ideas y en la fenomenología de los hechos. La Revolución india estallará como una ley natural" (*La revolución*, 71).

12. I clarify that my understanding of the concept *Global South* does not refer to a geographical zoning of the planet nor to the international relations between

the so-called third world countries. From decolonial thought, I understand the Global South as those spaces in which oppressed subjects—whether oppressed by colonialism, slavery, or coloniality (we know that it is not necessary to go through the colonial experience to suffer the onslaught of coloniality)—struggle for liberation from the Western rhetoric that justifies the cultural, economic, and political domination of their ways of life. Thus, in the geographic Northern Hemisphere, there are multiple experiences of struggle that, from my understanding, are positioned in the Global South as a place of enunciation (e.g., the Indigenous nations of North America and Canada; oppressed racialized sectors, and so on). Although there is no consensus on the definition of Global South, I find myself more closely aligned with the definition of Boaventura de Sousa Santos (2016) who conceptualizes it as a metaphorical space where epistemological struggles are waged against Western centralism.

13. Although *El Moudjahid* is currently one of the main newspapers in Algeria, at the time of the war of independence it served as the propaganda organ of the National Liberation Front.

14. "El indigenismo era una corriente reivindicativa. El indianismo es un movimiento liberatorio. El indigenismo fue una idea pura de reivindicación. El indianismo es una fuerza política de liberación. Es más. El indigenismo fue un movimiento del cholaje blanco-mestizo; en tanto que el indianismo es un movimiento indio, un movimiento indio revolucionario, que no desea asimilarse a nadie; se propone, liberarse" (*La revolución*, 136).

15. It can be inferred that Reinaga is responding to the pathologizing arguments of Alcides Arguedas who, in his essay *Pueblo enfermo* (1910) and his novels, re-creates Bolivian Indigenous people as an inert and demobilized subject.

16. In fact, part of the political program of the Cuban Revolution contained an anticolonial discourse that in the cultural sphere was propagated through the influential magazine *Casa de las Américas*, at that time directed by Haydée Santamaría.

17. Somehow, it is the recognition of this blind spot in the globalizing geopolitical panorama that runs through the nonaligned countries and political actors gathered in what is known as the Spirit of Bandung, where transnational ideas of decolonization were forged, identifying limitations in the ideological imperatives of the polarized world. For more information on the emancipatory logic of the Spirit of Bandung, I suggest consulting Jeong Eun Annabel We's "Spirit of Bandung beyond Colonial Mobility" (2019).

18. I am especially interested in Waskar Ari's interpretation of the movement of Indigenous activists that, from the 1920s, mobilized in rural Bolivia claiming rights such as education, land titling, and access to water with a rhet-

oric that sought to counteract the colonial legacy in force in their societies. For more information, consult his book *Earth Politics: Religion, Decolonization, and Bolivia's Indigenous* (2014).

19. Katarismo is a political current forged in Bolivia during the second half of the twentieth century. Inspired by the figure and anticolonial demands of the Indigenous leader Túpac Katari, it was constituted as a political movement that coincided dialectically on many points with indianismo, Marxism, and some nationalist formulations. Javier Hurtado affirms that "in Katarism there coexisted indigenista, leftist nationalist, and exacerbated indianista positions" ("en el katarismo convivían posiciones indigenistas, nacionalistas de izquierda e indianistas exacerbadas") (*El katarismo*, 86). For further information, I recommend consulting *Movimientos y poder indígena en Bolivia, Ecuador y Perú* (2008) by Xavier Albó.

20. *Mallku* is a term of Aymara origin with several connotations. In the religious sphere, it refers to a deity that dwells in the heights and is usually represented as a condor. In the community political sphere, it refers to the political authorities whose jurisdiction reaches a particular group of communal organizations.

21. Jichha, "No quiero que mi hija sea su sirvienta." https://www.youtube.com/watch?v=rlyHHG6ayf0&t=22s/.

22. The Guerra del Agua (The Bolivian Water War) is the name given to the Indigenous uprising that took place in early 2000 in Cochabamba against a water privatization project financed by the World Bank. The radical protests, which lasted three months, were allied with the coca leaf farmers' unions and led by then congressman Evo Morales. The protests brought about, on the one hand, the repeal of the project that ordered the privatization of the supply and, on the other hand, the consolidation of Morales as an Indigenous leader with national scope.

23. Another perspective on this disjunction is offered by Álvaro García Linera in his article "Indianismo y Marxismo. El desencuentro de dos razones revolucionarias" in *La potencia plebeya* (2015).

CHAPTER 5. MARCOS AND THE ZAPATISTA WRITING

1. NAFTA is a free commercial treaty that involves Canada, the United States, and Mexico. The main promoter on the Mexican side was former President Carlos Salinas de Gortari, who has always been associated with the most neoliberal and conservative wing of the Institutional Revolutionary Party (PRI).

2. The *declaraciones* are statements made by EZLN and zapatista municipali-

ties to an external audience. Although they are essentially communiqués, which may have some narrative passages, they serve to inform their allies and enemies about their actions, internal changes, and positions on certain issues. The last one issued was the *Sexta Declaración de la Selva Lacandona* (Sixth Declaration of the Lacandon Jungle), which dates from 2005.

3. The postrevolutionary Mexican state institutionalized mestizaje as the articulating ideology of its national project. To explore how this instrumentalization was progressively represented in Mexican literary production, I suggest seeing *The Mestizo State: Writing Race in Modern Mexico* (2012) by Joshua Lund.

4. Here I refer specifically to the faction led by Emiliano Zapata and the claims embodied in the Plan de Ayala. For more information, see Mark Wasserman, *The Mexican Revolution: A Brief History with Documents* (2012).

5. The ejido system is a model of farmland distribution that can be traced back to the agrarian demands formulated by the Indigenous communities that participated in the Mexican Revolution. However, the indigenista policies of the Mexican state privileged mestizos as owners of these lands (ejidatarios), continuing the legacy of dispossession of the Indigenous peoples.

6. Yetman accurately illustrates how, at different times in Mexican history, land distribution within the ejido system was corruptly manipulated by the ruling party PRI, which ended up subjecting ejidatarios to a neoliberal reform that reversed the initial purposes of the agrarian reform ("Ejidos," 215–19).

7. During the postrevolutionary administrations, the Mexican state identified cinema as an effective instrument of propaganda for its national project and its pro-mestizaje discourse. A foundational example of this dynamic was the endorsement given to *¡Que viva México!* directed by Soviet filmmaker Sergei Eisenstein with the support and supervision of the state apparatus. One of the most iconic cases was that of Emilio Indio Fernández, an indigenista director. Several of his films portray the vicissitudes of rural Indigenous life and often promote the idea of mestizaje and education as avenues for the development of Mexican Indigenous peoples. Many of his films were produced and circulated with the financial support of the Mexican state. For more information, see Dolores Tierney, *Emilio Fernández: Pictures in the Margins* (2007), and Julia Tuñón, "Emilio Fernández: A Look behind the Bars" (1995).

8. "El Ejército Zapatista de Liberación Nacional, a través de él [el viejo Antonio], a través de esos líderes políticos y de los jefes de comunidades, empieza a entender su historia de fundación política, su consciencia, su consciencia histórica. Y el resultado es que no estábamos hablando con un movimiento indígena que estaba esperando un salvador, sino con un movimiento indígena de mucha tradición de lucha, con mucha experiencia, muy resistente, muy inteligente tam-

bién, al que simplemente le servíamos de algo así como brazo armado" (Marcos and Le Bot, *El sueño*, 147).

9. Enlace Zapatista, "Sobre el PFCRN y la ofensiva militar del gobierno," January 11, 1994. Retrieved from https://enlacezapatista.ezln.org.mx/1994/01/11/sobre-el-pfcrn-y-la-ofensiva-militar-del-gobierno/.

10. "Y así vieron los más primeros dioses que el uno es necesario, que es necesario para aprender y para trabajar y para vivir y para amar. Pero vieron también que el uno no es suficiente. Vieron que se necesitan los todos y solo los todos son suficientes para echar a andar al mundo. Y así fue como se hicieron buenos sabedores los primeros dioses, los más grandes, los que nacieron el mundo. Se supieron hablar y escuchar los dioses estos. Y sabedores eran. No porque supieran muchas cosas o porque supieran mucho de una cosa, sino porque se entendieron que el uno y los todos son necesarios y suficientes" (Marcos, *Desde las montañas*, 389).

11. "Nuestros más grandes abuelos tuvieron que enfrentar al extranjero que vino a conquistar estas tierras. Vino el extranjero a ponernos otro modo, otra palabra, otra creencia, otro dios y otra justicia. Era su justicia sólo para tener él y despojarnos a nosotros. Era su dios el oro. Era su creencia su superioridad. Era su palabra la mentira. Era su modo la crueldad. Los nuestros, los más grandes guerreros se enfrentaron a ellos, grandes peleas hubo entre los naturales de estas tierras para defender la tierra de la mano del extranjero. Pero grande era la fuerza que traía la mano extraña" (Marcos, *Relatos*, 70–71).

12. The reference is to the famous book *Visión de los vencidos* (1959), which is a compilation of Nahua stories from the sixteenth century edited by the Mexican scholar Miguel León-Portilla.

13. Another possible interpretation is that this zapatista slogan reemphasizing "democracy, liberty and justice" is a reappropriation of the slogan that articulated the French Revolution: *Liberté, Égalité, Fraternité*. After all, it is a common strategy of Zapatista discourse to appropriate and resignify Western political symbols, as noted by Di Paramo in "Beyond Modernity" (2011).

14. Enlace Zapatista. "Fourth Declaration of the Lacandon Jungle," January 1, 1996. Retrieved from https://enlacezapatista.ezln.org.mx/1996/01/01/cuarta-declaracion-de-la-selva-lacandona/.

The source is a communique from the Zapatista Army of National Liberation (EZLN), with Subcomandante Marcos as the primary spokesperson, and the website is a primary archive for EZLN documents.

15. "Cualquier intento de 'reforma' o 'equilibrio' de esta deformación es imposible desde dentro del sistema de partido de Estado. No hay 'cambio sin ruptura.' Es necesario un cambio profundo, radical, de todas las relaciones sociales

en el México de hoy. Es necesaria una revolución, una nueva revolución. Esta revolución sólo será posible desde fuera del sistema de partidos de Estado" (*Don Durito*, 56).

16. Although I will elaborate further on the concept of *ontologies* in the context of Indigenous studies in chapter 6, here I am following the ideas of ontologies as existential perspective-building processes articulated by Amerindian cosmologies. Accordingly, in the various Indigenous contexts, ontological engagement—which defines what exists and what does not exist—is defined by communal life praxis (world-making processes). For more information, see "Anthropology of Ontologies" (2015) by Eduardo Kohn and "Ontology and Indigeneity: On the Political Ontology of Heterogeneous Assemblages" (2014) by Mario Blaser.

CHAPTER 6. POETICS OF *BUEN VIVIR*

1. *Buen Vivir*, loosely translated, means "Good living" or "Living well."

2. In "Development as Buen Vivir: Institutional Arrangements and (De) Colonial Entanglements" (2018), Catherine Walsh provides a convincing argument about the manipulation of this concept in the policies of interculturality carried out by Rafael Correa's administration in Ecuador. For his part, in "Teología de los extractivismos" (2016), Eduardo Gudynas describes a similar situation in the staging of indigeneity through which Evo Morales's administration imposed extractive projects in Bolivia.

3. I would not rule out that the notion of "alternative" or "multiple modernities" as defined by Grossberg (2010) can be a useful analytical framework. However, the basis of his conceptualization of modernity is grounded in the productive capacity of non-Euro/Atlantic spaces conditioned by their cultural conjunctures (territoriality, geography), which he renders in ontological form—that is, the ontology of modernity as multiplicity. It is possible that Grossberg's nomenclature is the main barrier to bringing the many iterations of Buen Vivir into this debate.

4. The term *oralitura* is a neologism coined by the Senegalese cultural historian Yoro K. Fall to describe African literary practices rooted in orality. The concept was later adopted by the Mapuche Chilean poet and intellectual Elicura Chihuailaf, who used *oralitura* to explain the literary formations of Mapuche poetry. For further exploration, I recommend consulting Chihuailaf's *Recado confidencial a los chilenos* (1999).

5. Alberto Acosta has been a key actor in the historiography of Buen Vivir in the Andes since he served as minister of energy and mines during the early stag-

es of Rafael Correa's administration. He also chaired the National Constituent Assembly, which drafted the Ecuadorian Constitution of 2008, known as the Constitution of Montecristi, a document where *Sumak Kawsay* was introduced through the inclusion of nature as a subject of rights.

6. The *wakcha* is a Quechua term that describes orphaned or lonely people. In Andean literature, it is generally represented in characters subjected to a situation of orphanhood derived from some vital misunderstanding. I suggest, for example, exploring the orphaned or lonely characters that appear abundantly in the literature of José María Arguedas or Carlos Eduardo Zavaleta.

7. Although Ninawaman's identity is crucial to this study, I acknowledge that her academic background and familiarity with the indigenista literary tradition place her within the category of what Marisol de la Cadena terms *indigenous mestizos*. This authentic identity formation does not require her to de-indigenize herself; rather, it stands in opposition to subordinate forms of mestizaje that are heavily conditioned by acculturation processes. For further exploration, please refer to de la Cadena's *Indigenous Mestizos* (2000).

8. The Quechua and the Spanish are by Ninawaman. All English translations of her poems are mine.

9. Although Ninawaman's description might resemble Jane Bennett's concept of vital materialism, here I focus specifically on how the connection Ninawaman describes with coca is necessarily grounded in the material, rather than solely through spiritual means. This does not reduce coca to vibrant matter (Bennett, 2010), an approach that refers to objects that interact with humans in a quasi-independent way, the main tenet of Bennett's theory.

10. This highlights a difference between the role of coca in Andean Indigenous literature and activism and the role it plays in its own cultural representation in the Amazon. Juan R. Duchesne Winter has made interesting metaphysical inquiries into the role of coca cultural representation in his *Plant Theory in Amazonian Literature* (2019).

11. Rodolfo Cerrón-Palomino (2006) has comprehensively explained the distortions suffered by the term *Qosqo*, which, besides being a term of Aymara origin and not Quechua, is not among any of its most widespread etymological versions. Cerrón-Palomino proves the inaccuracy of Inca Garcilaso's version ("navel of the world") and that of the Spanish chronicler Fernando Montesinos ("flattened land"), tracing the historiography of this word in its Aymara origins (Cerrón-Palomino, "Cuzco," 156, 158).

12. Emerging from the city of Puno, high in the southern Peruvian Andes, the Grupo Orkopata was a collective of indigenista intellectuals who bridged the gap between indigenismo and artistic vanguards. Their most significant

publication, the magazine known as *Boletín Titikaka*, became a platform for their work. Among the group's prominent members were Alejandro Peralta and Gamaliel Churata. For further exploration, I recommend consulting *Indigenismo de vanguardia en el Perú* (2000) by Cynthia Vich.

13. Córdova completed doctoral studies in the Environment and Sustainable Development program at the Universidad Nacional Federico Villarreal where in 2019 he defended the thesis entitled "Modelo operativo componente social para optimizar proyectos en riego en la provincia de Espinar-Cusco."

14. Since Correa's and Morales's administrations introduced Buen Vivir in their constitutions, some political measures were implemented to mitigate the impact of the expansion of extractive industries in Indigenous territory. This never implied the incorporation of Indigenous cosmopolitical variables in the public debate, however, but ended up instead being measures to demobilize Indigenous organizations allied to these administrations. For more information on this type of manipulation, I recommend reading Catherine Walsh's "Development as Buen Vivir: Institutional Arrangements and (De)colonial Entanglements" (2018).

AFTERWORD: AN INDIGENOUS DECOLONIAL CRITIQUE

1. For example, I am thinking of some ideas formulated and popularized by influential cultural critics such as the anthropologist Guillermo Bonfil Batalla who in his *México Profundo* (1987) establishes a dualistic, almost dichotomous, vision between what he calls México profundo, embodied in the Indigenous cultural tradition, versus an imaginary Mexico, incarnated in a mestizo national aspiration; both sectors that, in his perspective, barely touch each other. Such dualism, which I deliberately avoid, overlooks the kind of symbolic connections that are exhibited in my work's genealogy. In the Peruvian case, a similar view is offered by literary critic Tomás G. Escajadillo who, throughout his several books devoted to the indigenista literary tradition (I highly value his texts on Ciro Alegría and Enrique López Albújar), offers a constrained perspective on the formal limits of literary indigenismo. Perhaps his vision is best condensed in the article "Aves sin nido, ¿novela indigenista?" (2004) where he explains his reasons for thinking the writer Clorinda Matto de Turner is not an indigenista writer.

2. The GTANW is a sui generis autonomous administration project in Peru that involves the recognition by the Peruvian State of the territorial autonomy of the Wampís Nation in the basins of the Santiago and Morona Rivers, currently occupying three hundred thousand hectares that overlap with the regions of Amazonas and Loreto. Since 2017, approximately fifteen thousand people

in this space are ruled by an Indigenous constitutional statute that frames the degree of autonomy available to them. For more information, I recommend consulting "Autonomías indígenas en la Amazonía peruana" (2019) by Wrays Pérez and Deborah Delgado.

3. Scholars and activists such as Silvia Rivera Cusicanqui and Catherine E. Walsh have revisited on more than one occasion the scope and limitations of mesocratic decolonial scholarship and have argued for the necessity of problematizing the privileges of decolonial theorists.

4. Some scholars who have already opened analyses on this corpus of Mesoamerican writers (both in Mexico and Central America) are Arturo Arias (2007, 2017) and Gloria E. Chacón (2018).

BIBLIOGRAPHY

Acosta, Alberto. "El Buen Vivir en el camino del post-desarrollo. Una lectura desde la Constitución de Montecristi." Fundacion Fredrich Ebert, 2010.

Acosta, Yamandú. *Sujeto, transmodernidad, interculturalidad. Tres tópicos utópicos en la transformación del mundo.* Universidad de la República, 2020.

"Acta Final del Primer Congreso Indigenista Interamericano." *Congreso Indigenista Interamericano*, Pátzcuaro, Michoacán, Mexico, April 1940.

"Acta Final del Tercer Congreso Indigenista Interamericano." *Congreso Indigenista Interamericano*, La Paz, Bolivia, September 1954.

Adamson, Joni. "People of the Water: *El Río*, *The Shape of Water*, and the Rights of Nature." *ISLE: Interdisciplinary Studies in Literature and Environment* 3 (2020): 1–17.

Aguilar Gil, Yásnaya. "(Is There) an Indigenous Literature?" Translated by Gloria E. Chacón. *Diálogo* 19, no. 1 (2016): 157–59.

Albó, Xavier. *Movimientos y poder indígena en Bolivia, Ecuador y Perú*. Centro de Investigación y Promoción del Campesinado (CIPCA), 2008.

Alegría, Ciro. *El mundo es ancho y ajeno*. Farrar and Rinehart, 1941.

Alejo Ticona, Esteban. *Saberes, conocimientos y prácticas anticoloniales del pueblo aymara-quechua en Bolivia*. AGRUCO/Plural, 2010.

Allen, Catherine J. "To Be Quechua: The Symbolism of Coca Chewing in Highland Peru." *American Ethnologist* 8, no. 1 (1981): 157–71.

Allen, Catherine J. "When Utensils Revolt: Mind, Matter, and Modes of Being in the Pre-Columbian Andes." *RES: Anthropology and Aesthetics*, no. 33 (1998): 18–27.

Alvin Martin, Percy. "El Primer Congreso Interamericano de Indianistas." *Hispanic American Historical Review* 19, no. 2 (1939): 223–25.

BIBLIOGRAPHY

Anzaldúa, Gloria. *Borderlands/La Frontera: The New Mestiza*. 1987. Aunt Lute Books, 2012.

Aparicio, Juan, and Mario Blaser. "The 'Lettered City' and the Insurrection of Subjugated Knowledges in Latin America." *Anthropological Quarterly* 81, no. 1 (2008): 59–94.

Arguedas, Alcides. *Pueblo enfermo. Contribución á la psicología de los pueblos hispano-americanos*. 1909. Casa Editorial de Vda. De Luis Tasso, 1910.

Arguedas, Alcides. *Raza de bronce*. 1919. Biblioteca Ayacucho, 2006.

Arguedas, Alcides. *Vida criolla. (La novela de la ciudad)*. Sociedad de Ediciones Literarias y Artísticas, 1905.

Arguedas, José María. *Canto quechua. Con un ensayo sobre la capacidad de creación artística del pueblo indio y mestizo*. 1938. Dendro Ediciones, 2021.

Arguedas, José María. *Formación de una cultura nacional indoamericana*. 1975. Siglo XXI, 1987.

Arguedas, José María. *Indios, mestizos y señores*. Horizonte, 1989.

Arguedas, José María. *El zorro de arriba y el zorro de abajo*. 1971. Horizonte, 1988.

Ari, Waskar. *Earth Politics: Religion, Decolonization, and Bolivia's Indigenous*. Duke University Press, 2014.

Arias, Arturo. *Recovering Lost Footprints*. Vol. 1 of *Contemporary Maya Narratives*. SUNY Press, 2017.

Arias, Arturo. *Taking Their World: Literature and the Signs of Central America*. University of Minnesota Press, 2007.

Aricó, José. *Mariátegui y los orígenes del marxismo latinoamericano*. Siglo XXI, 1978.

Aronna, Michael. *"Pueblos Enfermos": The Discourse of Illness in the Turn-of-the-Century Spanish and Latin American Essays*. University of North Carolina Press, 1999.

Arroyo Reyes, Carlos. *Nuestros años diez. La Asociación Pro-Indígena, el levantamiento de Rumi Maqui y el incaísmo modernista*. LibrosEnRed, 2005.

Arteaga, Claudia A. "Función poética y política en la poesía Quechua peruana escrita por mujeres." *Revista Iberoamericana* 89, no. 282–83 (2023): 561–84.

Augé, Marc. *Non-Places: Introduction to an Anthropology of Supermodernity*. Translated by John Howe. Verson, 1995.

Barthes, Roland. "The Death of the Author." In *Image, Music, Text*, translated by Stephen Heath, 142–48. 1967. Fontana Press, 1977.

Bartra, Armando. "Mitos en la aldea global." In *Relatos de El Viejo Antonio*, Subcomandante Insurgente Marcos, 7–17. Centro de Información y Análisis de Chiapas, 1998.

BIBLIOGRAPHY

Baschet, Jérôme. *¡Rebeldía, resistencia y autonomía! La experiencia zapatista.* Eón, 2018.

Baxmeyer, Martin. "El mito universal. Reconstrucción y deconstrucción de la identidad indígena en 'Relatos de El Viejo Antonio' del Subcomandante Marcos." *Kamchatka. Revista de Análisis Cultural* 12 (2018): 175–86.

Becker, Marjorie. *Setting the Virgin on Fire: Lazaro Cardenas, Michoacan Peasants and the Redemption of the Mexican Revolution.* University of California Press, 1995.

Bennett, Jane. *Vibrant Matter: A Political Ecology of Things.* Duke University Press, 2010.

Bennett, Oliver. *Cultural Pessimism: Narratives of Decline in the Postmodern World.* Edinburgh University Press, 2001.

Beverly, John. *Subalternity and Representation: Arguments in Cultural Theory.* Duke University Press, 1999.

Blaser, Mario. "Conflicts and the Stories of Peoples in Spite of Europe: Toward a Conversation on Political Ontology." *Current Anthropology* 54, no. 5 (2013): 547–68.

Blaser, Mario. "Is Another Cosmopolitics Possible?" *Cultural Anthropology* 31, no. 4 (2016): 545–70.

Blaser, Mario. "Ontology and Indigeneity: On the Political Ontology of Heterogeneous Assemblages." *Cultural Geographies* 21, no. 1 (2014): 49–58.

Blaser, Mario. "Political Ontology: Cultural Studies without 'Cultures'?" *Cultural Studies* 23, no. 5–6 (2009): 873–96.

Blaser, Mario. "Reflexiones sobre la ontología política de los conflictos medioambientales." *América Crítica* 3, no. 2 (2019): 63–80.

Boas, Franz. *The Mind of Primitive Man.* Macmillan, 1911.

Bonfil Batalla, Guillermo. "Del indigenismo de la revolución a la antropología crítica." In *La quiebra política de la antropología social en México (Antología de una polémica)*, edited by Andrés Medina and Carlos García Mora, 141–64. Universidad Nacional Autónoma de México, 1983.

Bonfil Batalla, Guillermo. *México profundo. Una civilización negada.* Grijalbo, 1987.

Branding, David A., and María Urquidi. "Manuel Gamio y el indigenismo oficial en México." *Revista Mexicana de Sociología* 51, no. 2 (1989): 267–84.

Burdette, Hannah. *Revealing Rebellion in Abiayala: The Insurgent Poetics of Contemporary Indigenous Literature.* University of Arizona Press, 2019.

Burman, Anders. *Indigeneity and Decolonization in the Bolivian Andes: Ritual Practice and Activism.* Lexington Books, 2016.

Campuzano Arteta, Álvaro. *La modernidad imaginada. Arte y literatura en el pensamiento de José Carlos Mariátegui (1911–1930)*. Iberoamericana/Vervuert, 2017.

Castaño Pareja, Yoer Javier. "Estrategias de fomento y desarrollo de la actividad agropecuaria durante el sexenio cardenista. El papel desempeñado por el Banco Nacional de Crédito Ejidal, 1934–1940." *Secuencia: Revista de Historia y Ciencias Sociales* 89 (2014): 119–40.

Castro Pozo, Hildebrando. *Nuestra comunidad indígena*. El Lucero, 1924.

Cerrón-Palomino, Rodolfo. "Cuzco: la piedra donde se posó la lechuza. Historia de un nombre." *Lexis* 30, no. 1 (2006): 143–94.

Chacón, Gloria. "Cultivating Nichimal K'op (Poetry) from the Heart: Indigenous Women of Chiapas." *Revista Canadiense de Estudios Hispánicos* 39, no. 1 (2014): 165–80.

Chacón, Gloria. *Indigenous Cosmolectics: Kab'awil and the Making of Maya and Zapotec Literatures*. University of North Carolina Press, 2018.

Chakrabarty, Dipesh. *Provincializing Europe: Postcolonial Thought and Historical Difference*. Princeton University Press, 2000.

Chang-Rodríguez, Eugenio. *Poética e ideología en José Carlos Mariátegui*. José Purrúa Turanzas, 1983.

Chihuailaf, Elicura. *Recado confidencial a los chilenos*. LOM, 1999.

Chivi, Idón. "Buen Vivir. Una democracia altamente igualitaria." (2010). https://movimientos.org/pt-br/node/16980/.

Choque Quispe, María Eugenia. "Principios para la construcción de una democracia intercultural." In *Intelectuales indígenas piensan América Latina*, edited by Claudia Zapata, 273–84. Universidad Andina Simón Bolívar/Ediciones Abya-Yala/Centro de Estudios Culturales Latinoamericanos, Universidad de Chile, 2007.

Contreras, Manuel E. "A Comparative Perspective of Education Reforms in Bolivia: 1950–2000." In *Proclaiming Revolution: Bolivia in Comparative Perspective*, edited by Merilee S. Grindle and Pilar Domingo, 259–86. University of London Press, 2003.

Córdova Delgado, Washington. "Efecto de un programa de capacitación en la gestión administrativa de los docentes de la Universidad Nacional Mayor de San Marcos, 2019." Dissertation, Universidad Nacional Federico Villarreal, 2020. https://www.scribd.com/document/430444265/Cordova-Huaman-Washington-Doctorado

Córdova Delgado, Washington. *Parawayraq chawpinpi/Entre la lluvia y el viento*. Pakarina, 2019.

Cornejo Polar, Antonio. *Escribir en el aire. Ensayo sobre la heterogeneidad sociocultural en las literaturas andinas*. Horizonte, 1994.

Coronado, Jorge. *The Andes Imagined: Indigenismo, Society, and Modernity*. University of Pittsburgh Press, 2009.

Coronado, Jorge. *Portraits in the Andes: Photography and Agency, 1900–1950*. University of Pittsburgh Press, 2018.

Dalton, David S. *Mestizo Modernity: Race, Technology, and the Body in Postrevolutionary Mexico*. University of Florida Press, 2018.

Davies, R. W. *The Industrialization of Soviet Russia 2: The Soviet Collective Farm, 1929–1930*. Macmillan, 1980.

De Ávila, Francisco. *Dioses y hombres de Huarochirí*. Translated by José María Arguedas. Instituto de Estudios Peruanos, 1966.

De Castro, Juan E. *Bread and Beauty: The Cultural Politics of José Carlos Mariátegui*. Brill, 2021.

De Castro, Juan E. *Mestizo Nations: Culture, Race, and Conformity in Latin American Literature*. University of Arizona Press, 2002.

De la Cadena, Marisol. *Earth Beings: Ecologies of Practice across Andean Worlds*. Duke University Press, 2015.

De la Cadena, Marisol. "Indigenous Cosmopolitics in the Andes: Conceptual Reflections beyond 'Politics.'" *Cultural Anthropology* 25, no. 2 (2010): 334–70.

De la Cadena, Marisol. *Indigenous Mestizos: The Politics of Race and Culture in Cusco, Perú, 1919–1991*. Duke University Press, 2000.

De la Cadena, Marisol, and Mario Blaser. "Introduction. Pluriverse: Proposals for a World of Many Worlds." In *A World of Many Worlds*, edited by Marisol de la Cadena and Mario Blaser, 1–22. Duke University Press, 2018.

De la Cadena, Marisol, and Mario Blaser, eds. *A World of Many Worlds*. Duke University Press, 2018.

De Quesada, Alejandro. *The Chaco War, 1932–35: South America's Greatest Modern Conflict*. Osprey, 2011.

Descola, Philippe. *Beyond Nature and Culture*. University of Chicago Press, 2013.

Di Paramo, Daniela. "Beyond Modernity: Irony, Fantasy, and the Challenge to Grand Narratives in Subcomandante Marcos's Tales." *Mexican Studies/Estudios Mexicanos* 27, no. 1 (2011): 177–205.

Díaz Zanelli, José Carlos. "Writing Machu Picchu: Epistemological Extractivism and the Citadel through the Lens of *indigenismo cusqueño*." *Journal of Latin American Cultural Studies* 30, no. 4 (2021): 569–85.

Duchesne Winter, Juan R. *Plant Theory in Amazonian Literature*. Palgrave, 2019.

Dussel, Enrique. *1492. El encubrimiento del otro. Hacia el origen del "mito de la modernidad."* Antropos, 1992.

Dussel, Enrique. *Ética de la liberación*. Trotta, 1998.

Dussel, Enrique. *Filosofía del Sur y Descolonización*. Docencia, 2014.

Dussel, Enrique. *The Invention of the Americas: Eclipse of "the Other" and the Myth of Modernity*. Translated by Michael D. Barber. Continuum, 1995.

Dussel, Enrique. "Transmodernity and Interculturality: An Interpretation from the Perspective of the Philosophy of Liberation." *Transmodernity: Journal of Peripheral Cultural Production of the Luso-Hispanic World* 1, no. 3 (2012): 28–59.

Escajadillo, Tomás G. "'Aves sin nido' ¿novela 'indigenista'?" *Revista de Crítica Literaria Latinoamericana* 30, no. 59 (2004): 131–54.

Escárzaga, Fabiola. *La comunidad indígena insurgente. Perú, Bolivia y México (1980–2000)*. Plural Editores/Universidad Autónoma Metropolitana, 2017.

Escobar, Arturo. *Designs for the Pluriverse: Radical Interdependence, Autonomy, and the Making of Worlds*. Duke University Press, 2018.

Escobar, Arturo. *Territories of Difference: Place, Movements, Life, Redes*. Duke University Press, 2008.

Escobar, Arturo. "Transition Discourses and the Politics of Relationality: Toward Designs for the Pluriverse." In *Constructing the Pluriverse*, edited by Bernd Reiter, 63–89. Duke University Press, 2018.

Fallaw, Ben. *Cárdenas Compromised: The Failure of Reform in Postrevolutionary Yucatán*. Duke University Press, 2001.

Fanon, Frantz. *Black Skin, White Masks*. 1952. Grove Press, 2008.

Fanon, Frantz. *Sociología de una revolución*. Ediciones Era, 1976.

Fanon, Frantz. *Toward the African Revolution*. 1964. Grove Press, 1967.

Fanon, Frantz. *The Wretched of the Earth*. 1961. Grove Press, 1963.

Fatheuer, Thomas. "Buen Vivir: A Brief Introduction to Latin America's New Concepts for the Good Life and the Rights of Nature." *Heinrich Böll Stiftung—Publication Series on Ecology* 17 (2011): 7–30.

Favre, Henri. *El indigenismo*. Fondo de Cultura Económica, 1996.

Feldman, Irina Alexandra. *Rethinking Community from Peru: The Political Philosophy of José María Arguedas*. University of Pittsburgh Press, 2014.

Flores Galindo, Alberto. *La agonía de Mariátegui*. Instituto de Apoyo Agrario, 1989.

Flores Galindo, Alberto. *Buscando un inca. Identidad y utopía en los Andes*. Casa de las Américas, 1986.

Forns-Broggi, Roberto. "Los retos del ecocine en nuestras Américas. Rastreos del buen vivir en tierra sublevada." *Revista de Crítica Literaria Latinoamericana* 40, no. 79 (2014): 315–32.

Foucault, Michel. "Nietzsche, Genealogy, History." In *Language, Counter-Memory, Practice: Selected Essays and Interviews*, edited by D. F. Bouchard, 139–64. Cornell University Press, 1977.

Foucault, Michel. *El poder, una bestia magnífica*. Translated by Horacio Pons. Siglo XXI, 2012.

Foucault, Michel. "What Is an Author?" 1969. In *Michel Foucault: Aesthetic, Method, and Epistemology*, edited by James D. Faubion, 205–22. The New Press, 1998.

Franco, Jean. "Some Reflections on Contemporary Writing in the Indigenous Languages of America." *Comparative American Studies* 3, no. 4 (2005): 455–69.

García Liendo, Javier. *El intelectual y la cultura de masas. Argumentos latinoamericanos en torno a Ángel Rama y José María Arguedas*. Purdue University Press, 2017.

García Linera, Álvaro. "Introducción al cuaderno de Kovalevsky." In *La potencia plebeya. Acción colectiva e identidades indígenas, obreras y populares en Bolivia*, 31–52, CLACSO/Siglo XXI, 2015.

García Linera, Álvaro. *La potencia plebeya. Acción colectiva e identidades indígenas, obreras y populares en Bolivia*. CLACSO/Siglo XXI, 2015.

Gamio, Manuel. *Arqueología e indigenismo*. Instituto Nacional Indigenista, 1986.

Gamio, Manuel. *Consideraciones sobre el problema indígena*. Instituto Indigenista Interamericano, 1948.

Gamio, Manuel. *Forjando patria*. Ediciones Porrúa, 1916.

García-Canclini, Néstor. *Culturas híbridas. Estrategias para entrar y salir de la modernidad*. Grijalbo, 1990.

Geertz, Clifford. "The Uses of Diversity." *The Tanner Lectures on Human Values*, edited by Sterling M. McMurrin, 7:251–75. Cambridge University Press, 1986.

Gonzales, Odi. *Nación anti. Ensayos de antropología lingüística andina, lenguaje y pensamiento quechua, traducción cultural y resistencia*. Pakarina, 2022.

Gordon, Lewis R. *What Fanon Said: A Philosophical Introduction to His Life and Thought*. Fordham University Press, 2015.

Grijalva, Juan Carlos. "Paradoxes of the Inka Utopianism of José Carlos Mariátegui's *Seven Interpretative Essays on Peruvian Reality*." *Journal of Latin American Cultural Studies* 19, no. 3 (2010): 317–34.

Grijalva, Juan Carlos. "Vasconcelos o la búsqueda de la Atlántida. Exotismo, arqueología y utopía del mestizaje en 'La raza cósmica.'" *Revista de Crítica Literaria Latinoamericana* 30, no. 60 (2004): 333–49.

Grosfoguel, Ramón. "Colonial Difference, Geopolitics of Knowledge, and Global Coloniality in the Modern/Colonial Capitalist World-System." *Review (Fernand Braudel Center)* 25, no. 3 (2002): 203–24.

Grosfoguel, Ramón. "El concepto de 'racismo' en Michel Foucault y Frantz Fanon. ¿Teorizar desde la zona del ser o desde la zona del no-ser?" *Tabula Rasa* 16 (2012): 79–102.

Grossberg, Lawrence. *Cultural Studies in the Future Tense*. Duke University Press, 2010.

Grupo Resurgimiento. "La violenta situación de los indios en el departamento de Cusco." *Amauta*, no. 6 (1927): 37–38.

Gudynas, Eduardo. "Buen Vivir: Today's Tomorrow." *Development* 54, no. 4 (2011): 441–47.

Gudynas, Eduardo. "Extracciones, extractivismos y extrahecciones. Un marco conceptual sobre la apropiación de los recursos naturales," *Observatorio del Desarrollo* 18 (2013): 1–18.

Gudynas, Eduardo. "Teología de los extractivismos." *Tabula Rasa*, no. 24 (2016): 11–23.

Gutiérrez Aguilar, Raquel. *Rhythms of the Pachakuti: Indigenous Uprising and State of Power in Bolivia*. Duke University Press, 2014.

Haya de la Torre, Víctor Raúl. *Por la emancipación de América Latina*. M. Gleizer, 1927.

Hurtado, Javier. *El katarismo*. 1986. Biblioteca del Bicentenario de Bolivia, 2016.

Iubini Vidal, Giovanna. "*Tinkuy* de la palabra y la imagen. Migración estética eimaginarios visuales en la neovanguardia andina." *Literatura. Teoría, Historia, Crítica* 24, no. 2 (2022): 167–200.

Jolly, Jennifer. *Creating Pátzcuaro, Creating Mexico: Art, Tourism, and Nation Building under Lázaro Cárdenas*. University of Texas Press, 2018.

Keme', Emil. "For Abiayala to Live, the Americas Must Die: Toward a Transhemispheric Indigeneity." *Native American and Indigenous Studies* 5, no. 1, translated by Adam Coon (2018): 42–68.

Kline, Curtis. "The Open Marxism of José Carlos Mariátegui." *Latin American Perspectives* 49, no. 4 (2022): 94–109.

Kohn, Eduardo. "Anthropology of Ontologies." *Annual Review of Anthropology* 44 (2015): 311–27.

Kristal, Efraín. *The Andes Viewed from the City: Literary and Political Discourse on the Indian in Peru, 1848–1930*. Peter Lang, 1987.

Kristal, Efraín. *Una visión urbana de los Andes. Génesis y desarrollo del indigenismo en el Perú, 1848–1930*. Instituto de Apoyo Agrario, 1991.

Krögel, Alison. "'Sara mamacha, papa mamacha'. Representaciones alimenticias en la poesía quechua." *Revista de Crítica Literaria Latinoamericana* 38, no. 75 (2012): 331–61.

Lamana, Gonzalo. *How "Indians" Think: Colonial Indigenous Intellectuals and the Question of Critical Race Theory.* University of Arizona Press, 2019.

Lander, Edgardo. "Modernidad, colonialidad y posmodernidad." *Estudios Latinoamericanos* 4, no. 8 (1997): 31–46.

Latour, Bruno. *Politics of Nature.* Harvard University Press, 2004.

Latour, Bruno. *We Have Never Been Modern.* Harvard University Press, 1993.

Lauer, Mirko. *Andes Imaginarios. Discursos del indigenismo-2.* CBC/Sur Casa de Estudios del Socialismo, 1997.

Leibner, Gerardo. *El mito del socialismo indígena. Fuentes y contextos peruanos de Mariátegui.* Fondo Editorial de la Universidad Católica del Perú, 1999.

León-Portilla, Miguel. *Visión de los vencidos: Relaciones indígenas de la conquista.* Universidad Nacional Autónoma de México, 1959.

Lomnitz, Claudio. *Deep Mexico, Silent Mexico.* University of Minnesota Press, 2001.

López-Albújar, Enrique. *Cuentos andinos.* 1920. Peisa, 2007.

López-Baralt, Merdeces. "El retorno del Inca rey en la memoria colectiva andina. Del ciclo de Inkarri a la poesia quechua urbana de hoy." *América. Cahiers du CRICCAL* 2, no. 31 (2004): 19–26.

López Intzín, Juan. "*Ich'el ta muk'*: La trama en la construcción del Lekil kuxlejal (vida plena-digna-justa)." In *Senti-pensar el género. Perspectivas desde los pueblos originarios*, edited by Georgina Méndez Torres, Juan López Intzín, Sylvia Marcos, and Carmen Osorio Hernández, 73–110. Red Interdisciplinaria de Investigadores de los Pueblos Indios de México, 2013.

Lora, Guillermo. *A History of Bolivian Labour Movement, 1848–1971.* Cambridge University Press, 1977.

Losurdo, Domenico. *Il marxismo occidentale.* Sagittari Laterza, 2017.

Lugones, María. "Colonialidad y género." *Tabula Rasa*, no. 9 (2008): 73–101.

Lugones, María. "Heterosexualism and the Colonial/Modern Gender System." *Hypatia* 22, no. 1 (2007): 186–209.

Lugones, María. "The Inseparability of Race, Class, and Gender in Latino Studies." Translated by Joshua Price. *Latino Studies* 1 (2003): 329–32.

Lugones, María. "Toward a Decolonial Feminism." *Hypatia* 24, no. 4 (2010): 742–59.

Lund, Joshua. *The Impure Imagination: Toward a Critical Hybridity in Latin American Writing.* University of Minnesota Press, 2006.

Lund, Joshua. *The Mestizo State: Reading Race in Modern Mexico*. University of Minnesota Press, 2012.

Macusaya Cruz, Carlos. *Del indianismo al pensamiento amáutico. La decadencia de Fausto Reinaga*. Katari Indian Movement, 2015.

Maldonado, Ezequiel. "Los relatos zapatistas y su vínculo con la oralidad tradicional." *Convergencia. Revista de Ciencias Sociales* 8, no. 24 (2001): 141–53.

Maldonado-Torres, Nelson. *Against War: Views from the Underside of Modernity*. Duke University Press, 2008.

Maldonado-Torres, Nelson. "On the Coloniality of Being." *Cultural Studies* 21, no. 2–3 (2007): 240–70.

Maldonado-Torres, Nelson. "Outline of Ten Theses on Coloniality and Decoloniality." *Frantz Fanon Foundation* (2016): 1–37. https://fondation-frantzfanon.com/outline-of-ten-theses-on-coloniality-and-decoloniality/.

Maldonado-Torres, Nelson. "Post-continental Philosophy: Its Definition, Contours, and Fundamental Sources." *Worlds and Knowledges Otherwise* 1, no. 3 (2006): 1–29. https://globalstudies.trinity.duke.edu/sites/globalstudies.trinity.duke.edu/files/file-attachments/v1d3_NMaldonado-Torres.pdf.

Mallon, Florencia E. "Introduction: Decolonizing Knowledge, Language, and Narrative." In *Decolonizing Native Histories: Collaboration, Knowledge, and Language in the Americas*, edited by Florencia E. Mallon, 1–20. Duke University Press, 2012.

Mamani Macedo, Mauro. "Literatura quechua contemporánea de Perú. Continuidades y aperturas en la poesía." *Latinoamérica. Revista de Estudios Latinoamericanos* 77 (2023): 133–62.

Manrique, Nelson. "Historia y utopía en los Andes." *Debates en Sociología* 12, no. 14 (1988): 201–11.

Marcone, Jorge. "Filming the Emergence of Popular Environmentalism in Latin America." In *Global Ecologies and the Environmental Humanities: Postcolonial Approaches*, edited by Elizabeth DeLoughrey, Jill Didur, and Anthony Carrigan, 207–25. Routledge, 2015.

Marcone, Jorge. "Latin American Literature at the Rise of Environmentalism: Urban Ecological Thinking in José María Arguedas's *The Foxes*." *Comparative Literature Studies* 50, no. 1 (2013): 64–86.

Marcone, Jorge. "The Stone Guests: *Buen Vivir* and Popular Environmentalisms in the Andes and Amazonia." In *The Routledge Companion to the Environmental Humanities*, edited by Ursula K. Keise, Jon Christensen, and Nichelle Niemann, 227–35. Routledge, 2017.

Marcos, Subcomandante Insurgente. *Los colores de la tierra. Textos insurgentes desde Chiapas*. Txalaparta, 2001.

Marcos, Subcomandante Insurgente. *Cuentos para una soledad desvelada. Textos del Subcomandante Insurgente Marcos.* Frente Zapatista de Liberación Nacional, 1998.

Marcos, Subcomandante Insurgente. *Desde las montañas del sureste mexicano.* Plaza y Janés, 1999.

Marcos, Subcomandante Insurgente. *Don Durito de la Lacandona.* Centro de Información y Análisis de Chiapas, 1999.

Marcos, Subcomandante Insurgente. *La historia de los colores/The Story of Colors.* Translated by Anne Bar Din. Cinco Puntos Press, 1999.

Marcos, Subcomandante Insurgente. *Relatos de El Viejo Antonio.* Centro de Información y Análisis de Chiapas, 1998.

Marcos, Subcomandante, and Ejército Zapatista de Liberación Nacional (EZLN). "Cuarta Declaración de la Selva Lacandona." *Enlace Zapatista*, January 1, 1996. https://enlacezapatista.ezln.org.mx/1996/01/01/cuarta-declaracion-de-la-selva-lacandona/.

Marcos, Subcomandante Insurgente, and Yvon Le Bot. *El sueño Zapatista. Entrevistas con el Subcomandante Marcos, el Mayor Moisés y el Comandante Tacho, del Ejército Zapatista de Liberación Nacional.* Plaza y Janés, 1997.

Marcos, Subcomandante Insurgente, and Paco Ignacio Taibo II. *Muertos incómodos (falta lo que falta).* Joaquín Mortiz/Planeta, 2005.

Mariátegui, José Carlos. "Hombre y mito." *El alma matinal y otras estaciones del hombre de hoy.* Amauta, 1970. https://www.marxists.org/htm/.

Mariátegui, José Carlos. *Ideología y política.* 1969. Biblioteca Amauta, 1987.

Mariátegui, José Carlos. *La novela y la vida. Siegfried y el profesor Canella. Obras completas de José Carlos Mariátegui, vol. 4.* Amauta, 1979.

Mariátegui, José Carlos. *Seven Interpretive Essays on Peruvian Reality.* Translated by Marjory Urquidi. University of Texas Press, 1971.

Mariátegui, José Carlos. *Siete ensayos de interpretación de la realidad peruana.* 1928. Biblioteca Amauta, 1952.

Martínez Estrada, Ezequiel. *Radiografía de la pampa.* Babel, 1933.

Matto de Turner, Clorinda. *Aves sin nido.* Universo, 1889.

Mayer, Enrique. *Ugly Stories of the Peruvian Agrarian Reform.* Duke University Press, 2009.

Mignolo, Walter. *The Darker Side of the Renaissance: Literacy, Territoriality, Colonization.* University of Michigan Press, 1995.

Mignolo, Walter. "Decoloniality and Phenomenology: The Geopolitics of Knowing and Epistemic/Ontological Colonial Differences." *Journal of Speculative Philosophy* 32, no. 3 (2018): 360–87.

Mignolo, Walter. "Delinking. The Rhetoric of Modernity, the Logic of Coloniality, and the Grammar of Decoloniality." *Cultural Studies* 21, no. 2–3 (2007): 449–514.

Mignolo, Walter. "The Geopolitics of Knowledge and the Colonial Difference." *South Atlantic Quarterly* 101, no. 1 (2002): 57–96.

Mignolo, Walter. "The Global South and World Dis/Order." *Journal of Anthropological Research* 67, no. 2 (2011): 165–88.

Mignolo, Walter. *Local Histories/Global Designs: Coloniality, Subaltern Knowledges, and Border Thinking*. Princeton University Press, 2000.

Mignolo, Walter. "On Pluriversality and Multipolar World Order: Decoloniality after Decolonization; Dewesternization after the Cold World." In *Constructing the Pluriverse*, edited by Bernd Reiter, 90–116. Duke University Press, 2018.

Mignolo, Walter. "The Zapatistas's Theoretical Revolution: Its Historical, Ethical, and Political Consequences." *Review (Fernand Braudel Center)* 25, no. 3 (2002): 245–75.

Mignolo, Walter D., and Walsh, Catherine E. *On Decoloniality: Concepts, Analytics, and Praxis*. Duke University Press, 2018.

Millones, Luis. "Mesianismo en la América Hispana. El Taki Onqoy." *Memoria Americana*, no. 15 (2007): 7–39.

Miro-Quesada, Francisco, ed. *Notas sobre la cultura latinoamericana y su destino*. Industrial Gráfica, 1966.

Miseres, Vanesa. *Mujeres en tránsito. Viaje, identidad y escritura en Sudamérica (1830–1910)*. University of North Carolina Press, 2017.

Mitrovic, Mijail, and Sebastián León. "Raza y clase en el materialismo histórico. Notas sobre América Latina." *Pacha: Revista de Estudios Contemporáneos del Sur Global* 3, no. 7 (2022): 1–19.

Moore, Melisa. "Rompiendo fronteras imaginadas. Retórica y 'revolución' en la narrativa de la nación peruana de José Carlos Mariátegui." In *Migración y frontera. Experiencias culturales en la literatura peruana del siglo XX*, edited by Javier García Liendo, 91–115. Iberoamericana/Vervuert, 2017.

Mora, Mariana. *Kuxlejal Politics: Indigenous Autonomy, Race, and Decolonizing Research in Zapatista Communities*. University of Texas Press, 2017.

Moraña, Mabel. *Arguedas-Vargas Llosa. Dilemas y ensamblajes*. Iberoamericana/Vervuert, 2013.

Muyolema, Armando. "América Latina y los pueblos indígenas. Para una crítica de la razón latinoamericana." In *Teorizando las literaturas indígenas contemporáneas*, edited by Emilio del Valle Escalante, 233–274. A Contracorriente, 2013.

Ninawaman, Ch'aska Anka. *Poesía en quechua. Chaskaschay*. Abya Yala, 2004.

Nishitani, Osamu. "Anthropos and Humanitas: Two Western Concepts of 'Human Being'." In *Translation, Biopolitics, Colonial Difference*, edited by Naoki Sakai and Jon Salomon, 259–73. Hong Kong University Press, 2006.

Oliva, María Elena. *La negritud, el indianismo y sus intelectuales. Aimé Césaire y Fausto Reinaga*. Editorial Universitaria, 2014.

Paz Soldán, Edmundo. *Alcides Arguedas y la narrativa de la nación enferma*. Plural, 2003.

Pease, Franklin. *Breve historia contemporánea del Perú*. Fondo de Cultura Económica, 1995.

Pérez, Wrays, and Deborah Delgado. "Autonomías indígenas en la Amazonía peruana. La experiencia del pueblo wampis." *Debates en Sociología* 49 (2019) 121–38.

Portocarrero, Gonzalo. *La urgencia por decir "nosotros". Los intelectuales y la idea de nación en el Perú republicano*. Fondo Editorial de la PUCP, 2015.

Quijano, Aníbal. "Prólogo." In *Siete ensayos de interpretación de la realidad peruana* by José Carlos Mariátegui, ix–cxxix. Fundación Biblioteca Ayacucho, 2007.

Quijano, Aníbal. "Prólogo. Colonialidad del poder y clasificación social." In *Cuestiones y horizontes. De la dependencia histórico-estructural a la colonialidad/descolonialidad del poder*, edited by Danilo Assis Clímaco, 285–327. CLACSO, 2014.

Quijano, Aníbal. "Prólogo. Colonialidad del poder y clasificación social." *Journal of World-System Research* 6, no. 2 (2000): 342–88.

Quijano, Aníbal. "Prólogo. Colonialidad y modernidad/racionalidad." *Perú Indígena* 13, no. 29 (1992): 11–20.

Quijano, Aníbal. "Prologue: Coloniality of Power, Eurocentrism, and Latin America." Translated by Michael Ennis. *Nepantla: Views from South* 1, no. 2 (2000): 533–80.

Quijano, Aníbal. "Prologue: The Challenge of the 'Indigenous Movement' in Latin America." *Socialism and Democracy* 19, no. 3 (2010): 55–78.

Quijano, Aníbal, and Immanuel Wallerstein. "Americanity as a Concept; or, the Americas in the Modern World-System." *International Journal of Social Sciences* 124 (1992): 549–57.

Quintana-Navarrete, Jorge. "José Vasconcelos's Plant Theory: The Life of Plants, Botanical Ethics, and the Cosmic Race." *Hispanic Review* 89, no. 1 (2021): 69–92.

Rabasa, José. *Without History: Subaltern Studies, the Zapatista Insurgency, and the Specter of History*. University of Pittsburgh Press, 2010.

Rama, Ángel. *Transculturación narrativa en América Latina*. Siglo XXI, 1982.

Ramos, Gabriela, and Yanna Yannakakis, eds. *Indigenous Intellectuals: Knowledge, Power, and Colonial Culture in Mexico and the Andes.* Duke University Press, 2014.

Reinaga, Fausto. *El indio y los escritores de América.* Partido Indio de Bolivia, 1968.

Reinaga, Fausto. *Obras completas. Tomo II. Vol. IV.* Vicepresidencia del Estado Plurinacional de Bolivia, 2014.

Reinaga, Fausto. *El pensamiento amáutico.* Partido Indio de Bolivia, 1978

Reinaga, Fausto. *La revolución india.* 1970. Fundación Amáutica "Fausto Reinaga," 2001.

Reinaga, Fausto. *Tierra y libertad.* Rumbo Sindical, 1952.

Reiter, Bernd, ed. *Constructing the Pluriverse.* Duke University Press, 2018.

Rivera Cusicanqui, Silvia. "La raíz: colonizadores y colonizados." *Violencias encubiertas en Bolivia,* edited by Silvia Rivera Cusicanqui, Raúl Barrios Morón, and Xavier Albó, 27–42. *CIPCA-Aruwiyiri,* 1993.

Rivera Cusicanqui, Silvia. *Sociología de la imagen. Miradas ch'ixi desde la historia andina.* Tinta Limon/Plural/Piedra Rota, 2018.

Rivera Cusicanqui, Silvia. *Violencias (re)encubiertas en Bolivia.* La mirada salvaje–Piedra Rota, 2010.

Rocha Vivas, Miguel. *Mingas de la palabras. Textualidades oralitegráficas y visione de cabeza en las oralituras y literaturas indígenas contemporáneas.* 2016. Pontificia Universidad Javeriana/Universidad de los Andes, 2018.

Romero-Ibarra, María Eugenia. "La reforma agraria de Cárdenas y la agroindustria azucarera de México, 1930–1960." *Historia Agraria: Revista de Agricultura e Historia Rural* 52 (2010): 103–127.

Rowe, William. "Arguedas. Música, conocimiento y transformación social." *Revista de Crítica Literaria Latinoamericana* 25 (1987): 97–107.

Saldaña-Portillo, María Josefina. *The Revolutionary Imagination in the Americas and the Age of Development.* Duke University Press, 2003.

Sánchez-Prado, Ignacio M. *Intermitencias americanistas. Estudios y ensayos escogidos (2004–2010).* Universidad Nacional Autónoma de México, 2012.

Sánchez-Prado, Ignacio M. "El mestizaje en el corazón de la utopía. *La raza cósmica* entre Aztlán y América Latina." *Revista Canadiense de Estudios Hispánicos* 33, no. 2 (2009): 381–404.

Sanjinés C., Javier. *Embers of the Past: Essays in Times of Decolonization.* Translated by David Frye. Duke University Press, 2013.

Sanjinés C., Javier. "Foundational Essays as 'Mestizo-Criollo Acts': The Bolivian Case." *Latin American and Caribbean Ethnic Studies* 11, no. 3 (2016): 266–86.

Sanjinés C., Javier. *Mestizaje Upside-Down: Aesthetic Politics in Modern Bolivia*. University of Pittsburgh Press, 2004.

Santos, Boaventura de Sousa. *Epistemologies of the South: Justice against Epistemicide*. Routledge, 2016.

Solón, Pablo. *¿Es posible el Buen Vivir? Reflexiones a quema de ropa sobre alternativas sistémicas*. Fundación Solón, 2016.

Sorel, Georges. *Reflections on Violence*. Cambridge University Press, 1999.

Stahler-Sholk, Richard. "Resisting Neoliberal Homogenization: The Zapatista Autonomy Movement." *Latin American Perspectives* 34, no. 2 (2007): 48–63.

Tavárez, David. "Zapotec Time, Alphabetic Writing, and the Public Sphere." *Ethnohistory* 57, no. 1 (2010): 73–85.

Taylor, Analisa. "The Ends of Indigenismo in Mexico." *Journal of Latin American Cultural Studies* 14, no. 1 (2005): 75–86.

Taylor, Analisa. *Indigeneity in the Mexican Cultural Imagination: Thresholds of Belonging*. University of Arizona Press, 2009.

Thomson, Sinclair. "'Cuando sólo reinasen los indios'. Recuperando la variedad de proyectos anticoloniales entre los comuneros andinos (La Paz, 1740–1781)." *Argumentos* 19, no. 59 (2006): 15–47.

Ticona, Esteban Alejo. "La producción del conocimiento descolonizador en contextos del colonialismo interno." *Revista Integra Educativa* 3, no. 1 (2010): 37–48.

Tierney, Dolores. *Emilio Fernández: Pictures in the Margins*. Manchester University Press, 2007.

Trujillo Bautista, Jorge Martín. "El ejido, símbolo de la Revolución Mexicana." *Estudios Agrarios* 58 (2015): 125–151.

Tuñón, Julia. "Emilio Fernández: A Look behind the Bars." In *Mexican Cinema*, edited by Antonio Paranaguá, translated by Ana M. López, 179–92. British Film Institue/IMCINE, 1995.

Vanden Berghe, Kristine. *Narrativa de la rebelión zapatista. Los relatos del Subcomandante Marcos*. Iberoamericana/Vervuert, 2005.

Vanden Berghe, Kristine. "Nativismo y alter/natividad en los *Relatos del viejo Antonio* del Subcomandante Marcos." *Caravelle. Cahiers du Monde Hispanique et Luso-Brésilien*, no. 78 (2002): 197–209.

Valcárcel, Luis E. *Del ayllu al imperio. La evolución político-social en el antiguo Perú y otros estudios*. Editorial Garcilaso, 1925.

Valcárcel, Luis E. *Mirador indio. Apuntes para una filosofía de la cultura incaica*. 1941. Universidad Inca Garcilaso de la Vega, 2015.

Valcárcel, Luis E. *Tempestad en los Andes*. Editorial Minerva, 1927. Rey de Abastos, 2020.

Vargas Llosa, Mario. *La utopía arcaica. José María Arguedas y las ficciones del indigenismo*. Fondo de Cultura Económica, 1996.

Vasconcelos, José. *The Cosmic Race/La raza cósmica*. 1925. Translated by Didier T. Jaén. Johns Hopkins University Press, 1997.

Vasconcelos, José. *La raza cósmica*. Agencia Mundial de Librería, 1925.

Vich, Cynthia. *Indigenismo de vanguardia en el Perú. Un estudio sobre el Boletín Titikaka*. Fondo Editorial de la Pontificia Universidad Católica del Perú, 2000.

Villoro, Luis. *Los grandes momentos del indigenismo en México*. Fondo de Cultura Económica, 1996.

Viveiros de Castro, Eduardo. "Exchanging Perspectives: The Transformation of Objects into Subjects in Amerindian Ontologies." *Common Knowledge* 10, no. 3 (2004): 463–84.

Vucinich, Alexander. "The Kolkhoz: Its Social Structure and Development." *American Slavic and East European Review* 8, no. 1 (1949): 10–24.

Wade, Peter. "Multiculturalismo y racismo." *Revista Colombiana de Antropología* 47, no. 2 (2011): 15–35.

Walker, Charles F. *The Tupac Amaru Rebellion*. Harvard University Press, 2014.

Wallerstein, Immanuel. "The Inventions of TimeSpace Realities: Towards an Understanding of Our Historical Systems." *Geography* 73, no. 4 (1988): 289–97.

Walsh, Casey. "Eugenic Acculturation: Manuel Gamio, Migration Studies, and the Anthropology of Development in Mexico, 1910–1940." *Latin American Perspectives* 138, vol. 31, no. 5 (2004): 118–45.

Walsh, Catherine E. "Development as Buen Vivir: Institutional Arrangements and (De)colonial Entanglements." In *Constructing the Pluriverse: The Geopolitics of Knowledge*, edited by Bernd Reiter, 184–94. Duke University Press, 2018.

Walsh, Catherine E. "'Other' Knowledges, 'Other' Critiques: Reflections on the Politics and Practices of Philosophy and Decoloniality in the 'Other' America." *Transmodernity: Journal of Peripheral Cultural Production of the Luso-Hispanic World* 1, no. 3 (2012): 11–27.

Walsh, Catherine E. *Rising Up, Living On: Re-existences, Sowings, and Decolonial Cracks*. Duke University Press, 2023.

Ward, Thomas. *La resistencia cultural. La nación en el ensayo en las Américas*. Editorial Universitaria–Universidad Ricardo Palma, 2004.

Wasserman, Mark. *The Mexican Revolution: A Brief History with Documents*. Bedford/St. Martin's, 2012.

We, Jeong Eun Annabel. "Spirit of Bandung beyond Colonial Mobility." *Bandung: Journal of Global South* 6, no. 2 (2019): 190–209.

Weber, Heloise, and Poppy Winanti. "The 'Bandung Spirit' and Solidarist Internationalism." *Australian Journal of International Affairs* 70, no. 4 (2016): 391–406.

Yetman, David. "Ejidos, Land Sales, and Free Trade in Northwest Mexico: Will Globalization Affect the Commons?" *American Studies* 41, no. 2/3 (2000): 211–34.

Zapata, Claudia, and María Elena Oliva. "Frantz Fanon en el pensamiento de Fausto Reinaga. Cultura, revolución y nuevo humanismo." *Alpha (Osorno* 42 (2016): 177–96.

Zavaleta Mercado, René. *La caída del M.N.R. y la conjuración de noviembre. Historia del golpe militar del 4 de noviembre de 1964 en Bolivia*. Los Amigos del Libro, 1995.

Zavaleta Mercado, René. *Lo nacional-popular en Bolivia*. Siglo XXI, 1986.

Zevallos Aguilar, Ulises. "Peruvian Quechua Poetry (1993–2008): Cultural Agency in Central Andes." *A Contracorriente* 10, no. 3 (Spring 2013): 54–73.

INDEX

Note: References following "n" refer notes.

Acosta, Alberto, 161–70, 216n5
Acosta Cárdenas, Miguelina, 6
Acosta, Yamandú, 59–61, 71
acculturation, 26, 41, 62, 97
agriculturism, 72
altiplano, 28–30, 116. *See also* indio del altiplano
Allin Kawsay, 163–66, 180
Amauta (journal), 6, 74, 92, 94–95, 202n1, 207n17
Amazonian Rainforest, 58, 62, 65, 72, 190–95, 209n11, 217n10, 218n2
andinismo, 14–15, 63–64, 68–69, 116–17, 191
anthropology, 10, 22–23, 34–38, 103
Anzaldúa, Gloria, 58
Aparicio, Juan, 120, 153
Araucanía, 43, 195
Arguedas, Alcides, 7, 35, 55, 84, 146, 191, 199n5; anti-mestizaje, 41, 68; on pessimistic indigenismo, 27–33, 104; pluriversality, 42–47; *Pueblo enfermo*, 15, 21–23, 27–32, 199n5 201n17, 212n15; *Raza de bronce*, 30–31; *Vida criolla*, 31–32, 200n7, 200n8
Arguedas, José María, 16, 75–76, 93–97, 100, 169–72, 191, 199n9; *Canto Quechua*, 93, 97, 167; "El indigenismo en el Perú," 95, 207n17; Indo-Marxism, 83, 92; "La cultura. Un patrimonio difícil de colonizar," 96; *Manuscrito de Huarochirí*, 207n18; mestizaje, 68; "No soy un aculturado," 94, 207n16; poem "Apu Inka Atawallpaman," 180
Arias, Arturo, 14, 160, 172, 219n4
assimilation, 23, 33, 41–42, 45, 112–14, 127, 149, 200n10. *See also* cultural assimilation
author theory, 17, 137, 145–46
ayllu, 69–70, 76–77, 90, 96, 111, 117, 205n5, 205n7; as a proto-communist form, 78–79, 81–84;

INDEX

as revolutionary myth, 87, 182. *See also* Ayllus Rojos
Ayllus Rojos, 121, 128
Aymara Nation, 21, 28, 41–45, 89, 127, 130, 166, 192; Túpac Katari, 52–54; uprisings, 66, 127

Bánzer Suarez, Hugo, 128
Barthes, Roland, 145
Bartra, Armando, 148–49, 152
Bingham, Hiram, 204n9
Blaser, Mario, 11, 120, 153, 166–67, 201n16, 216n16
Boas, Franz, 34, 199n1
Bolivian Revolution (1952), 6, 16, 33, 54, 100, 104, 209n11; MNR administration, 120, 133, 209n12; Reinaga, 111. *See also* MNR (Movimiento Nacionalista Revolucionario)
Bonfil Batalla, Guillermo, 8, 38–39, 218n1
Brecht, Bertolt, 157–58
Buen Vivir, 17, 70, 139, 161–69, 191, 216n2, 216n5; as a literary trope, 11, 132, 172–89; as public policy, 218n14

Cadena, Marisol de la, 11, 43, 161, 201n16, 217n7; *earth-beings*, 184; on indigenismo cuzqueño, 50, 65; on indigenous cosmopolitics, 165
campesinización, 101, 104–5, 124
capitalism, 25, 69–70, 77–80, 83, 145, 154, 163, 191–92; anti-capitalism, 87–88, 96, 205n4; capitalist modernity, 9, 12; modern/capitalist system, 9; neoliberalism, 25, 135–36, 138, 154, 161, 165, 188

Cárdenas del Río, Lázaro, 16, 100–105, 107–8, 202n19, 209n10
Castro Pozo, Hildebrando, 81–82, 205n5
Central Obrera Boliviana (COB), 105
Chacón, Gloria E., 14, 145, 188, 201n14
Chihuailaf, Elicura, 217
Chikangana, Fredy, 216n4
Ch'aska Anka Ninawaman, 17, 97, 162, 167–70, 187–88, 192, 207n20, 217n7; *Poesía en quechua*, 163, 171–78
Chiapas, 40, 43, 107, 135–36, 138, 140–43, 152, 166, 193. *See also* EZLN and Zapatista communities
Chivi, Idón, 181
cholo, 27–32, 112, 114, 121, 123–25; *cholificación*, 124; cholismo, 3
Choque Quispe, María Eugenia, 52
coca leaf, 128, 130–32, 167, 173, 213n22. *See also* K'intu
colonialism, 8, 51, 55, 67, 72, 86–88, 114, 130–31, 145, 191–92; anticolonialism, 122–25, 212n16; "colonial difference," 25–26, 147; critique of colonialism, 79, 98, 211n8; internal colonialism, 137–40
coloniality, 8–14, 23, 75, 87, 114, 145, 159; coloniality of being, 125; coloniality of knowledge, 118; coloniality of power, 13, 40, 76, 87, 161; cultural coloniality, 54–56, 76, 89–92, 93–98. *See also* trinomial modernity/coloniality/capitalism
colonial matrix of power, 17, 86, 125, 130, 140, 193
communism, 77–80, 84–85, 90, 114;

INDEX

Communist International (Comintern), 16, 75–76, 81, 85–88, 191; Inca communism, 70, 75–81; indigenista communism, 7, 10, 104, 107

Córdova Huamán, Washington, 2, 97, 162, 167, 178–80, 187–88, 192, 207n20, 218n13; *Parawayraq Chawpinpi / Entre la lluvia y el viento*, 163, 180–86

Cornejo Polar, Antonio, 78, 197n2

Coronado, Jorge, 5, 14, 50, 78, 81

Correa, Rafael, 103, 184, 216n2, 218n14

cosmic race (concept), 14, 49, 56–63, 68, 73. *See also La raza cósmica*

cosmology, 147–48, 160, 166, 187, 216n16; Andean cosmology, 71, 118, 129, 132–34, 162, 168–78; Mayan cosmology, 141, 152–54, 157

criollo elites, 22–23, 29–30, 45, 74, 100

cultural assimilation, 26, 35, 140. *See also* assimilation

cultural relativism, 25, 124–25, 139, 147, 158, 199n1

Cuzco, 6, 50–55, 68, 116, 127, 168–69, 177, 195, 202n1; as literary trope, 174–76, 188; in *Tempestad en los Andes*, 63–67. *See also* Qosqo

decolonial cracks, 7, 14, 23, 43, 46, 75, 82, 88; *indigenista decolonial cracks*, 7, 13–16, 142, 157, 160, 179, 182, 186, 191–92,

decolonial theory, 14, 17, 56, 71, 194. *See also* Indigenous Decolonial Critique

decoloniality, 9–12, 76, 118, 194, 197n1. *See also* coloniality

De Castro, Juan, 49, 58, 78, 87

degenerative discourse, 13, 21–23, 27

dialectical bypass, 76, 88, 98

Dussel, Enrique, 10, 51–55, 59–60, 71, 192. *See also* transmodernity

Ejército Guerrillero Túpac Katari (EGTK), 128–29

ejido system, 101, 107, 138, 202n19, 208n5, 214n5

encomendero, 24

epistemology, 18, 25–26, 43–47, 68, 79, 90, 95–98, 113, 147–53, 190–92; epistemological difference, 7, 23, 54, 76, 194; epistemological superiority, 26, 118; Indigenous epistemologies, 17, 106, 114–17, 119–20, 122–24, 128–30, 134, 184, 193; Maya epistemology, 160

Escobar, Arturo, 11, 120, 153, 156

Eurocentrism, 9, 17, 34, 40–42, 48–56, 59–62, 73, 79, 87–90, 119, 137, 149; anti-Eurocentrism, 58, 73

evangelization, 24–26, 34

EZLN (Ejército Zapatista de Liberación Nacional), 17, 135–43, 149, 154, 159, 192, 213n2, 215n14; Comité Revolucionario Clandestino Indígena (CCRI), 143–45, 153–58

Fanon, Frantz, 114, 118, 121–25, 133, 157; *The Wretched of the Earth*, 121–22, 133; *Black Skin, White Masks*, 121–24; on national liberation, 123, 212n13

Favre, Henri, 4

INDEX

Flores Galindo, Alberto, 75, 77, 85–87, 180–86, 206n11
Forjando patria, 22–23, 34–46, 62, 147, 201n13, 202n18. *See also* Manuel Gamio
Foucault, Michel, 145, 198n8
French Revolution, 53

Galeano, Juan Carlos, 165
Gamio, Manuel, 15, 21–23, 27, 34–47, 103, 137–38, 157, 191. *See also* Forjando patria
gamonalismo, 69, 76, 79
García, José Uriel, 51, 100, 202n1
García Calderón, Ventura, 90
García Canclini, Néstor, 203n5
García Linera, Álvaro, 128–30, 205n4, 213n23
Gordon, Lewis R., 123
Grosfoguel, Ramón, 25, 29, 90, 192
Grupo Resurgimiento, 66, 100, 202n1
Gudynas, Eduardo, 161–62, 165, 216n2

hacendados, 98
Haya de la Torre, Víctor Raúl, 50, 73
historical-structural heterogeneity, 80–90. *See also* Aníbal Quijano
historical materialism, 79
historicism, 40, 48–49, 62
Huarochirí Manuscript, 97, 172, 217n19
Hurtado, Javier, 127, 213n19

Ibero-American race, 49–59
incaismo, 64–66, 68, 177
indianismo, 7, 17, 89, 105–107, 111–20; concomitance with Fanon and *negritude*, 121–25, 211n10; indianismo-katarismo, 54, 127; in Indigenous movements, 126–30; indianista revolution, 114–19, 125, 131, 185; *La revolución india* (Reinaga), 113–18, 121–23, 131–34, 210n2; Reinaga philosophy, 4, 131, 133–34
indigenismo, 3–16, 35, 38–39, 55–57, 75–78, 84–97, 113, 119–24, 133–37, 166, 174, 184–87; Cuzqueño indigenista school, 50, 64–68, 115; definition, 4–5, 212n14; pessimistic indigenismo, 27–33, 104; as public policies, 39, 99–108, 127–33, 138–40, 183–84; transmodernist indigenismo, 49, 71–3. *See also* Indigenista decolonial cracks
indigenista decolonial cracks, 7, 13–16, 142, 157, 160, 179, 182, 186, 191–92
Indigenous authorship, 137–40, 144–46, 165
Indigenous Decolonial Critique, 4, 16, 18, 100, 153, 156, 190–94
Indigenous literatures, 5–9, 14–17, 37, 76, 90–92, 146, 190–95; Buen Vivir literature, 186–89; Maya literature, 37, 144, 160; Quechua poetry, 97, 162–72, 178–86
Indigenous intellectuals, 5, 71, 100–101, 127, 133, 191–94, 208n3, 211n9
indio del altiplano, 22, 41
Inkarri, 180–85, 188
Inter-American Indigenista Congress, 16, 100–106
Instituto Nacional Indigenista (INI), 38–39, 42, 138–39

katarismo, 126–29, 134, 213n19

INDEX

Keme,' Emil, 178
k'intu, 171–77

La raza cósmica, 15, 35, 49–62, 71
Latin American Communist Conference (1929), 184
Latin American eco-cinema, 164
Latour, Bruno, 11, 172, 198n7
Las Casas, Bartolomé de, 24–26, 34–35, 199n2
Lauer, Mirko, 94
lekil kuxlejal, 139–40, 145, 160, 166
lettered city (*ciudad letrada*), 37, 120
Lienhard, Martin, 169–70
Lugones, María, 10, 192
López Albújar, Enrique, 82, 90, 205n6
López Intzin, Juan, 139

Machu Picchu, 6, 65, 99, 204n9
Maldonado-Torres, Nelson, 24–26, 118, 124
Mamani, Mauro, 179
mandar obedeciendo, 136, 144–46, 151, 160
Mariátegui, José Carlos, 3–7, 10, 16, 41, 50, 64, 74–79, 84–89, 148, 191, 205n5, 206n11; on Ayllu, 70, 80–84, 182; "El problema de las razas en América Latina," 86; in Fausto Reinaga, 111–13, 117, 133, 210n3; Indo-Marxism, 80–83, 90–93; in J.M. Arguedas, 93–99; in *Perricholi* (magazine), 92; *Siete ensayos de interpretación de la realidad peruana*, 3, 74–82, 84–85, 89; in *Tempestad en los Andes*, 65
Marcone, Jorge, 164, 173
Marcos, Subcomandante (Galeano), 17, 135–36, 149–51, 154, 192; *Desde las montañas del sureste mexicano*, 149, 157; *Don Durito de la Lacandona*, 141, 154–58; Marcos-author, 137, 140–48, 156–59; *Relatos del viejo Antonio*, 148–53
Marxism, 74–79, 88, 115–17, 125, 132, 147, 205n3, 206n14; Indo-Marxism, 14–16, 76–77, 81–88, 92–98, 191
Matto de Turner, Clorinda, 6, 90, 197n2
Maya literature, 37, 144, 160
Melgar, Mariano, 92
Menchú, Rigoberta, 144
Mesoamerica, 4–5, 39–41, 48, 99–100, 135, 164, 191, 195; Mesoamerican civilization, 35–36, 153; Mesoamerican literatures, 38, 145–46, 157, 201n14, 219n4
mestizaje, 37, 41, 50, 56–63, 106, 138–40, 204n11, 214n3, 214n7; anti-mestizaje, 68–73
Mexican Revolution, 6, 22, 35–38, 91, 101–4, 138, 153, 214n5
Mignolo, Walter, 10–12, 25, 43, 79, 115–18, 147, 155, 192
modernity, 9, 14–15, 23, 34–35, 51–59, 96, 120, 143; colonial modernity, 68; modernity/coloniality/capitalism, 9–13, 18, 46, 192–94, 198n3; in pluriversality, 40–46. *See also* transmodernity
Mora, Mariana, 136, 139, 146, 166
Morales, Evo, 17, 33, 103–5, 128–33, 167, 173, 184, 210n1, 213n22
Moraña, Mabel, 94
Movimiento Indio Katari, 126
Movimiento Indio Túpac Katari, 126

INDEX

MNR (Movimiento Nacionalista Revolucionario), 6, 16, 100, 104–8, 111–13, 127, 133, 209n12, 210n2. *See also* Bolivian Revolution

Movimiento Revolucionario Tupaj Katari, 126

Muyolema, Armando, 33, 187

myth (as revolutionary force), 76, 81–87, 90, 180–82, 185; indigenous myths, 148–54, 166, 179, 181

nationalism, 38–39, 49, 53; Mexican nationalism, 22, 34–38, 40; modern nationalism, 36, 40–74

National literature, 37, 144

nayrapacha, 49, 52–53, 66, 116–19, 130–34, 176–77, 185, 202n4

neoliberalism, 25, 135–38, 154, 161, 165, 188

Netzahualcoyotl, 37

Nuevas Leyes de Indias, 24

nuevo indio, 65–67, 71–72, 112

ontology, 43–45, 70, 77, 132, 152–57, 164, 172–73, 192, 216n16; ontological domination, 29–30; ontological turn, 11, 158, 167; political ontology, 162–67, 177–78

oralitura, 162, 216n4

Orkopata Group, 179, 217n12

Pachamama, 117

pachakuti, 119, 129–34, 164, 177–79

Partido Comunista de Bolivia, 111

Partido Indio de Bolivia (PIB), 126–27

Partido de Indios Aymaras y Keswas (PIAK), 126

Partido Revolucionario Institucional (PRI), 102, 107, 138–39, 213n1, 214n6

Paz Soldán, Edmundo, 21, 28, 199n5

pessimism, 14, 21, 27, 32–33, 69, 104; pessimistic indigenismo, 27–33, 104

phenomenology, 26, 118, 121

Plan de Ayala, 138

pluriversality, 40–43, 153–58

political ontology, 162–67, 177–78

Poma de Ayala, Guamán, 136, 180

pongueaje, 28–30, 33, 129; *pongos*, 28–29, 114, 199n6

positivism, 48–51, 56–58, 63, 88

postcoloniality, 8, 194

Qosqo, 174, 217n11

Quechua Nation, 53–54, 89, 125–30, 160–63, 177–78, 188, 192; Quechua poetry, 97, 162–72, 178–86

Quijano, Aníbal, 8–10, 29, 54, 80, 88, 192, 197n1, 198n6; coloniality of power, 13, 40, 76, 87, 161

Quispe, Felipe "El Mallku," 121, 126–29

racism, 12, 28–29, 79, 87, 121–25, 129, 138, 193; cultural racism, 25–26, 90; misanthropic skepticism, 24–26, 30; scientific racism, 34, 199n1

Rama, Ángel, 5, 207n8

Raza de bronce, 30–31

Reinaga, Fausto, 3–7, 17, 88–89, 105–7, 111–34, 155, 176–77, 185, 191–94; *El indio y los escritores de América*, 3, 17, 112–14; indianismo, 7, 17, 89, 105–7, 111–20; *La revolución india*, 113–18, 121–23, 131–34, 210n2; *Tierra y libertad*, 111, 114

Rivera, Diego, 91

INDEX

Rivera Cusicanqui, Silvia, 52–54, 59, 66, 71, 106, 130, 192, 202n4

Sabogal, José, 91
Said, Edward, 188
Saldaña-Portillo, María Josefina, 156
Sánchez-Prado, Ignacio, 34–35, 58–59
San Cristóbal de las Casas, 135
Sanjinés, Javier C., 28, 68, 79, 130, 192, 204n11
Sarmiento, Domingo Faustino, 28
Sepúlveda, Juan Ginés de, 24–30
skepticism: misanthropic skepticism, 24–26, 30
Social Darwinism, 27, 57, 63, 199n1
Sorel, Georges, 80, 84
Subalternity, 9; subaltern studies, 203n5
Sumak Kawsay, 163–66
Suma Qamaña, 163–66

Tahuantinsuyo (Tawantinsuyo), 79–80, 113, 116
Taylor, Analisa, 136, 140
technocracy, 45–46, 94, 150, 184
Tiwanaku Manifesto, 126
tellurism, 13–15, 64, 68–71, 117, 122, 174, 181–85
transculturation, 137, 143–44, 179
transmodernity, 51, 54–56, 59–63, 71
transmodern subject, 51, 59–63, 67–72
transmodernist indigenismo, 49, 71–73
trinomial modernity/coloniality/capitalism, 9–13, 18, 46, 192–94, 198n3
Túpac Amaru II, 52–54, 116, 127

Túpac Katari, 52, 116, 126–28. *See also* katarismo
Tzotzil myth, 148

Valcárcel, Luis E., 7, 16, 48–51, 54–56, 70–73, 82, 90, 115–20, 142, 174–77, 1991; *Del ayllu al imperio*, 69–70; *Mirador indio*, 73; *Tempestad en los andes*, 15, 50–15, 56, 63–70, 112, 133, 183. *See also* Grupo Resurgimiento.
Valladolid, 24–26, 35
Vasconcelos, José, 15, 41, 48–51, 54, 65–68, 112, 137–40, 191, 200n10, 203n7; Cosmic race (concept), 14, 49, 56–63, 68, 73; *La raza cósmica*, 15, 35, 49–62, 71
Vida criolla, 31–32, 200n7, 200n8
Villoro, Luis, 23
Viveiros de Castro, Eduardo, 198n7

Wallerstein, Immanuel, 9, 119, 211n7
Walsh, Catherine E., 11–14, 46, 115, 142, 161, 192, 216n2
Wampis Nation, 5, 43, 193, 218n2
world-making process, 153–59
world-system, 89, 155

zapatismo (movement), 5, 17, 43, 107, 135–60, 191–95, 213n2, 215n13; Comité Revolucionario Clandestino Indígena (CCRI), 143–45, 153–58; zapatista literature, 17, 140–60. *See also* Marcos, Subcomandante.
zapatista communities, 17, 140–46, 150, 166
Zavaleta Mercado, René, 105–6
Zulen, Pedro, 6